Scuba D̶ [barcode: D0867894]

Explained

Questions and Answers on
Physiology and Medical Aspects
of Scuba Diving

BEST PUBLISHING COMPANY

Scuba Diving Explained

Questions and Answers on
Physiology and Medical Aspects
of Scuba Diving

By
Lawrence Martin, M.D.

BEST PUBLISHING COMPANY

Cover design by Debra Shirley

Publisher's Cataloging in Publication Data
        Martin, Lawrence
Scuba Diving Explained: Questions and Answers on Physiology and Medical Aspects of
Scuba Diving/Lawrence Martin
p. cm.
Includes bibliographical references and index.

1. Scuba diving. 2. Scuba diving - Physiological aspects. 3. Scuba diving - Medical
aspects. 4. Diving - Recreational.
        I. Title

                GV840.S78L43
                797.2'3—dc20

Text design by Linda Longnaker.

ISBN: 0-941332-56-X
Library of Congress catalog card number : 93-079817

Composed, printed and bound in the United States of America.

Best Publishing Company
2355 North Steves Boulevard
P.O. Box 30100
Flagstaff, Arizona 86003-0100 USA

ACKNOWLEDGMENTS

Several scuba divers reviewed the draft of this manuscript. They made many useful suggestions, most of which I readily incorporated, and caught some errors, for which I am grateful. For their efforts I thank (in alphabetical order): Pam Alderman, Anne Cath, M.D., Jolie Bookspan, Ph.D., John Comley, Bernard Martin, Robert Martin, M.D., Ruth S. Martin, M.D., and Lorain Rimko. I would also like to thank Debra Shirley for her many excellent line drawings; and Diver's Alert Network and the Diving Historical Society for permission to use some of their photos.

DEDICATION

To Ruth, my wife and dive buddy.

TABLE OF CONTENTS

SECTION	Page

A. A Brief History of Diving, from Antiquity to the Present

B. Recreational Scuba Diving: An Overview

C. The Respiratory System: A Brief Review

D. An Explanation of Pressure and the Laws of Boyle, Charles, Dalton, and Henry

E. Water and the Physical Laws That Affect All Divers

F. Effects of Unequal Air Pressures While Scuba Diving: Ear Squeeze, Sinus Squeeze, Air Embolism and Other Forms of Barotrauma

G. Effects of Increased Dissolved Nitrogen From Scuba Diving: Decompression Sickness

H. Oxygen Therapy for Diving Accidents : At Atmospheric and Hyperbaric Pressure

I. Effects of Gas Pressures at Depth: Nitrogen Narcosis, CO and CO_2 Toxicity, Oxygen Toxicity and "Shallow-Water Blackout"

J. Dive Tables and Dive Computers: Their History and Utility

K. Stress, Hyperventilation, and Hypothermia

L. Diving with Non-air Gas Mixtures: Nitrox, Heliox, Trimix, et. al.

M. Women and Diving

N. Medical Fitness for Diving: Guidelines Real and Imagined

O. Should Asthmatics Not Scuba Dive?

P. But Is Recreational Scuba Diving Safe? The Great Debate

GLOSSARY AND APPENDICES

DIVING ODDS N' ENDS

PREFACE

Unless you score 80% or better on the short scuba quiz (page xvii), you can probably benefit from reading this book. Knowledge of basic underwater physiology is critical to diving safety, of course, and the subject is taught in every certification class. For example, the first rule of diving - *don't hold your breath* - is based on Boyle's law of gas pressures, which predicts that a scuba diver's lungs will expand if breath is held on ascent. The consequence can be a serious and even fatal over-expansion injury.

Although all certification manuals and general scuba books review underwater physiology, the coverage is necessarily limited. Typically, one chapter is devoted to the subject. Important effects of altered physiology, such as decompression sickness and arterial gas embolism, are covered only briefly.

As a recreational diver and pulmonary physician, I believe there is need for a book that more fully explains this material. Not a textbook for the doctor, engineer or scientist, but a book any recreational diver can understand. A book that answers questions frequently pondered by the recreational diver. After searching and finding no such book, I decided to write one! *Scuba Diving Explained* is intended for all sport divers because the material is important for all of us, from beginner to people with years of experience.

Subjects include: the concept of pressure, the four major gas laws as they apply to diving, composition of air, changes in gas pressures with depth, ear and sinus squeeze, lung barotrauma, air embolism, decompression sickness, nitrogen narcosis, oxygen toxicity, carbon monoxide and carbon dioxide toxicity, stress, hypothermia, hyperventilation, and oxygen therapy.

I also answer some questions on "deep diving" (below 130 feet), and diving with non-air mixtures such as Nitrox. Both activities are outside the realm of recreational diving (as defined by the scuba training agencies), but their physiology is fascinating and germane to all diving. If you understand, for example, what Nitrox is and why it does *not* allow one to dive deeper than with ordinary air, you can better appreciate the effects of water pressure on nitrogen and oxygen in any gas mixture, including ordinary air.

A separate section answers some commonly-asked questions about women and diving, e.g., "Do women have an increased risk of the bends?" and, "Is diving safe during pregnancy?" A section on medical fitness for diving explains the rationale of some published guidelines, most of which are based on theory rather than hard data. Another section reviews perhaps the most controversial of all conditions for scuba diving, asthma.

Scuba Diving Explained is designed to increase your understanding and enjoyment of the sport. However, this book is not an instruction manual; it contains relatively little information about scuba equipment (better taught with hands-on instruction in a scuba course), diving skills or marine life. Instead, emphasis is on the physiology vital to all sport divers. I go to great length to explain changes in gas pressures with depth because, quite simply, that singular feature most affects the diver's safety.

In sections B through L are brief questions to 'test your understanding' of the material. Placement of some questions within the text is preferable to putting all of them at the end of a section or in an appendix. Each question is germane to the proceeding paragraphs; answers are at the end of the section. For diversion, you will find paragraphs of 'Diving Odds N' Ends' at the end of each section, in grey boxes. Some of this information is gleaned from various popular periodicals and non-technical books. Because scuba magazines are a prime source of information for the sport diver, I have prepared a list of nationally-circulated periodicals published in the U.S., along with addresses, circulation figures and phone/fax numbers (Section T). Section U lists U.S. distributors of scuba books and dive videos and internet addresses of comprehensive scuba sites. Also included for most sections is an extensive bibliography, covering both quoted sources and other books and articles that may be of interest to recreational divers.

Although you will probably get more out of *Scuba Diving Explained* if you have some scuba experience, it should also be useful to anyone interested in diving who has yet to don scuba gear. There seem to be as many "wannabe" divers as there are the certified kind. If you don't dive but plan to learn, it is not too soon to begin your exposure to underwater physiology.

There is no substitute for basic training from one of the national scuba certification agencies. These agencies, listed in Section S, teach the basic scuba skills and provide a general introduction to underwater physiology. *Scuba Diving Explained* should help you better understand this physiology and the effects of breathing compressed air underwater.

Happy and safe diving!

Lawrence Martin, M.D.

DISCLAIMER

Most books about scuba diving carry disclaimers and this one is no exception. Information provided in this book is not infallible, and it should in no way be accepted or used as specific advice or recommendation for any specific individual. The purpose of this book is to increase your understanding of scuba diving, not to tell you what to do when, including how deep to dive, what equipment to use, how quickly to ascend, or whether to take up the sport in the first place.

Although I make specific recommendations in some areas, particularly about some medical conditions as they relate to diving, these are not specific for any individual and should not be construed as such. Any question about any activity related to an actual dive should be discussed directly with the dive professional involved (instructor, dive master, a dive store owner, etc.) or, if appropriate, a qualified physician.

AN INVITATION

This book is written for the recreational diver who wishes to learn more about medical and physiologic aspects of scuba diving. Inevitably, some aspects are discussed more than others, some topics are omitted, some subjects are treated less than the reader might wish. I invite any feedback from readers about the book's content. Please let me know about any information or subject you think should be included, augmented, or deleted. Also, by all means tell me about any errors found in the text. I will read and carefully consider all suggestions for a future edition. You can send any suggestion or comment to the publisher, or directly to me (Pulmonary Division, Mt. Sinai Medical Center, One Mt. Sinai Drive, Cleveland, OH 44106). I can also be reached via the internet (martin@lightstream.net).

Lawrence Martin, M.D.

MYTHS AND MISCONCEPTIONS

Some information in this book will no doubt challenge myths or misconceptions held by many recreational divers. For people who prefer to browse I have made a list of some common myths and misconceptions; they are in the form of statements, with sections where each subject is mentioned or discussed. Each of these statements is: 1) accepted as fact by many recreational divers (personal survey), and 2) either not true or there is no basis for believing it is true.

There was no scuba diving before invention of the aqua lung by Jacques Cousteau and Emil Gagnan in 1943. **Section A**

The maximum recreational diving depth of 130 feet is based on studies of divers at various depths. **Section A**

Recreational diving is 'no decompression' diving ; the three minute safety stop is not a decompression stop. **Section B**

When diving with compressed air, the percentage of inhaled oxygen increases with depth. **Section D**

Inflation and deflation of the buoyancy compensator is the main method by which to achieve buoyancy control underwater. **Section E**

The most venomous sea creature is the sea snake (or some snake) found in the Pacific Ocean. **Section E** *(Diving Odds n' Ends)*

The great white shark can grow to over 30 feet in length. **Section E** *(Diving Odds n' Ends)*

Decompression sickness only occurs in divers who exceed the limits of the dive tables. **Section G**

Decompression sickness and decompression illness are the same. **Section G**

Decompression sickness is an entity easily distinguishable from arterial gas embolism. **Section G**

The main reason for having oxygen available at any dive site is to treat hypoxia (low oxygen) in dive accident victims. **Section H**

Pure oxygen inhaled at sea level can cause seizures. **Section H**

MYTHS AND MISCONCEPTIONS
(continued)

The cause of shallow-water blackout in breath-hold divers is buildup of CO_2 in the body. **Section I**

All sharks are known to attack humans. **Section I** *(Diving Odds n' Ends)*

Dive computers generally provide for safer diving than printed dive tables. **Section J**

All dive computers use essentially the same algorithm and give essentially the same dive times for a given depth. **Section J**

Nitrox allows dives deeper than the recreational depth limit of 130 feet. **Section L**

Women are more prone to decompression sickness than men. **Section M**

Women risk shark attack if they dive during their menstrual period. **Section M**

Diving while pregnant is safe for the fetus if the diver stays shallow (less than 33 fsw). **Section M**

Proper cooking of fish can prevent ciguatera food poisoning. **Section M** *(Diving Odds n' Ends)*

Most medical prohibitions to diving (e.g., for asthma, diabetes) are based on documented data or clinical experience. **Section N**

Diabetes is a clear prohibition for scuba diving. **Section N**

Asthma is a clear prohibition for scuba diving. **Section M**

Asthmatics who dive can minimize risk by staying shallow (less than 33 fsw). **Section M**

Scuba diving is safe. **Section P**

Scuba diving is unsafe. **Section P**

SHORT SCUBA QUIZ

This multiple-choice quiz should take only about 10 to 15 minutes. There is only one correct answer for each question. Correctly answer 12 or more of the 15 questions and you likely know a great deal about scuba diving already; after reading sections that interest you, pass the book along to a friend. Answers are at the end of the Quiz.

1. The gas composition of ordinary air is:
   a) 15% oxygen, 80% nitrogen, 5% other
   b) 20% oxygen, 75% nitrogen, 5% other
   c) 21% oxygen, 78% nitrogen, 1% other
   d) 24% oxygen, 79% nitrogen, 3% other
   e) 26% oxygen, 81% nitrogen, 3% other

2. Compressed air in a scuba tank filled to capacity, compared to ordinary air, has:
   a) the same composition
   b) a greater percentage of oxygen
   c) a greater percentage of nitrogen
   d) a greater percentage of both oxygen and nitrogen
   e) varying composition of oxygen and nitrogen, depending on the tank pressure

3. Compared to sea level air pressure, air pressure in a scuba tank with 3000 psi is approximately how many times higher?
   a) 10
   b) 50
   c) 100
   d) 200
   e) 400

4. The total number of atmospheres of absolute pressure on a scuba diver at 99 feet of sea water is:
   a) 2
   b) 3
   c) 4
   d) 5
   e) 6

5. Nitrogen narcosis ("rapture of the deep") results from:
   a) nitrogen forming bubbles in the nervous system
   b) lack of oxygen to the brain from excess nitrogen pressure
   c) a direct effect of high nitrogen pressure on the nervous system

d) diving with an elevated blood alcohol level

e) staying too long underwater

6. Which of the following problems is *least related* to diving deeper than the limits allowed by standard dive tables?

    a) nitrogen narcosis

    b) type I decompression sickness (pain only, or "the bends")

    c) type II decompression sickness (major physical deficit, such as paralysis)

    d) air embolism

    e) running out of air

7. The reason scuba divers should never hold breath underwater has to do with effects explained by:

    a) Boyle's law

    b) Dalton's law

    c) Henry's law

    d) lack of oxygen that occurs when you stop breathing

    e) the buildup of carbon dioxide when you stop breathing

8. At a depth of 66 feet sea water, air breathed from a scuba tank as it enters the diver's lungs is how much denser than air breathed at sea level?

    a) same density

    b) twice as dense

    c) three times as dense

    d) four times as dense

    e) depends on amount of air left in scuba tank at that point

9. Which one of the following factors is the same for air embolism and for decompression sickness?

    a) composition of the gas bubbles

    b) principal location of gas bubbles in the body

    c) cause of the bubbles

    d) time of onset of symptoms in relation to the end of the dive

    e) method of treatment

10. Air embolism occurs on:

    a) descent only

    b) ascent or descent, depending on where the diver holds his or her breath

    c) ascent or descent, depending on where the diver runs out of air

    d) ascent only, and only with breath holding

    e) ascent only, and depends on factors such as breath-holding and state of the diver's lungs

11. "Shallow-water blackout," as may be seen in breath-hold divers, is due to:
    a) elevated carbon dioxide from prolonged breath holding
    b) lack of oxygen from prolonged breath holding
    c) both elevated carbon dioxide and lack of oxygen
    d) nitrogen buildup from prolonged time underwater
    e) seizures brought on by the breath hold in susceptible people

12. First aid treatment for a victim of decompression illness should always include 100% inhaled oxygen because:
    a) it stimulates the heart to pump harder
    b) it hastens the elimination of nitrogen
    c) it hastens the elimination of carbon dioxide
    d) it helps to keep victims from hyperventilating
    e) the victim's blood is usually low in oxygen

13. All of the following are forms of barotrauma except one:
    a) pneumothorax
    b) mask squeeze
    c) air embolism
    d) the bends
    e) ear squeeze

14. Dive tables are based on the assumption that:
    a) the diver will make no more than three dives a day
    b) all bottom time is spent at the deepest depth reached
    c) the surface interval will be at least one hour between dives
    d) any subsequent dive will be shallower than the one before
    e) there will be no multi-level diving

15. The principal reason people with asthma are advised not to dive is the risk of:
    a) the bends
    b) running out of air due to over breathing
    c) arterial gas embolism
    d) an asthma attack from breathing dry compressed air
    e) aspirating sea water from coughing at depth

END OF QUIZ

ANSWERS

1. c	5. c	9. e	13. d
2. a	6. d	10. e	14. b
3. d	7. a	11. b	15. c
4. c	8. c	12. b	

__NOTES__

A Brief History of Diving, From Antiquity to the Present

WHAT IS THE EARLY HISTORY OF DIVING?

Men and women have practiced breath-hold diving for centuries. Indirect evidence comes from thousand-year-old undersea artifacts found on land (e.g., mother-of-pearl ornaments), and depictions of divers in ancient drawings. In ancient Greece breath-hold divers are known to have hunted for sponges and engaged in military exploits. Of the latter, the story of Scyllis (sometimes spelled Scyllias; about 500 B.C.) is perhaps the most famous. As told by the 5th century B.C. historian Herodotus (and quoted in numerous modern texts),

> During a naval campaign the Greek Scyllis was taken aboard ship as prisoner by the Persian King Xerxes I. When Scyllis learned that Xerxes was to attack a Greek flotilla, he seized a knife and jumped overboard. The Persians could not find him in the water and presumed he had drowned. Scyllis surfaced at night and made his way among all the ships in Xerxes' fleet, cutting each ship loose from its moorings; he used a hollow reed as snorkel to remain unobserved. Then he swam nine miles (15 kilometers) to rejoin the Greeks off Cape Artemisium.

The desire to go underwater has probably always existed: to hunt for food, uncover artifacts, repair ships (or sink them!), and perhaps just to observe marine life. Until humans found a way to breathe underwater, however, each dive was necessarily short and frantic.

How to stay underwater longer? Breathing through a hollow reed allows the body to be submerged, but it must have become apparent right away that reeds more than two feet long do not work well; difficulty inhaling against water pressure effectively limits snorkel length. Breathing from an air-filled bag brought underwater was also tried, but it failed due to rebreathing of carbon dioxide.

In the 16th century people began to use diving bells supplied with air from the surface, probably the first effective means of staying underwater for any length of time. The bell was held stationary a few feet from the surface, its bottom open to water and its top portion containing air compressed by the water pressure. A diver standing upright would have his head in the air. He could leave the bell for a minute or two to collect sponges or explore the bottom, then return for a short while until air in the bell was no longer breathable.

In 16th century England and France, full diving suits made of leather were used to depths of 60 feet. Air was pumped down from the surface with the aid of manual pumps. Soon helmets were made of metal to withstand even greater water pressure and divers went deeper. By the 1830s the surface-supplied air helmet was perfected well enough to allow extensive salvage work.

Starting in the 19th century, two main avenues of investigation - one scientific, the other technologic - greatly accelerated underwater exploration. Scientific research was advanced by the work of Paul Bert and John Scott Haldane, from France and Scotland, respectively. Their studies helped explain effects of water pressure on the body, and also define safe limits for compressed air diving. At the same time, improvements in technology - compressed air pumps, carbon dioxide scrubbers, regulators, etc. - made it possible for people to *stay* underwater for long periods.

WHAT ARE THE DIFFERENT TYPES OF DIVING?

There are really four 'mini-histories' in the fascinating story of man's desire to explore beneath the sea; they correspond to four separate methods of diving, of which scuba is but the latest.

a) ***Breath-hold diving (free diving, skin diving).*** This earliest form of diving is still practiced for both sport and commercial purposes (e.g., ama divers of Japan and Korea, pearl divers of the Tuamoto Archipelago). The breath-hold diver's compressible air spaces are squeezed by the increased water pressure throughout the dive. Each dive, limited by the individual's tolerance for breath-hold and the risk of drowning from hypoxia, is usually a minute or less.

b) ***Diving in a heavy-walled vessel.*** Heavy-walled vessels can maintain their internal atmosphere at or near sea level pressure ('one atmosphere' or 'one atm.'), and so prevent the surrounding water pressure from affecting the occupants. Such vessels include: the *bathysphere*, an unpowered hollow steel ball lowered from the mother ship by steel cable; the *bathyscaphe*, a bathysphere with buoyancy control so that cable is not needed for descent and ascent; and the *submarine*, which can travel great distances in any direction under its own power. All one-atmosphere vessels require a system to both provide fresh air (usually by adding oxygen to the existing air) and get rid of exhaled carbon dioxide (with soda lime, lithium hydroxide, or a similar compound that takes up CO_2). A modern extension of the one-atmosphere vessel is the self-contained armored diving suit, flexible yet able to withstand pressures at depth: in effect, the diver becomes almost like a small submarine. With these one-atmosphere suits, a diver can work at a depth of several hundred meters for hours.

c) ***Diving with compressed air supplied from the surface.*** The diver is separated from the supply of fresh air, which is kept on the surface. Air reaches the diver through a long umbilical, which in its simplest form ends in a regulator and mouthpiece carried by the diver. In more sophisticated systems, the umbilical leads into a dive suit or some larger enclosed space containing the diver. Devices in this category include caissons (huge spaces supplied with compressed air, employed mainly for bridge and tunnel work), underwater habitats used for saturation diving, diving bells, and rigid-helmet diving suits. In all these devices, the diver breathes air at the same pressure as the surrounding water pressure, and so is at risk for decompression problems (bends, air embolism, etc.) if ascent is too fast. Special 'high tech' mixtures, such as hydrogen-oxygen, helium-oxygen and helium-nitrogen-oxygen, are used to dive deeper than possible with compressed air.

d) ***Diving with compressed air or other gas mixture that is carried by the diver (scuba diving).*** There are two principle types of scuba: open and closed circuit. Open circuit vents all expired air into the water, and is the mode used in recreational diving. Closed circuit systems, in which exhaled air is re-breathed after carbon dioxide is absorbed and oxygen added, were widely used before open circuit became available, particularly by military divers who wished to avoid showing any air bubbles. As with divers using surface-supplied compressed air, scuba divers are at risk for decompression problems if they ascend without proper decompression. Helium-oxygen and other mixtures can be used to go deeper than possible with compressed air.

WHAT ARE SOME IMPORTANT EVENTS IN THE HISTORY OF DIVING?

The remainder of this chapter is a chronologic recounting of some important events in the four mini-histories of diving, with emphasis on scuba. There are many legends attached to diving history, some based on isolated woodcuts or the storyteller's art. This list includes selected inventions, discoveries and achievements documented and accepted by historians as fact. Following each date is the type of diving to which the described event is most relevant. (Events that advanced knowledge of diving physics and decompression sickness are relevant to all compressed air diving.) To summarize, the four types of diving are:

a) Breath-hold diving ("breath-hold")
b) Diving in a heavy-walled vessel ("vessel")
c) Diving with compressed air or other gas supplied from the surface ("surface air")
d) Diving with compressed air or other gas in a container carried by the diver ("scuba")

A BRIEF CHRONOLOGY OF DIVING HISTORY

500 B.C. (breath-hold). Scyllis demonstrates practical use of breath-hold diving by performing military exploits for the King of Persia (see above).

1530 (surface air). First diving bell is invented.

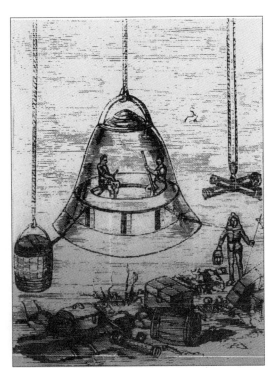

Figure 1. Halley's diving bell, late 17th century. Weighted barrels of air replenished the bell's atmosphere. (Best Publishing Files)

1667 (surface air). *Robert Boyle,* English physicist and originator of Boyle's law, observes gas bubble in eye of viper that had been compressed and then decompressed. He writes: "I have seen a very apparent bubble moving from side to side in the aqueous humor of the eye of a viper at the time when this animal seemed violently distressed in the receiver from which the air had been exhausted." This is the first recorded observation of decompression sickness or "the bends."

1690 (surface air). *Edmund Halley* (of comet fame) patents a diving bell which is connected by a pipe to weighted barrels of air that can be replenished from the surface. Both barrel and bell (the latter with men in it) are lowered to depth; dives to over 60 feet for 90 minutes are recorded. Diving bells are thus shown to be practicable devices.

1715 (surface air). Englishman *John Lethbridge* builds a "diving engine," an underwater oak cylinder that is surface-supplied with compressed air. Inside this device a diver can stay submerged for 30 minutes at 60 feet, while protruding his arms into the water for salvage work. Water is kept out of the suit by means of greased leather cuffs, which seal around the operator's arms. The diving engine is claimed to be used successfully for many years.

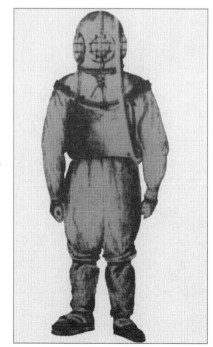

Figure 2. Siebe's early diving suit. (U.S. Navy Diving Manual)

1776 (vessel).   First authenticated attack by military submarine – American *Turtle* vs. *HMS Eagle*, New York harbor.

1788 (surface air).   American *John Smeaton* refines diving bell; incorporates an efficient hand-operated pump to supply fresh compressed air and a non-return valve to keep air from going back up the hose when pumping stops.   In 1790 Smeaton's diving bell is used at Ramsgate Harbor, England, for salvage work.   In another 10 years his bell is found in all major harbors.

1823 (surface air).   *Charles Anthony Deane*, an English inventor, patents a "smoke helmet" for fighting fires.   At some point in the next few years it is used for diving as well.   The helmet fits over a man's head and is held on with weights; air is supplied from the surface through a hose.   In 1828 Charles and his brother *John Deane* market the helmet with a "diving suit."   The suit is not attached to the helmet but only secured with straps; thus the diver cannot bend over without risking drowning.   Even so, the apparatus is used successfully in salvage work, including the removal of some cannons from the *HMS Royal George* in 1834-35 (see also 1839).

1825 (scuba).   "First workable, full-time SCUBA" is invented by an Englishman, William James.   It incorporates a cylindrical belt around the diver's trunk that serves as an air reservoir, at 450 psi.   (It is unclear if this equipment was ever actually used for diving; see Marx 1990 and Brylske 1994 in the Bibliography).   Other inventors about this time are also working on self-contained underwater breathing apparatus.

1837 (surface air).   German-born inventor *Augustus Siebe*, living in England, seals the Deane brothers' diving helmet (see 1823) to a water-tight, air-containing rubber suit.   The closed diving suit, connected to an air pump on the surface, becomes the first effective standard diving dress, and the prototype of hard-hat rigs still in use today.   In his obituary Siebe is described as the father of diving.

1839 (surface air).   Siebe's diving suit is used during salvage of the British warship *HMS Royal George*. The 108-gun ship sank in 65 feet of water at Spithead anchorage in 1783.   The "Siebe Improved Diving Dress" is adopted as the standard diving dress by the Royal Engineers. During this salvage, which continues through 1843, the divers report suffering from "rheumatism and cold," no doubt symptoms (among the first recorded) of decompression sickness.   Also of note in this salvage is the first recorded use of the buddy system for diving.

1843 (surface air). As a result of experience gained salvaging the *HMS Royal George*, the first diving school is set up by the Royal Navy.

1865 (surface air, scuba). Frenchmen *Benoît Rouquayrol* and *Auguste Denayrouse*, a mining engineer and naval lieutenant, respectively, patent an apparatus for underwater breathing. It consists of a horizontal steel tank of compressed air (about 250-350 psi) on a diver's back, connected through a valve arrangement to a mouth-piece. Patented as the "Aerophore," the device delivers air only when the diver inhales, via a membrane that is sensitive to outside water pressure: in effect, the first demand regulator for underwater use. With this apparatus the diver is tethered to the surface by a hose that pumps fresh air into the low pressure tank, but he is able to disconnect the tether and dive with just the tank on his back for a few minutes. The aerophore is a forerunner of modern scuba equipment. The apparatus is used by the French and other navies for several years, and also appears prominently in Jules Verne's 1870 novel, *20,000 Leagues Under The Sea* (see Diving Odds N' Ends).

Figure 3. Aerophore patented in 1865 by Benoît Rouquayrol and Auguste Denayrouse. (Courtesy Historical Diving Society)

1873 (surface air). *Dr. Andrew H. Smith* presents his formal report as Surgeon to the New York Bridge Company, builders of the Brooklyn Bridge, about workers who suffered the bends after leaving the pressurized caisson. (The bends was a common problem among caisson workers. The condition also afflicted chief engineer Washington Roebling; he developed a severe, non-fatal case of decompression sickness, permanently impairing his health.) By the time of Smith's report, which recommends chamber recompression for future projects, all Brooklyn Bridge caisson work is completed. Smith's report makes no mention of the true cause of decompression sickness: nitrogen bubbles.

1876 (scuba). An English merchant seaman, *Henry A. Fleuss*, develops the first workable, self-contained diving rig that uses compressed oxygen (rather than compressed air). In this prototype of closed circuit scuba, which is the forerunner of modern closed circuit scuba units used by military divers, carbon dioxide is absorbed by rope soaked in caustic potash, so that exhaled air can be re-breathed (no bubbles enter the water). Although depths are limited (pure oxygen is toxic below about 25 feet of sea water, a fact not known at the time), the apparatus allows for relatively long bottom times, up to three hours. In 1880 Fleuss's apparatus is used by the famous English diver, Alexander Lambert, to enter a flooded tunnel and seal a hatchway door; the hatchway is 60 feet down and 1000 feet back into the tunnel.

1878 (surface air; scuba). Frenchman *Paul Bert* publishes *La Pression Barometrique*, a 1000-page work containing his physiologic studies of pressure changes. He shows that decompression sickness is due to formation of nitrogen gas bubbles, and suggests gradual ascent as one way to prevent the problem. He also shows that pain can be relieved by recompression. Bert provides the link between Boyle's 17th century observation of decompression sickness in a viper and the symptoms of compressed air workers first recorded in the 19th century.

1908 (surface air; scuba). In 1906, the British Government asks *John Scott Haldane*, an eminent Scottish physiologist, to do research in the prevention of decompression sickness. Two years later Haldane, *Arthur E. Boycott* and *Guybon C. Damant*, publish their landmark paper on decompression sickness (from hyperbaric experiments done on goats). "The Prevention of Compressed-Air Illness" lays the groundwork for staged decompression. Tables based on this work are soon adopted by the British Royal Navy and later the United States Navy, and save many divers from the bends. (See Section J)

1912 (surface air; scuba). The U.S. Navy tests tables published by Boycott, Damant and Haldane.

1917 (surface air). The U.S. Bureau of Construction & Repair first introduces the Mark V Diving Helmet. When attached to a deep sea dress and umbilical, the Mark V becomes the underwater work horse for decades to come. It is used for "practically all salvage work undertaken during World War II...the MK V Diving Helmet becomes the standard U.S. Navy Diving equipment until succeeded by the MK12 in 1980." (U.S. Navy Diving Manual). "So sound was its design that very few modifications were ever incorporated, and recent models vary only slightly from the 1917 version." (Leaney 1993)

1920s (surface air; scuba). Research is begun in United States into the use of helium-oxygen mixtures for deep dives. To the beginning of World War II, the U.S. maintains a monopoly on helium.

1924 (surface air; scuba). First helium-oxygen experimental dives are conducted by U.S. Navy and Bureau of Mines.

1930 (vessel). *William Beebe*, a diving pioneer and "oceanographic naturalist" descends 1426 feet in a round, 4'9" bathysphere; it is attached to a barge by a 7/8" non-twisting steel cable to the mother ship. Of this dive Beebe later writes:

...There came to me at that instant [1426 feet down] a tremendous wave of emotion, a real appreciation of what was momentarily almost superhuman, cosmic, of the whole situation; our barge slowly rolling high overhead in the blazing sunlight, like the merest chip in the midst of the ocean, the long cobweb of cable leading down through the spectrum to our lonely sphere, where, sealed tight, two conscious human beings sat and peered into the abysmal darkness as we dangled in mid-water, isolated as a lost planet in outermost space.

1930s (breath-hold). *Guy Gilpatric*, an American ex-aviator living in southern France, pioneers use of rubber goggles with glass lenses for skin diving. By the mid-1930s, face masks, fins, and snorkels are in common use. Fins are patented by a Frenchman, *Louis de Corlieu*, in 1933 (called "Swimming Propellers") and later popularized world-wide by an American entrepreneur, *Owen Churchill* (see 1940). The modern mask (covering eyes and nose, as opposed to simple eye goggles), evolves from the ideas of various people, including the Russian *Alec Kramarenko*, and the Frenchmen *Yves Le Prieur* and *Maxime Forjot*. In 1934 Gilpatric writes of his Mediterranean exploits for *The Saturday Evening Post*, and in **1938**

publishes *The Compleat Goggler*, the first book on amateur diving and hunting. Among the book's readers: a French naval lieutenant named Jacques Cousteau.

1933 (breath-hold). First sport divers club is started in California, called the Bottom Scratchers; a year later an amateur diving group, Club des Sous-l'Eau, is founded in Paris. A primary purpose of these and similar clubs is underwater spear fishing.

1933 (scuba). French navy captain *Yves Le Prieur* modifies the Rouquayrol-Denayrouse invention by combining a specially designed demand valve with a high pressure air tank (1500 psi) to give the diver complete freedom from restricting hoses and lines. The apparatus contains no regulator; the diver receives a breath of fresh air by opening a tap, while exhaled air escapes into the water under the edge of the diver's mask. (In the late 1930s Cousteau used this apparatus but, as he wrote in *The Silent World*, "the continuous discharge of air allowed only short submersions.") In 1935 Le Prieur's SCUBA is adopted by the French navy.

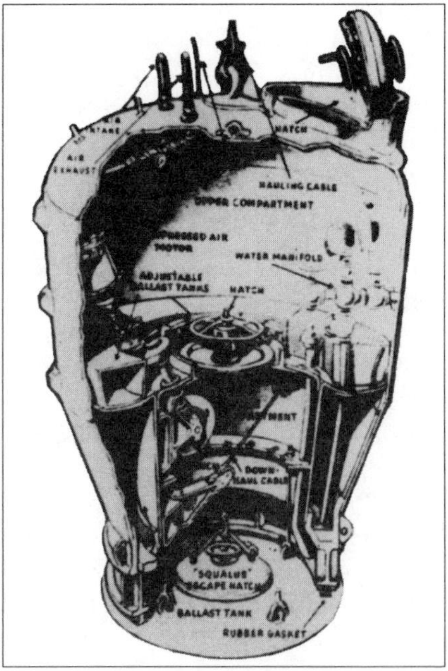

Figure 4. Vertical cross section of the McCann-Erickson Rescue Chamber. (Courtesy U.S. Navy Diving Manual.)

1934 (vessel). On August 15 *William Beebe* and *Otis Barton* descend 3028 feet in a bathysphere near Bermuda. This dive sets a depth record that remains unbroken for 14 years.

1936 (scuba). Le Prieur founds the world's first SCUBA diving club, called the "Club of Divers and Underwater Life."

1938 (surface air; scuba). *Edgar End* and *Max Nohl* make the first intentional saturation dive, spending 27 hours at a depth of 101 feet in a Milwaukee hospital hyperbaric chamber. Decompression takes five hours and one of the divers (Nohl) suffers the bends.

1939 (vessel). The first completely successful rescue of submarine-trapped men is carried out. On May 23 the *USS Squalus*, a new 310-foot submarine, sinks in 243 feet of water during a checkout dive in the North Atlantic. Twenty-six of the crew die instantly in the flooded aft compartments. The forward, unflooded area holds 33 men (including the captain) with enough air and water to last several days. Within hours the largest submarine rescue in history is underway. By midnight of May 25 all 33 men are rescued by a new diving bell, the *McCann-Erickson* Rescue Chamber. The chamber fits over an escape hatch on the submarine; when the chamber and submarine hatches are opened the men enter the bell under one atmosphere of pressure. Four separate trips are used to rescue the men. The submarine is later salvaged and renovated, and enters World War II duty as the *USS Sailfish*.

1940 (breath-hold; scuba). First year of production of Owen Churchill's swim fins. Initially, only 946 pairs are sold, but in later years production increases substantially, and tens of thousands are sold to the Allied forces.

1941-1944 (scuba). During World War II Italian divers, working out of midget submarines, use closed circuit scuba equipment to place explosives under British naval and merchant marine ships. Later in the war the British adopt this technology to sink German battleship *Tirpitz*.

1942-43 (scuba). *Jacques-Yves Cousteau* (a French naval lieutenant) and *Emile Gagnan* (an engineer for Air Liquide, a Parisian natural gas company) work together to redesign a car regulator that will automatically provide compressed air to a diver on his slightest intake of breath. (Prior to this date, all self-contained apparatus still in use supplied air continuously, or had to be manually turned on and off. For unclear reasons, the

19th century demand regulator of Rouquayrol-Denayrouse had long been abandoned.) Cousteau and Gagnan attach their new demand valve regulator to hoses, a mouthpiece and a pair of compressed air tanks. In January 1943 Cousteau tests the unit in the cold Marne River outside Paris. After a modification (placing the intake and exhaust valves at the same level), they patent the Aqua Lung. One of Cousteau's biographers later writes:

The Gagnan-Cousteau regulator fundamentally altered diving. Its simple design and solid construction provided a reliable and low-cost unit for sport diving. Air Liquide put the equipment into commercial production, but it couldn't keep up with the demand. Competitors tried to capture the growing market by producing imitations or making slight adjustments... The devices revolutionized man's perception of the planet. Not unlike the Portuguese, Spanish, and Chinese explorers of the fifteenth century who doubled their knowledge of the size of the world, Cousteau and Gagnan helped open a vast portion of the globe to human exploration. They offered the opportunity for extensive undersea investigation to enthusiastic scientists, engineers, and sportsmen. (Munson, 1989; page 41)

Summer and fall 1943 (scuba). Cousteau and two close friends, *Frédéric Dumas* and *Philippe Tailliez*, make over five hundred dives with the aqualung, gradually increasing the depths to which they plunge. They have developed the first workable, open-circuit demand-type scuba apparatus. In October Dumas, in a carefully planned dive, descends to 210 feet in the Mediterranean Sea and experiences *l'ivresse des grandes profondeurs* - "rapture of the great depths."

1946 (scuba). Cousteau's Aqua Lung is marketed commercially in France. (It is marketed in Great Britain in 1950, Canada in 1951 and the USA in 1952.)

1947 (scuba). In August, Dumas makes a record dive with the Aqua Lung to 307 feet in the Mediterranean Sea.

1948 (vessel). Otis Barton descends in a modified bathysphere to a depth of 4500 feet, off the coast of California.

1950 (scuba). Despite the technical success of the aqua lung, it has yet to catch on in the U.S. So far only 10 aqua lung units have been shipped to the U.S. because, the distributor tells Cousteau, "the market is saturated."

1950s (vessel). Famed Swiss balloonist *August Picard* turns his attention to the deep sea. With son Jacques, he pioneers a new type of vessel called the bathyscaphe (deep boat). The bathyscaphe is completely self-contained (not tethered to the surface), and designed to go deeper than any bathysphere. On February 15, 1954, off the coast of French West Africa, a bathyscaphe containing *Georges S. Houot* and *Pierre-Henri Willm* exceeds Barton's 1948 diving record, reaching a depth of 13,287 feet.

1950s (breath-hold; scuba). The sport of diving gradually changes from breath-hold to mainly scuba. Dive stores open up around the U.S.

1951 (breath-hold; scuba). The first issue of *Skin Diver Magazine* appears in December.

1953 (scuba). *The Silent World* is published. Written in English by Jacques Cousteau, with the assistance of Frédéric Dumas, the book chronicles the development and early testing of the Cousteau-Gagnan Aqua Lung.

1957 (scuba). First segment of *Sea Hunt* airs on television, starring *Lloyd Bridges* as Mike Hunt, underwater adventurer. The series inspires thousands of people to take up scuba diving.

1959 (scuba). YMCA begins the first nationally organized course for scuba certification.

1960 (vessel). On January 23, *Jacques Picard* and Navy lieutenant *Don Walsh* descend to 35,820 feet (10,916 meters, 6.78 miles) in the August Picard-designed, Swiss-built, US Navy-owned bathyscaphe *Trieste*. This dive takes place in the Pacific Ocean's Mariana Trench, 250 miles southwest of Guam, one of the deepest parts of the world ocean. Water pressure at this depth is 16,883 psi, temperature 37.4°F. Picard observes what he later calls "a flatfish at the very nadir of the earth" but no specimens can be collected. Trieste leaves the surface at 8:22 a.m., reaches maximum depth at 1:10 p.m. and surfaces at 4:30 p.m. No one will ever go deeper (unless, of course, oceanographers discover a deeper spot than the Mariana trench).

1960s (scuba). As accident rates for scuba divers climb, the first national training agencies are formed to train and certify divers; NAUI is formed in 1960, PADI in 1966.

1962 (surface air; scuba). Beginning in 1962 several experiments are conducted whereby people live in underwater habitats, leaving the habitat for exploration (using scuba equipment) and returning for sleeping, eating and relaxing. The habitats are supplied by compressed air from the surface. The first such experiment, Conshelf (Continental Shelf) One, takes place in September 1962. Under the watchful eye of Jacques Cousteau and his team, *Albert Falco* and *Claude Wesley* spend seven days under 33 feet of water near Marseilles, in a habitat they name Diogenes. *Diogenes was an enormous Aqua-lung into which Falco and Wesley retreated for warmth and food, sleep and hygiene. It was like the air bubble that a water spider takes down to sustain itself in its activities beneath the surface. For our men, the five daily hours outside were more important than the nineteen hours within.* (Cousteau 1963)

1963-1965 (surface air; scuba). In 1963, eight divers live in Conshelf Two under the Red Sea for a month. Other habitats of this period: Sealab I (1964); Sealab II (1965); and Conshelf Three (1965), in which former astronaut *Scott Carpenter* and other divers spend a month at 60 meters off the coast of southern France.

1967 (scuba). PADI, Professional Association of Diving Instructors, trains 3226 divers in its first year of operation.

1968 (scuba). On October 14, *John J. Gruener* and *R. Neal Watson* dive to 437 feet breathing compressed air, off coast of Grand Bahama Island. This record is not broken until 1990 (see Diving Odds N' Ends).

1970s (scuba). Important advances relating to scuba safety that began in the 1960s become widely implemented in the 1970s, including: adoption of certification cards to indicate a minimum level of training and as a requirement for tank refills and rental of scuba equipment; change from J-valve reserve systems to non-reserve K valves and adoption of submersible pressure gauges; adoption of the buoyancy compensator and single hose regulators as essential pieces of diving equipment (replacing the dual hose, non-BC equipment initially in widespread use).

1980 (scuba). Divers Alert Network is founded at Duke University as a non-profit organization to promote safe diving.

1981 (scuba). Record 2250 foot-dive is made in a Duke Medical Center chamber. *Stephen Porter, Len Whitlock* and *Erik Kramer* live in the eight-foot diameter spherical chamber for 43 days, breathing a mixture of nitrogen, oxygen and helium. They beat their own previous record set in 1980.

1983 (scuba). The first commercially available dive computer, the Orca Edge, is introduced. In the next decade many manufacturers market dive computers, and they become common equipment among recreational divers.

1985 (vessel). U.S.-French team headed by Woods Hole researcher, *Robert Ballard*, using a remote controlled camera attached to the mother ship, finds the wreck of the *Titanic*. The ship sits broken into two sections at 12,500 feet depth, some 400 miles northeast of New York. On April 15, 1912, five days into its maiden voyage, *Titanic* hit an iceberg and sank in less than three hours. At the time she was the largest ship in the world. A total of 1522 passengers and crew died. Since 1985 both the U.S. and France have revisited the site, and the French have recovered artifacts from the ship.

1993 (scuba). The 50th anniversary of the invention of modern scuba diving is celebrated around the world. PADI, the largest of the national training agencies, certifies 515,000 new divers worldwide.

1990s (scuba). An estimated 500,000 new scuba divers are certified yearly in the U.S., new scuba magazines form, dive computers proliferate, new liveaboards ply the waters and scuba travel is transformed into a big business. In North America alone recreational diving becomes a multi-billion dollar industry. At the same time there is expansion of "technical diving" - diving by non-professionals who use advanced technology, including mixed gases, full face masks, underwater voice communication, propulsion systems, etc.

REFERENCES AND BIBLIOGRAPHY
(For both SECTION A and DIVING ODDS N' ENDS)

Quoted sources and general references are listed by section or sections, in alphabetical order. An asterisk indicates references that are especially recommended. Medical textbooks and journal articles can be obtained from most public libraries via inter-library loan. For a list of companies that distribute free catalogs of diving books and videos, see Section U.

Ballard RD. Epilogue for *Titanic*. National Geographic, Vol. 172, October 1987, page 454.

Brylske A. Brief History of Diving, Parts I and II. *Dive Training Magazine*. Aug. & Sept. 1994.

Cardone B, editor. *The Fireside Diver*. Menasha Ridge Press, Birmingham, 1992.

Carlisle N. *Riches of the Sea*. Sterling Publishing Co., New York, 1967.

*Cousteau JY and Dumas F. *The Silent World*. Ballantine Books, New York, 1953.

Cousteau JY, with Dugan J. *The Living Sea*. Harper & Row, New York, 1963.

Cousteau JY, Dugan J. *World Without Sun*. Harper & Row, New York, 1965.

Crichton M. *Spere*. Alfred A. Knopf, New York, 1987.

Cussler C. *Pacific Vortex*. Bantam Books, New York, 1982.

Davis J. Bikini's Silver Lining. NY Times Magazine, May 1, 1994. Pg. 43.

DeLoach N. Eagles Fly Alone. aquaCorps N8, 1994; page 65.

Dugan J. *Man Under the Sea*. Harper & Brothers, New York, 1956.

*Ellis RE. *The Book of Sharks*. Alfred A. Knopf, New York, 1989.

*Ellis RE, McCosker JE. *Great White Shark*. HarperCollins Publishers, New York, 1991.

Ellis RE. *Monsters of the Sea*. Alfred A. Knopf, New York, 1994.

Exley S. Max Head Room. aquaCorps N7, 1994; pages 64-65.

Gilliam B, Von Maier R. History of Diving, in *Deep Diving. An Advanced Guide to Physiology, Procedures and Systems*. Watersport Publishing, Inc. San Diego; 1992.

Gilpatric G. The Compleat Goggler. Saturday Evening Post, October 6, 1934, p. 10.

Groves D. *The Oceans. A Book of Questions and Answers*. John Wiley & Sons. New York, 1989.

Guinness Book of Records, Bantam Books, New York. Published annually.

Hamilton B, Daughtery G, Kristovich A. What happened to Sheck Exley? Pressure November/December 1994 (part 1) and January/February 1995 (part 2).

Hamner WM. Australia's Box Jellyfish. A Killer Down Under. National Geographic 86:2, August, 1994; p. 116.

*Hendrickson R. *The Ocean Almanac*. Doubleday, New York, 1984.

Hong, et. al. Daily diving pattern of Korean and Japanese breath-hold divers (ama). Undersea Biomedical Research 1991;18:433-443.

Holliday L. *Coral Reefs*. Tetra Press, Morris Plains, NJ, 1989.

Huehner JC. The Call of the Deep. The Cleveland Plain Dealer, August 2, 1994, page 1.

Leaney L. The Mark V Column. Historical Diver, No. 2, Winter 1993; p. 17.

*Madsen A. *Cousteau. An Unauthorized Biography*. Beaufort Books Publishers, New York, 1986. Manion DJ: IANTD Journal, 9628 N.E. 2nd Avenue, Suite D, Miami Shores, Florida 33138-2767; issue of May-July 1994, page 8.

Martin M, Porter M. *Video Movie Guide 1995*. Ballantine Books, New York, 1994.

Marx RF, with Marx J. *The Search for Sunken Treasure. Exploring the World's Great Shipwrecks*. Key-Porter Books, Toronto, 1993.

Marx RF. *Into the Deep*. Van Nostrand Reinhold, New York, 1978.

*Marx RF. *The History of Underwater Exploration*. Dover Publications, Inc., New York, 1990.

*McCullough D. *The Great Bridge. The Epic Story of the Building of the Brooklyn Bridge*. Simon and Schuster, New York, 1972.

*Munson R. *Cousteau: the Captain and His World*. Wm. Morrow & Co., New York, 1989.

Nichols G. History of Diving, in *Alert Diver*, Divers Alert Network, May/June 1993.

Protasio J. *To the Bottom of the Sea. True Accounts of Major Ship Disasters*. Carol Publishing Group, New York, 1990.

Roessler C. *Underwater Wilderness: Life Around the Great Reefs*. Chanticleer Press, New York, 1986.

*Sammon R. *Seven Underwater Wonders of the World*. Thomasson-Grant, Inc. Charlottesville, VA, 1992.

Sheard B. *Beyond Sport Diving! Exploring the Deepwater Shipwrecks of the Atlantic*. Menasha Ridge Press, Birmingham, AL, 1991.

Sterba JP. Klutzy Scuba Divers Love the Coral Reefs A Bit Too Vigorously. Wall Street Journal, May 7, 1993. Page 1.

Talyor MR. Deep, Dark and Deadly. The perils of cave diving didn't spare even the sport's greatest star. Sports Illustrated, Vol 81, No. 14, October 3, 1994.

Verne J. *20,000 Leagues Under the Sea*. 1925; Charles Scribner's Sons, New York

Whittingham. *The Rand McNally Almanac of Adventure*. Rand McNally, Chicago, 1982.

Zumrick J. Sheck Exley: Preliminary Accident Report. aquaCorps N8, 994; page 71.

DIVING ODDS N' ENDS

Scuba in Jules Verne's *20,000 Leagues Under The Sea*

A limited scuba apparatus was developed by Frenchmen Rouquayrol and Denayrouse in 1865 (see Figure 3). Verne was aware of this invention and incorporated it into his 1870 novel. Although the actual Rouquayrol-Denay-rouse invention could only function as true scuba (i.e., untethered) for a few minutes at a time, Verne extended this to several hours in his novel. Inside the submarine Nautilus, just prior to a long underwater hike using the scuba apparatus, Captain Nemo explains how it works to Professor Aronnax, a French naturalist (and the novel's narrator):

"You know as well as I do, Professor, that man can live underwater, providing he carries with him a sufficient supply of breathable air. In submarine works, the workman, clad in an impervious dress, with his head in a metal helmet, receives air from above by means of forcing pumps and regulators."

"That is a diving apparatus," said I.

"Just so, but under these conditions the man is not at liberty; he is attached to the pump which sends him air through an india-rubber tube, and if we were obliged to be thus held to the Nautilus, we could not go far."

"And the means of getting free?"

"It is to use the Rouquayrol apparatus, invented by two of your own country-men, which I have brought to perfection for my own use, and which will allow you to risk yourself under these new physiological conditions, without any organ whatever suffering. It consists of a reservoir of thick iron plates, in which I store the air under a pressure of fifty atmospheres. This reservoir is fixed on the back by means of braces, like a soldier's knapsack. Its upper part forms a box in which the air is kept by means of a bellows, and therefore cannot escape unless at its normal tension. In the Rouquayrol apparatus such as we use, two india-rubber pipes leave this box and join a sort of tent which holds the nose and mouth; one is to introduce fresh air, the other to let out the foul, and the tongue closes one or the other according to the wants of the respirator. But I, in encountering great pressures at the bottom of the sea, was obliged to shut my head, like that of a diver, in a ball of copper; and it is to this ball of copper that the two pipes, the inspirator and the expirator, open."

"Perfectly, Captain Nemo; but the air that you carry with you must soon be used; when it only contains fifteen per cent. of oxygen, it is no longer fit to breathe."

"Right! but I told you, M. Aronnax, that the pumps of the Nautilus allow me to store the air under considerable pressure and on these conditions the reservoir of the apparatus can furnish breathable air for nine or ten hours."

"I have no further objections to make," I answered.

Recreational Scuba Diving: An Overview

WHAT DOES 'SCUBA' STAND FOR?

Scuba is an acronym for 'self-contained underwater breathing apparatus.' There are several ways one can go underwater (breath-hold, helmet diving, submarine, etc.). "Diving with scuba" signifies using apparatus that is completely carried by the diver and not connected to the surface, hence self-contained.

HOW POPULAR IS SCUBA DIVING?

An estimated 2.5-3.5 million Americans participate in recreational scuba diving. Another 500 thousand become certified each year in the United States. In the early days of scuba diving (roughly 1950-1970), participants were predominately young men. Today the sport is enjoyed by people in all age groups and both sexes. And why not? Just about any teenager or adult who enjoys the water and can swim, and who does not have heart or lung impairment, can learn to scuba dive. It does not take great physical strength or unusual exercise tolerance. All it takes is the desire, plus some basic classroom and in-water training.

Scuba originally began with military and commercial applications, where it is still employed. However, by far its widest use, in terms of number of participants, is recreational. Recreational scuba today is like other any other sport that requires specialized equipment and training, such as snow skiing, sailing, mountain climbing and horseback riding. This section will provide an overview of recreational scuba diving, and explain how it differs from other forms of diving with scuba equipment.

WHAT MAKES UP SCUBA EQUIPMENT?

Scuba apparatus for the recreational diver consists of (Figure 1):
- a tank of compressed air carried by the diver on his or her back.
- a first stage regulator attached to the tank that serves to lower air pressure delivered to the diver.
- a second stage demand regulator and mouthpiece, that delivers air on inhalation and closes on exhalation.

Figure 1. Front and side view of scuba diver equipped ready to jump into the water. She is carrying a compressed air tank, and is wearing a buoyancy compensator (BC), mask with snorkel, and fins. Her mouthpiece is attached to the second stage regulator, and it in turn is attached by hose to the first stage regulator on top of the tank. The alternate second stage regulator is shown over her left arm. Note: this diver is not wearing a weight belt; weights are carried inside her BC.

- a face mask that covers the diver's eyes and nose, to allow for both underwater vision and equalization of air pressure within the mask.
- an extra second stage regulator and mouthpiece, carried by the diver in case of emergency (when attached to a long hose, this extra second stage is called an octopus).
- two submersible gauges, one to display an accurate depth and the other to show how much air remains in the tank (or, alternatively, a single gauge that combines both functions, e.g., as part of a dive computer).
- an inflatable vest (buoyancy compensator, BC) worn to provide a means of establishing positive buoyancy when needed.
- a weight belt and weights (or some other type of weight system), worn to compensate for the positive buoyancy of the diver and scuba apparatus.
- fins to facilitate self-propulsion in the water.
- a wet suit or other type of body protection to prevent hypothermia (and secondarily to prevent cuts and abrasions underwater); in cold water, gloves and a hood may be worn for hypothermia protection also.

Optional equipment for scuba diving numbers many items, such as a snorkel, dive knife, small tank of extra air, dive computer, compass, dive lights, writing slate, whistle, and inflatable signaling device. Depending on the circumstances (e.g., lights for night diving, a snorkel for surface swimming) some of these items may at times be essential, but they are not part of basic scuba equipment.

With the basic scuba equipment, a qualified diver can safely remain underwater for anywhere from a few minutes to over two hours; the time limit for any given dive will depend on the depth of that dive, the rate of air consumption, and the profile of any dives made within the previous 6-12 hours.

WHAT IS SCUBA CERTIFICATION?

Potential hazards that every scuba diver must be aware of include decompression sickness, air embolism, hypothermia, physical exhaustion, injuries from marine life, boating accidents, sunburn, and out-of-air catastrophes. Despite the list of potential problems, recreational diving is actually a safe sport if the diver is healthy and trained properly, each dive is carefully planned and dive limits are followed. The most serious problems, and how to avoid them, are covered in the entry level scuba course.

The entry level course, also known as 'basic open water' or 'basic certification,' takes about 30 hours. About 10 hours is spent in classroom instruction and the remainder in supervised pool and open water diving. 'Open water' means a natural body of water open to the sky. Upon completion, a certification or 'C' card is issued. The C card contains the new diver's picture, date of course completion and signature of the instructor. The basic open water course is fairly standard and is given under the auspices of one of several national training agencies (see Section S).

Many people are first exposed to scuba through the "resort course." This is an introductory lesson offered at a resort or on a cruise, and is always taught by an instructor (i.e., one who is also qualified to teach the standard open water course). The resort course is highly variable; it may include only a brief lecture on a crowded bus on the way to the dive site, or a leisurely morning pool session before the afternoon open water dive (I have seen both methods). Because the resort course contains no textbook and very little in the way of theory or skills testing, it does not certify for independent diving. It is also good only for that resort and for the time you are a guest there. If you return six months or a year later to the same resort, you would have to start all over with another resort course. (One exception is the Club Med resort course, which offers 'Club Med Certification.' The student completing a Club Med resort course can dive at any other Club Med around the world, but always with a Club Med instructor and after an initial checkout dive.)

Resort courses are fine for introduction to scuba, but anyone who has enjoyed the experience is encouraged to take a standard certification course and learn the necessary skills and theory. Standard certification is also more practical. The C card allows one to rent or buy scuba equipment anywhere in the world, and to engage in recreational diving without supervision by an instructor.

The certification process distinguishes recreational scuba diving from most other sports that use specialized equipment (e.g., snow skiing, mountain climbing). Without a C card (i.e., without certification) one should not go scuba diving (unless accompanied by a professional scuba instructor).

WHO TEACHES SCUBA?

In college the lowest academic rank is the "instructor," usually someone in graduate school who is assigned to teach and work under a "professor." In the world of scuba, the instructor is the *highest* level. A scuba instructor is the only person trained and qualified to teach scuba diving. He or she works under the auspices of one of the national scuba training agencies (see Section S). The scuba instructor can be assisted by other scuba professionals who are in training to become a scuba instructor; they may have the title of dive master (the entry level position for a scuba professional) or assistant instructor. However, only someone with instructor status can teach the basic open water course.

HOW DOES RECREATIONAL SCUBA DIVING DIFFER FROM OTHER FORMS OF SCUBA DIVING?

Diving was revolutionized by the development of a workable demand regulator, co-invented in 1943 by Jacques Cousteau and Emil Gagnan. The "sport" of scuba diving did not catch on for another 10 years. Today the greatest use of scuba equipment is for recreational diving. Recreational scuba diving, as taught by national certifying agencies, is defined as diving that:

- Uses only compressed air as the breathing mixture.
- Is never done solo.
- Does not exceed a depth of 130 feet.
- Has a depth-time profile not requiring a decompression stop; if necessary one can ascend to the surface without stopping.
- Does not require specialized training beyond the basic open water course.

Scuba equipment is also widely employed by two other types of divers, loosely categorized as "professional" and "technical." By definition, these two groups are not constrained by the RSD criteria listed above.

Professional diving is done for military, governmental, commercial, or scientific purposes. Professional divers are paid to dive. They have a specific mission for each dive, e.g., lay a mine or recover a bomb (military), look for a body or a weapon (law enforcement agency), explore for oil (commercial), map an ancient wreck or examine a new species of fish (scientific).

Technical diving is the term for all diving that exceeds recreational limits but is not engaged in for profit. Although many, if not most, technical divers consider themselves involved in a recreational activity, the nature of their diving and type of equipment used exceed the boundaries of RSD. To be sure, there is not universal agreement on what constitutes technical diving, and any attempt to define it tends to degenerate into heated discussion and semantics. For the novice or basic open water diver, the following activities can be considered to be "technical diving."

THE REALM OF TECHNICAL DIVING

- cave diving
- ice diving
- very deep diving (to greater than 130 feet)
- mixed-gas diving (using gas mixtures other than air, such as nitrox or trimix)
- deep-penetration wreck diving
- diving with specialized life-support equipment (e.g., O_2 re-breathers)

Much of technical diving is taught by agencies other than the national open water certification agencies. However, recently PADI and other national agencies became involved in nitrox certification, although the activity is still not considered part of basic open water 'recreational diving.' Still, the trend is to expand the envelope of technology to encompass more and more divers, and it is conceivable that some of today's advanced technology (e.g., rebreathers) will one day be routinely used by open water recreational divers. Clearly, the distinction between 'technical' and 'recreational diving' is becoming less distinct over time. (No matter how diving activities are classified, no one should engage in any diving activity unless certified in that activity or else supervised by a qualified instructor.)

WHAT IS THE BUDDY SYSTEM?

RSD requires that each diver be accompanied underwater by a buddy who can share air or provide other assistance. Scuba apparatus is designed to carry an extra demand regulator. This is required in case one diver runs out of air and has to share a single tank with his or her buddy. Ideally, the buddies should have similar training and skill levels; it does no good to have a buddy who dives deeper or stays down longer than you do. Buddies should stay close together and always be aware of each other's location.

WHY IS 130 FEET THE MAXIMUM DEPTH IN RECREATIONAL DIVING?

The 130 foot limit is an arbitrary depth originally adopted by the U.S. Navy because it gave navy divers about 10 minutes of bottom time on compressed air; going any deeper on air made no sense to the Navy because the time available to do useful work was simply too short. As with many diving issues in the early days of scuba (e.g., the 'no decompression' limits), the Navy standard was also adopted by the recreational training agencies.

Some experienced recreational divers do go deeper than 130 feet, and yet still stay within no decompression limits. However, since the risks of the bends, running out of air, and nitrogen narcosis increase as you go deeper, the training agencies feel that some arbitrary limit must be set and have stayed with 130 feet. Thus, although one can dive deeper and stay within no decompression limits, diving deeper than 130 feet a) is not taught by the recreational training agencies, and b) must be undertaken with great care and an understanding of the increased risks.

WHAT IS MANDATORY DECOMPRESSION AND WHY IS IT NOT PART OF RECREATIONAL SCUBA DIVING?

"Decompression" always occurs when we go from a higher to a lower ambient pressure. Thus *all* compressed gas diving is decompression diving. When recreational diving is referred to as "no decompression diving" it really means "no *mandatory decompression stop* diving." A *decompression stop* should never be necessary within the guidelines of RSD.

A decompression stop is often necessary in dives deeper or longer than allowed in RSD; it provides time for some of the excess nitrogen that entered the tissues to "gas off " (diffuse into the blood stream and then be ventilated out by the lungs), thereby minimizing risk of decompression sickness (DCS). Based on experiments, plus much trial and error experience, the amount of excess nitrogen remaining in the tissues after a planned, mandatory decompression stop should not cause DCS.

Since professional and technical divers often spend longer periods underwater and/or dive deeper than recreational divers, they must know when to stop on ascent and how long to wait before surfacing. By contrast, each recreational dive is planned so that the diver can ascend *continuously* to the surface without encountering decompression sickness; the diver is still decompressing on the way up, but doesn't have to stop to allow further decompression. The basic assumption is that diving is inherently made safer by avoiding dives that require decompression stops. This is both the philosophy and practice of recreational diving today.

The "no decompression stop" limits in RSD are based on maximum depth, time underwater, and extent of any preceding dives, all factors which directly affect tissue nitrogen uptake. The limits are set in dive tables known to every certified diver, and are incorporated into all dive computers.

Excess nitrogen, which enters tissues due to the increased ambient pressure underwater, determines the "no decompression stop" limits. A non-repetitive dive (no previous dive within a specified time period, typically 6-12 hours) to 130 feet has an allowable "actual bottom time" (measured from the time dive commences to start of ascent) of only about 5-10 minutes for a dive to 130 feet. Beyond this brief time span the diver risks developing decompression sickness from a continuous ascent. In contrast, at 35 feet, on a non-repetitive dive, the 'no decompression' bottom time is about 205 minutes.

Although RSD is always planned for *no decompression stop required*, it is routine practice to make a 3 to 5 minute "safety stop" at 15 feet before surfacing from any dive deeper than about 40 feet. This *is* a decompression stop but it *is not* mandatory, just added for extra safety to the dive; hence the term safety stop. In theory, when adhering to the recreational diving tables one should not experience DCS if a safety stop is not made. Nonetheless, all dives deeper than about 40 feet should incorporate a safety stop, and it is universally practiced. If any dive *requires* a decompression stop for any reason, it has exceeded the limits of recreational diving.

TEST YOUR UNDERSTANDING

1. The reason RSD is limited to 130 feet is:
   a. compressed air won't support a diver below that level.
   b. there is not much to see below 130 feet.
   c. nitrogen narcosis begins to appear at that depth.
   d. decompression stop becomes mandatory.
   e. none of the above.

2. Which of the following items is(are) never *used while* scuba diving.

   a. eye goggles   c. snorkel
   b. ear plugs   d. gloves

3. If a diver inadvertently exceeds the recreational dive limits he should:

   a. prolong the safety stop, air permitting.
   b. surface and ask the divemaster/instructor what to do.
   c. begin exercising underwater to increase nitrogen off loading.
   d. not worry about it, and make the usual safety stop.

4. A diver goes to 50 feet depth for 30 minutes, then begins her ascent, stopping at 15 feet for three minutes. True or false: this is a decompression stop to lessen the risk of developing the bends.

5. True or false: a divemaster is qualified to teach the basic scuba certification course.

ARE THERE DIFFERENT LEVELS OF RECREATIONAL DIVING?

Within the universe of recreational diving there are many levels, based on extent of training, experience, or both. I have already commented on the resort course, which is not formal scuba training but just an introductory scuba experience. The following paragraphs pertain to the certified diver.

Training. One can take several courses beyond basic open water, and they can be divided into two "tracks." The first track is for people who want more training but have no intention of ever teaching scuba. With such courses as advanced diving, stress and rescue, underwater photography, ice diving, and deeper diving (60-130 feet), one can gain additional knowledge and skills, all under the purview of recreational diving.

The second track is for people who plan to turn professional (within the recreational purview) and teach scuba. They will take courses leading up to the instructor level (advanced diving, stress and rescue, divemaster, assistant instructor, instructor). Once an individual achieves instructor level he or she is a full-fledged professional within recreational scuba and can teach the basic certification course.

Unless they have taken special training, scuba instructors are not trained to exceed the recreational limits. Thus they are not technical divers and would need further training to do mixed gas diving, for example. Of course many scuba instructors do obtain training in these and other technical diving skills.

Experience. Most recreational divers never take more than the basic open water course. However, after making many dives over the years they become highly experienced and adept in all the important skills. In recent years scuba agencies have developed a way to recognize the more experienced divers, by creating "dive cards" showing the number of dives obtained, in round numbers. Thus, with proper documentation you can get a card that shows you have done anywhere from 50 to 5000 lifetime dives. The utility of this type of card is that it can quickly show your level of experience, such as when you go to rent equipment or sign on for a boat dive. Experience counts for much in scuba diving (as with any activity), and the cards are a way of acknowledging this.

WHAT IS SPORT SURFACE-SUPPLIED COMPRESSED AIR DIVING AND HOW DOES IT DIFFER FROM SCUBA?

As its name indicates, sport surface-supplied compressed air diving (sometimes shortened to 'sport surface-supplied air,' SSSA) separates the compressed air source from the diver. For this reason it is not "scuba," which is self-contained (the scuba diver always carries his/her own air source). SSSA uses a small gasoline-or electric-powered air compressor that can sit on a boat, dock or a floating inner tube, so it can literally go to any dive site and remain over the heads of the divers (Figure 2). The compressor can provide air to more than one diver at the same time.

Each SSSA diver is tethered to the compressed air source by a long hose. The entire apparatus is sometimes called a *hookah*, after the

Egyptian term for a pipe that cools water, but "surface-supplied compressed air" is the more correct term. At the end of each hose is a second stage regulator and mouth-piece, just like in scuba diving; exhaled air is expelled into the water. For recreational divers this technique has been pioneered by Brownie's Third Lung, Ft. Lauderdale, FL (1-800-327-0412).

SSSA diving is limited by the strength of the air compressor, the length of the hose and, as in scuba, the level of diver training. As sold by Brownies, each unit serves at least two divers; some can serve three or four divers at 30 feet. Other units allow deeper diving, up to 90 feet for two divers. In principle SSSA diving is the same as professional helmet diving, except that the depths are generally less, no helmet is worn by the diver, only compressed air is used (professionals may used mixed gases), and the amount of surface support (i.e., other people on the surface) may be minimal to none. The box on the next page lists advantages and disadvantages of SSSA compared to scuba.

SSSA diving is very popular in some areas. It is particularly useful for long, shallow, underwater tasks, such as lobster hunting, fish harvesting, cleaning a boat bottom, or examining a shallow wreck that doesn't require penetration.

Figure 2. Air compressor inside rubber tube, as used for surface-supplied compressed air diving for two people. (Courtesy Brownies' Third Lung.)

SSSA vs. Scuba

Principal advantages of SSSA diving

- Can provide unlimited supply of compressed air.
- Allows diving to full limit of dive tables without running out of air; only small amount of gasoline required for dives that would otherwise require several tank refills.
- Eliminates need to carry a heavy tank into the water.
- Eliminates need for first stage regulator.
- Each system designed to be used by at least two divers, fostering buddy system; buddy always close by and connected.
- Since there is no tank and therefore no changing tank pressure, diver's buoyancy tends to stay constant throughout dive.

Principal disadvantages of SSSA diving

- Requires purchase and maintenance of air compressor; requires use of hydrocarbon fuels (or access to source of electricity).
- Limited mobility underwater.
- Limited depths (depending on compressor size).
- Possible compressor failure; SSSA diver often encouraged to carry a small tank of compressed air for emergency surfacing.
- Cannot be used for wall or cave diving, or penetration wreck diving.
- Equipment is not resort based (as is scuba), so one usually has to travel with the compressor or make special arrangements to have it available.
- Unlimited air supply requires special diligence not to exceed dive table limits.

Although SSSA divers may stay shallow, and hence minimize the risk of DCS, they are still under the same risk of barotrauma inherent in all compressed air diving. For this reason people engaging in SSSA diving should be properly trained and certified. Unlike scuba, however, some proprietors allow purchase of equipment without evidence of proper certification (Brownies' Third Lung requires certification). It is a mistake to think that SSSA diving is somehow "safer" than scuba, or that it does not require training and learning about compressed air hazards. Anyone diving with surface-supplied air needs to fully understand the risks inherent in compressed air diving.

WHAT IS THE FUTURE OF RSD?

The future is now. The technology that exists today, mostly in the realm of technical diving, may become part of recreational diving tomorrow. There is unending debate within professional diving circles about most of this technology, and whether it should enter the realm of recreational diving sooner rather than later (see section on Nitrox diving, Section L). The future of RSD will likely see advances in two main areas.

Dive safety
- Spread of hyperbaric chambers to all popular dive sites; development of affordable, portable hyperbaric chambers that can be carried on a dive boat.
- Universal use of dive computers air integrated to the scuba tank, eliminating the high pressure hose connection.
- Use of full face masks that remain on the diver's face if there is any panic or loss of consciousness (absence of a mouthpiece reduces the risk of drowning in these situations).
- Implementation of underwater voice communication technology.
- Development of "heads up" displays for dive data; instead of data displayed on a wrist device or on a dangling console, all data will appear inside the diver's mask, available for reading with only a turn of the eye. Critical information may flash, assuring the diver's attention.
- Implementation of diver-specific algorithms (adjusted for the diver's age, weight, and perhaps other characteristics) for dive computers. Such algorithms may become available from studies that correlate dive accident experience with a wide range of dive profiles in a diverse group of divers.

Extension of bottom time or distance traveled underwater
- Use of nitrox, perhaps with a depth limiter to prevent diving too deep and incurring risk of oxygen toxicity.
- Use of stronger tanks (carbon fiber) that can hold higher pressures and thus more cubic feet of gas.
- Underwater scooters that allow the diver to range further on a given dive with the same amount of air.
- Use of re-breathing "closed circuit" scuba technology.

Much of this technology and equipment are available now, if not for the recreational diver than in technical circles. Just as other once-new technology gradually became accepted (e.g., dive computers), it seems likely that much of today's "cutting-edge" technology will be adopted by recreational divers in the coming years. Cost and complexity will certainly be a limiting factor, however. Many recreational divers may not want to be burdened with more equipment or ever more complicated and expensive technology. Only time and the marketplace will tell.

Answers to TEST YOUR UNDERSTANDING
1. e.
2. a,b,c
3. a
4. True
5. False

REFERENCES AND BIBLIOGRAPHY

For the sport diver, the training manuals of NAUI, PADI and SSI provide much useful information on physics and physiology of diving, as well as on all the diving skills. In addition, the following six books are highly recommended reference works for those who wish to read further on dive physics and physiology; the last three are textbooks marketed mainly to physicians and other medical professionals.

Richardson D., Shreeves J.T., van Roekel G., Hornsby A., *Encyclopedia of Recreational Diving*. International PADI, Inc., Santa Ana, CA.; 2nd edition, 1997.

NOAA Diving Manual, 3rd Edition. Best Publishing Co., Box 30100, Flagstaff, AZ; 1996.

U.S. Navy Diving Manual, Vol. 1 (Air Diving) and Vol 2 (Mixed-Gas Diving), Best Publishing Co., Box 30100, Flagstaff, AZ; 1996.

Bennett P., Elliott D., editors. *The Physiology and Medicine of Diving*. 4th edition. W.B. Saunders Co., Philadelphia; 1993.

Bove AA, Davis J.C., editors. *Diving Medicine*. 3rd Ed., W.B .Saunders., Philadelphia; 1997.

Edmonds C., Lowry L., Pennefather J. *Diving and Subaquatic Medicine*. Butterworth Heinemann, Oxford; 1992.

DIVING ODDS N' ENDS

Seven Underwater Wonders of the World

According to Rick Sammon, who has published a book by that name, they are:

Belize Barrier Reef
Lake Baikal in Siberia
Northern Red Sea
Galapagos Archipelago
Australia's Great Barrier Reef
Deep Ocean Vents of the Mid-Ocean Ridge
Palau, a Pacific Archipelago

Sammon's book contains full color photographs of each of these underwater wonders. Interestingly, only one site, Belize, is convenient to North American divers. All the sites are accessible to scuba enthusiasts except, of course, the deep ocean vents, reachable only by submarine (and the only site not personally visited by Sammon). This Ridge is a 40,000 mile long volcanic range and rift system that snakes across the bottom of the world's oceans "like the stitching on a baseball."

<u>NOTES</u>

The Respiratory System: A Brief Review

WHY THIS CHAPTER?

Virtually every book on scuba diving, including the open water teaching manuals, includes some information on anatomy and physiology of the respiratory system. Why is this material important to *explain* scuba diving? First, because it helps explain the origin of major problems that can result from pressure: decompression sickness and air embolism. Second, because it helps explain the one process vital to every dive: breathing compressed air underwater. If you already feel comfortable with basic anatomy and physiology of the respiratory system, please skip to Section D. If not, read on. (This material *is* germane to the rest of the book, which is why I don't put it in an Appendix.)

WHAT IS THE FUNCTION OF THE RESPIRATORY SYSTEM?

The function of the respiratory system is rather simple in concept: to bring in oxygen from the atmosphere and get rid of carbon dioxide from the blood. Since oxygen (O_2) and carbon dioxide (CO_2) are gases, the process of bringing one in and excreting the other is called *gas exchange*.

Oxygen is necessary for normal metabolism; lack of it leads to death in a few minutes. Carbon dioxide is a waste product of metabolism; if breathing stops, carbon dioxide will quickly accumulate to a toxic level in the blood. Thus our lungs, the organs that exchange O_2 and CO_2 with the atmosphere, are vital since their total failure is quickly fatal.

We have two lungs, one in the right side of our chest cage and one in the left (Figure l). Between them is the heart, a midline organ that tilts slightly to the left within the chest cage. (You can feel your heart beating by placing your finger tips under your left breast.) Although gas exchange takes place in the lungs, the respiratory system also includes two other components: the part of the central nervous system that controls our breathing, and the chest bellows.

The part of the nervous system that controls breathing is located in the mid-brain, also known as the brain stem. It is an area more primitive than the area of the brain responsible for thinking and motor move-

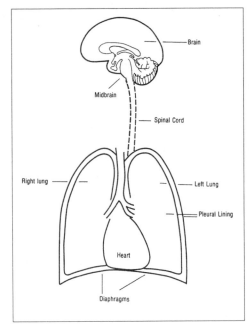

Figure 1. Schematic view of the respiratory system, which consists of: portions of the brain and spinal cord that send signals to the muscles of breathing; the thoracic cage, which includes the rib cage (not shown), pleural membranes and diaphragms; and the lungs and airways.

ments, known as the brain cortex. Brain stem control of breathing is automatic and functions whether we think about it or not. However, it may be altered by drugs or some diseases. A relatively common cause of respiratory depression is an overdose with narcotics or sedatives.

The chest bellows component of the respiratory system includes the bony *thoracic cage* that contains the lungs; the *diaphragms*, which are the major muscles of breathing; and *pleural membranes*, thin tissues that line both the outside of the lungs and the inside of the thoracic cage. The thoracic or chest cage consists of the ribs that protect the lungs from injury; the muscles and connective tissues that tie the ribs together; and all the nerves that lead into these muscles.

Approximately 10-12 times a minute, the brain stem sends nerve impulses that tell the diaphragms and thoracic cage muscles to contract. Contraction of these muscles expands the rib cage, leading to the expansion of the lungs contained within. With each expansion of the lungs we inhale a breath of fresh air containing 21 percent oxygen and almost no carbon dioxide. After full expansion the brain command to inhale ceases and the thoracic cage passively returns to its resting position, at the same time allowing the lungs to return to their resting size. As the lungs return to their resting position we exhale a breath of stale air, containing about 16 percent oxygen and 6 percent carbon dioxide.

In health this breathing cycle is silent, automatic, and effortless. In the process, oxygen is delivered from the atmosphere into our blood and carbon dioxide is excreted from our blood into the atmosphere.

Although "respiratory disease" is often thought of as only a lung problem, malfunction of any component of the respiratory system can cause a breathing problem. For example, if the brain stem center that controls breathing is depressed, as may occur with a drug overdose, failure of the respiratory system will occur (and the victim can die because of it) even though the lungs are normal. Polio, a common disease before discovery of the vaccine, can cause respiratory system failure by damaging the nerves leading to the thoracic cage muscles. In this situation the brain and lungs can be normal, but the chest may not be able to expand in order to move air into the lungs; as a result, the polio patient may have respiratory failure.

Thus *all* parts of the respiratory system must function properly for normal breathing to occur. Yet, despite the importance of all respiratory system components, there is good reason why the lungs are usually thought of when one hears about respiratory disease. Lung disease accounts for the vast majority of respiratory illness. Emphysema, bronchitis, asthma, pneumonia, lung cancer - all originate in the lungs. Our lungs are the only internal organ directly in contact with the atmosphere, making them vulnerable to all pollutants, including cigarette smoke, as well as airborne viruses and bacteria. *Our lungs are also the only internal organ in direct contact with the increased ambient pressure of diving, making them uniquely vulnerable to pressure changes.*

Because most serious diving-related injuries occur from pressure-related problems and/or from drowning, a more detailed discussion of gas exchange should enhance your understanding of scuba diving.

HOW DOES GAS EXCHANGE OCCUR?

Oxygen and carbon dioxide, symbolized O_2 and CO_2 respectively, are colorless, odorless gases. The atmosphere, or air around us, contains approximately 21 percent oxygen and 78 percent nitrogen. There is almost no CO_2 in air (about 0.03 percent); the carbon dioxide humans and animals exhale is a negligible part of the entire atmosphere. The nitrogen is inert and does not take part in gas exchange. (Except in altered-pressure environments nitrogen is of no consequence. Nitrogen takes on critical importance when breathing compressed air underwater.) The remainder of the air is made up of some rare inert gases, such as argon, that also play no role in gas exchange.

To accomplish gas exchange the air we inhale is delivered, via the mouth and nose and larger airways (Figure 2) to tiny sacs, called alveoli. Alveoli are the terminal or end units of the airways (Figures 3 and 4).

Oxygen from the air diffuses across a thin membrane into tiny blood capillaries surrounding the alveoli. At the same time CO_2 diffuses from the blood capillaries into the alveoli and out of the lungs with each exhalation. The combination of one alveolus (containing air) and its surrounding capillaries (containing blood) is called an alveolar-capillary unit. Both lungs contain an estimate 300,000,000 alveolar-capillary units; the surface area of the alveolar membranes, if placed end to end, would cover a tennis court!

This overview can be expanded by dividing gas exchange into the processes of alveolar ventilation (bringing air into the lungs for transfer of oxygen and carbon dioxide) and pulmonary circulation (bringing blood to the lungs to take up oxygen and excrete carbon dioxide).

Alveolar Ventilation. We inhale the air around us with each breath. The air enters the mouth and nose (Figure 2). In the nose and upper airway many of the dust particles are filtered out, purifying the air. Air from the mouth and nose come together in the throat and begin the journey into the lungs. First air enters the larynx (voice box) and then the trachea (just below the Adam's apple). The trachea divides into two air tubes, the right and left main bronchi. The trachea and bronchial tubes that branch from it are lined with cartilage. Cartilage provides a firm structure so the airways stay open when we inhale and exhale.

The trachea and air passages above it (i.e., mouth, throat, larynx) are collectively called the upper airways or upper respiratory system. Air entering the upper airways is warmed to body temperature and humidified (water vapor is added to it). (The right and left main bronchi and all airways that lead from them are collectively called the lower airway system, which is another term for our lungs.)

The right and left main bronchi represent the first of over 20 divisions of airways to come in the lower airway system (Figure 2). With each division the air passages become narrower, but the number of airways increases geometrically. By the 20th division there are a huge number of individual, tiny airways and air has been distributed to each of them. Also at the 20th division, where the diameter of each airway is less than 1 mm, air sacs (the alveoli) begin to appear; this is where gas exchange actually takes place. Eventually, each airway ends in a grapelike cluster of these alveoli.

At the alveolar-capillary membrane gas exchange takes place. Oxygen is delivered to, and carbon dioxide removed from, the capillary blood (Figures 3 and 4). This gas exchange converts the oxygen-poor blood entering the pulmonary capillary into oxygen-rich blood. At the same time the air we inhale (21 percent O_2, almost no CO_2) has been converted into stale air (16 percent O_2, 6 percent CO_2) that we exhale.

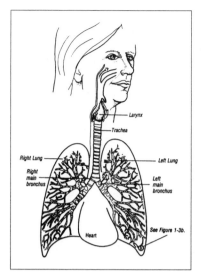

Figure 2. Diagram of upper airway and tracheobronchial tree. Air enters through the mouth and nose, then travels down the larynx (voice box) and trachea (windpipe). Air then enters the lungs, which consist (in part) of multiple branching airways called bronchi. These bronchi end in clusters of air sacs - the alveoli. Each alveolus is surrounded by blood capillaries, which take up the oxygen and give off carbon dioxide. A three-dimensional view and cross-section of alveoli are shown in Figures 3 and 4.

Figure 3. Each alveolar sac, or alveolus, is surrounded by one or more pulmonary capillaries. This alveolar-capillary unit is where oxygen (O_2) and carbon dioxide (CO_2) are exchanged with the atmosphere. See Figure 4.

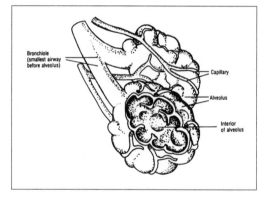

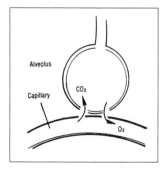

Figure 4. Cross-section of single alveolar-capillary unit. As blood flows past the alveolus, CO_2 is given off and O_2 is taken up.

Each minute, under resting conditions, we breathe in about six liters of fresh air. About 1/3 of this air stays in the mouth, throat, and large airways where no gas exchange takes place; this region (the upper airways and part of our lungs) is referred to as "dead space," because air in this space doesn't take part in gas exchange. The remaining four liters of fresh air breathed in each minute are distributed to the hundreds of millions of alveoli and it is this air that takes part in gas exchange and constitutes the alveolar ventilation.

Pulmonary Circulation. Each minute our heart pumps approximately five liters of blood through the lung capillaries, distributing blood among the hundreds of millions of alveoli so gas exchange can take place. Because the lungs are three dimensional, one alveolar sac may be surrounded by several pulmonary capillaries. Each alveolus and all of its accompanying capillaries constitute the gas exchange unit (Figure 3). If there was no blood flow around the alveolus or there was blood flow without an accompanying alveolus, there would be no gas exchange. Thus alveolar ventilation is but one part of respiration; the other necessary part, the delivery of blood to the capillaries surrounding the alveoli, is the pulmonary circulation.

The total circulation of the blood in our body is a circular affair. Blood flowing from one part of the heart to the lungs and back to another part of the heart constitutes one part of this circle; the other part is the systemic blood circulation, which is blood flowing from the heart to the rest of the body and then back to the heart (Figure 5). Arbitrarily, we can start this circle with one of the four chambers of the heart, the right atrium. Blood that enters the right atrium has given up much of its oxygen to the tissues, and is called venous blood (oxygen-poor or de-oxygenated blood). After collecting in the right atrium of the heart, venous blood then goes to the right ventricle from where it is pumped to the lungs in order to receive a fresh supply of oxygen.

Blood leaving the right ventricle is pumped into the lungs via one large blood vessel, the main pulmonary artery. This large artery divides into two smaller pulmonary arteries, one to each of the lungs. Each pulmonary artery gives rise to many divisions, and in short order the blood supply pumped from the heart is divided among millions of tiny pulmonary capillaries, the smallest unit of circulation. These capillaries are in contact with the hundreds of millions of alveoli, the tiny sacs that receives the fresh air we inhale. The distance between each alveolus or air sac, and its surrounding capillaries, is very short, only the diameter of a thin membrane; oxygen easily diffuses from the air sac into capillary blood while, at the same time, CO_2 diffuses out of the capillary blood

Figure 5. Pulmonary and systemic blood circulation. RL=right lung; RV =right ventricle; RA=right atrium; VC=vena cava; PA=pulmonary arteries; LL=left lung; LV=left ventricle; LA=left atrium; PV=pulmonary veins; AO=aorta.

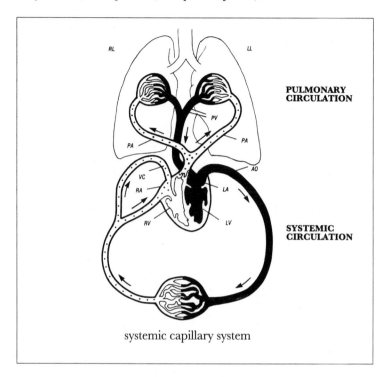

systemic capillary system

and into the air sac. The CO_2-laden stale air is then exhaled, and fresh air is brought into the lungs with the next breath.

Oxygenated blood leaving the millions of pulmonary capillaries enters the other side of the heart, first the left atrium and then the left ventricle. From the left ventricle oxygen-rich blood is pumped, via the body's arterial circulation, to all the muscles, tissues and organs. In this way our kidneys, brain, liver, heart, bones, and other tissues receive vital oxygen. (When an analysis of arterial blood gas is performed for oxygen measurements, the blood sample is obtained by inserting a small needle into the radial artery of the wrist, just behind the thumb. Unlike venous blood, arterial blood reflects the status of gas exchange in the lungs and is therefore useful to examine in patients with many types of lung disease.)

The pulmonary and systemic (non-pulmonary) circulation systems are schematically shown in Figure 5. The heart, normally between our two lungs (Figure 1), is here separated to show its four chambers and the vessels leading to and from them. Each pulmonary artery branches into millions of tiny capillaries before picking up oxygen and giving off CO_2 (gas exchange). Then the millions of capillaries merge to become the pulmonary veins. The pulmonary veins carry oxygenated blood back to the left heart, from where it is pumped, via the systemic arterial circulation, to the organs and tissues of the body. From these organs and tissues it then returns, via the systemic venous system, back to the right heart.

In Figure 5 the light stipple represents venous or de-oxygenated blood and the dark stipple, arterial or oxygenated blood. Arrows show the direction of blood flow. Note that pulmonary *arteries* carry venous blood, and pulmonary *veins* carry oxygenated blood. The role of veins and arteries is reversed in the systemic circulation, where veins carry oxygen-poor (venous) blood and arteries carry oxygen-rich (arterial) blood.

After entering the tissue, organ, or muscle, each systemic artery divides into smaller and smaller vessels, the smallest of which is the systemic capillary. These capillaries are structurally similar to the pul-

---

TEST YOUR UNDERSTANDING

1. Gas exchange, the main function of the lungs, refers to exchange of:
   a. oxygen in the atmosphere for nitrogen in the blood
   b. oxygen in the atmosphere for carbon dioxide in the blood
   c. carbon dioxide in the blood for nitrogen in the atmosphere
   d. none of the above

2. Below is a list of divisions or parts of the circulation. State whether each normally contains oxygenated or de-oxygenated blood.

   a. aorta   e. vein leaving the arm
   b. right atrium   f. pulmonary artery
   c. left atrium   g. pulmonary vein
   d. artery to leg

3. A diver forms nitrogen bubbles in his legs on ascent from a dive. Trace the path those bubbles will take after they enter the leg veins.

4. Some nitrogen bubbles from decompression enter the lung capillaries and, instead of being trapped, pass through and into the pulmonary veins. Trace the path those bubbles will take after entering the pulmonary veins.

monary capillaries and have the same function: to allow gas exchange to occur by simple diffusion. In the lung, oxygen diffuses into the capillaries and CO_2 diffuses out. In all other capillaries (non-pulmonary or systemic capillaries) oxygen diffuses out of the capillary into the cells of the organ, and CO_2 diffuses into the capillary from the cells of the organ. In this way oxygen is delivered for cellular metabolism and CO_2, a waste product of metabolism, is removed.

Gas exchange is a vital process; it occurs not only in the lungs but in all other tissues as well. Gas exchange requires both ventilation, provided by breathing adequate amounts of fresh air, and circulation, provided by the heart pumping blood to the lungs (pulmonary circulation) and then out to all other parts of the body (systemic circulation).

Blood entering the systemic (non-pulmonary) capillaries is oxygenated. When blood leaves these capillaries it has given up some (not all) of its oxygen, and is venous or de-oxygenated blood. Venous blood, which appears blue in our veins under the skin, is actually dark red in a test tube. Arterial blood is normally bright red (although if the patient is low on oxygen arterial blood will also look dark red).

The systemic capillaries, after delivering their oxygenated blood to the tissues, merge and form the veins that carry the venous blood; eventually all the systemic veins in the body come together to form the two great vena cavae, the superior, that carries blood leaving the head and neck, and the inferior, that carries blood leaving the rest of the body.

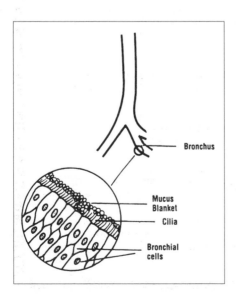

Bronchus

Mucus Blanket

Cilia

Bronchial cells

Figure 6. Each bronchus is lined with cells that are covered with tiny hairs, called cilia, that project into the airway. Cilia are covered with a blanket of mucus, which serves to collect dusts and other pollutants. This "mucus blanket," along with its collected dusts, is normally swept by the cilia up and out of the airways.

Both vena cavae enter the heart at the level of the right atrium. Blood from the right atrium enters the right ventricle and then is pumped to the lungs to once again begin the process of oxygenation.

The circle is completed.

DOES THE RESPIRATORY SYSTEM HAVE FUNCTIONS BESIDES GAS EXCHANGE?

Yes. A particularly important respiratory system function is body defense. A healthy respiratory system prevents many airborne particles from damaging the alveoli or from entering the blood stream. The nose filters large airborne particles out of the air we inhale. This efficient filtering mechanism is bypassed, however, during mouth breathing.

The trachea and main bronchi are also effective in keeping dusts and other large particles from reaching the alveoli. Coughing is one way we attempt to clear the large airways of noxious material.

Even when our nose and normal cough response are not helping keep out dusts, our bronchi function silently to move out any unwanted material. This is accomplished by a blanket of mucus that covers the bronchi, and tiny hairs (cilia) which sweep the mucus out of the airways (Figure 6). When this dust-laden mucus reaches the top of the trachea, it is usually swallowed.

Even if particles get past all of these defenses, special alveolar cells (called macrophages) are mobilized to help digest any foreign substances such as bacteria or tiny particles of dust. All of these normal defense mechanisms may be damaged from cigarette smoke, making smokers much more vulnerable to inhaled dusts and other impurities in the air.

Answers to TEST YOUR UNDERSTANDING

1. b. oxygen in the atmosphere for carbon dioxide in the blood

2. oxygenated blood: a, c, d, g
   de-oxygenated blood: b, e, f

3. leg vein —> inferior vena cava —> right atrium —> right ventricle —> lungs; normally these bubbles will be trapped by the lung capillaries. If any bubbles get through the lung capillaries they will take the path described in answer to the next question.

4. Pulmonary veins —> left atrium —> left ventricle —> aorta —> arterial circulation.

REFERENCES

Martin L: *Breathe Easy: A Guide to Lung and Respiratory Diseases for Patients and Their Families.* Prentice Hall, Englewood Cliffs, N.J., 1984.

Martin L. *Pulmonary Physiology in Clinical Practice.* C.V. Mosby Co., St. Louis, 1987.

Martin L. *All You Really Need to Know to Interpret Arterial Blood Gases.* Lea & Febiger, Malvern, PA, 1992.

Martin L. Pulmonary section in Berne, Levy: *Case Studies in Physiology*, C.V. Mosby Co., St. Louis, 1994.

DIVING ODDS N' ENDS

Do fish sleep?

For anyone who has ever done a night dive along a coral reef, the answer is apparent - many fish do sleep. The question is often raised because fish have no eyelids, so their eyes are always open (though they don't "see" while sleeping). During the day most fish will keep their distance from scuba divers (unless we feed them), but at night many species just hover in water, seemingly oblivious to the curious diver. At night some species, like the striped parrot fish, enclose themselves in an envelope of mucus. These and other fish seem to be in a state of suspended animation, i.e., asleep, and you can get as close as you want without touching. If touched, sleeping fish will wake up and dart away.

Other sea creatures sleep during the day and come out only at night (some species of octopus, some eels and most catfish, for example). And while all fishes must sleep or have periods of inactivity that serve the purpose of sleep, some species (notably sharks) appear to move constantly, and not to sleep at all.

DIVING ODDS N' ENDS

How long do fish live?

The answer varies, of course, depending on the species, but it is extremely rare for a fish to live more than 25 years. Many large fish live for 15-20 years, including barracuda, tarpon and herring. Smaller fish live anywhere from one to five years - unless they are caught and eaten by bigger fish (or by people).

Whales, which are not fish but mammals, may live up to 60 years.

DIVING ODDS N' ENDS

Great Lakes Shipwrecks

There are literally thousands of shipwrecks along America's coasts and in the Great Lakes. No one knows exactly how many but, increasingly, scuba divers are helping to locate and explore them. For Gerald Metzler charting the Great Lakes wrecks, especially those of Lake Erie, has become a lifetime passion. A high school science teacher in Lakewood, just outside Cleveland, Mr. Metzler has located and dove dozens of wrecks himself, and maintains an extensive file on Lake Erie wrecks, as well as detailed information on all 21000 ships ever built on the Great Lakes (Huehner 1994). As is well known among fresh water divers, cold temperatures and lack of wood worms favor preservation of Great Lakes wrecks. Metzler estimates there are 250-300 wrecks in Lake Erie, most of them known because of the Lake's shallow depth (av. about 60 ft., max. to about 200 ft.). The first Lake Erie wreck was a ship that went down in 1763.

An Explanation of Pressure and the Laws of Boyle, Charles, Dalton, and Henry

WHAT IS PRESSURE?

Key to understanding scuba diving is the concept of pressure, and how it varies with depth. We intuitively understand that pressure is some type of force, but how is it actually defined? Pressure is a force *or weight* per unit area. All matter, *including air*, has weight due to earth's gravity. Accordingly, anything exposed to air is under pressure - the weight of the atmosphere above it. This weight of air, due to gravity, is known as *atmospheric pressure* (Figure 1).

From experience just carrying a container of water, we also know that water is much heavier than air. Since pressure is related to weight, water pressure must be far greater than air pressure, and of course it is.

Gravity keeps the atmosphere wedded to the earth. Without gravity, earth's atmosphere would float away to outer space. Since gravity diminishes with distance from the center of the earth, air *weighs* less at altitude than at sea level. Literally, air at altitude is "thinner" (meaning less dense) compared to sea level, and air becomes *progressively* less dense with *increasing* altitude (Figure 1). A cubic foot of air on the summit of Mt. Everest contains only about a third as many molecules as a cubic foot at sea level, and hence weighs only about a third as much (Figure 2).

Figure 1. Earth is surrounded by a layer of atmosphere which is densest at sea level; the atmosphere becomes thinner - less dense - with altitude. Figure is not drawn to scale.

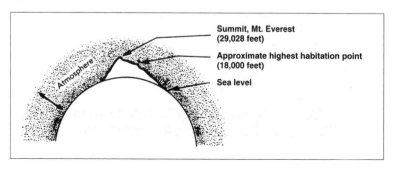

Summit, Mt. Everest
(29,028 feet)

Approximate highest habitation point
(18,000 feet)

Sea level

Atmosphere

(Everything weighs less at altitude, including people, but we don't notice the difference except in outer space. You would not feel lighter on the top of a high mountain. In outer space, miles from earth's center of gravity, weightlessness is experienced.)

WHAT IS AIR PRESSURE?

Air pressure can be specified in several ways; the most popular term used in scuba diving is "pounds per square inch" or "psi." At sea level the pressure exerted by the atmosphere is 14.7 psi. "Per square inch" refers to the surface area subjected to the weight of the air above it; the units could just as well be per "square foot," "square yard" or "square meter," but then the numbers would be correspondingly higher.

Stated another way, a column of air one inch square and about 50 miles high (a distance that encompasses virtually all of earth's atmosphere) weighs just 14.7 pounds (Figure 3). Not a lot of pounds for something fifty miles high, but not exactly weightless either. Most of the atmosphere's weight is actually contained in the first few miles, where gravity exerts its greatest effect. An air column one-inch square, from sea level and extending 3.4 miles high (18,000 feet), weighs about half that of the full air column, or 7.35 pounds. The remainder of the one-inch-square air column, from an altitude of 3.4 miles to outer space, weighs another 7.35 pounds.

To further consider the concept of air pressure, open your hand palm upward. The palm surface of an average-sized hand (with fingers closed) covers about 25 square inches. Now lift your hand quickly upward with the palm flat out (Figure 4). Assuming you are at sea level, and your hand is average-sized, you are lifting 25 x 14.7 or 368 pounds of air! Why, then, does your lifting seem so effortless? If you had to lift 368 pounds of anything with one hand you couldn't do it.

It feels effortless because air pressure is evenly distributed around your hand, and the molecules of air are easily movable. At sea level, air

Figure 2. A cubic foot of air at the summit of Mt. Everest contains only about a third the number of molecules as a cubic foot at sea level, and hence weighs a third as much.

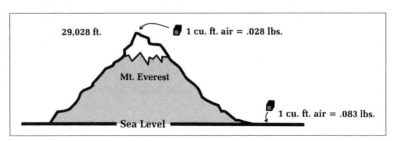

pressure is 14.7 pounds per square inch on top of your hand, underneath your hand, and on all sides. Thus you don't really 'lift' 368 pounds, though that is the weight of air on top of your hand.

As you lift your hand you move some air molecules out of the way and other molecules immediately come under and around your hand. The pressure surrounding your hand stays the same: 14.7 psi. Because the pressure is evenly distributed, you don't feel any weight in lifting your hand. (There is resistance, however, as it takes time for air molecules to get out of the way. Resistance in the face of equal pressures is much better appreciated underwater, since water is much denser than air.)

WHAT IS THE DIFFERENCE BETWEEN AMBIENT, BAROMETRIC AND ATMOSPHERIC PRESSURE?

It can be confusing when different terminology is used to describe the same thing. One example is the use of multiple terms to indicate the pressure around us *and* the different measurement units for that pressure.

Figure 3. A one-square-inch column of the entire atmosphere weighs 14.7 pounds; this is the atmospheric pressure at sea level. Since half the weight occurs in the first 18,000 feet (3.4 miles), air pressure at this altitude is one half the total, or 7.35 psi.

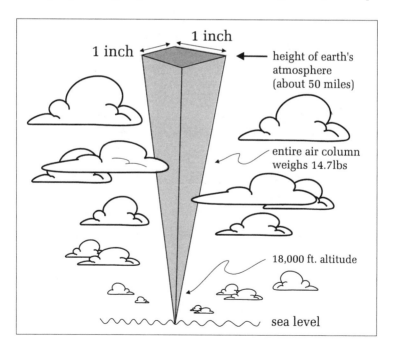

The surrounding pressure, on land or underwater, is referred to as the *ambient pressure*. If the surrounding pressure is from the weight of air, it is the *atmospheric* pressure. If the surrounding pressure is from the weight of water, it is the *water* pressure (Figure 5).

Weather forecasters usually report air pressure in terms of a barometer reading in inches, e.g., "the barometer is currently 30 inches of mercury and rising." A barometer is an instrument for measuring atmospheric pressure, so *barometric* pressure is just another term for atmospheric pressure.

TEST YOUR UNDERSTANDING

1. The weight of air over a square foot of earth's surface at sea level is:
    b. 14.7 lbs.
    a. 1470 lbs.
    c. 2117 lbs.

2. The weight of air over a square yard at sea level is:
    a. 144 lbs.
    b. 14440 lbs.
    c. 19051 lbs.

Choose 'True' or 'False' for each of the following statements:

3. A cubic foot of air weighs less in Denver (altitude 5280 ft.) than in Miami (sea level).

4. A cubic foot of air contains fewer molecules in Denver than in Miami.

5. A given volume of air contains fewer oxygen molecules in Denver than in Miami.

6. Each of the first three miles of atmosphere (where people live) exerts the same pressure over earth's surface.

WHAT ARE THE MEASUREMENT UNITS FOR THE AMBIENT PRESSURE?

There are several units of measurement for ambient pressure. None is universally used, as different groups seem to prefer different terms to describe this pressure. The various terms are listed in Table 1, arbitrarily subdivided according to whether or not they are commonly employed in diving. Note that "bar" is commonly used in European diving. North Americans who rent air gauges in other countries may find them calibrated in bars. Thus a tank filled to 3000 psi would register 206 bars.

Figure 4. Air pressure around your hand – or any object in the atmosphere – is evenly distributed.

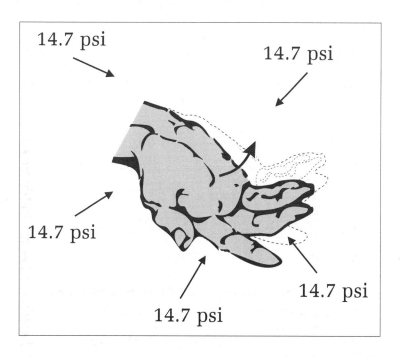

Figure 5. Ambient Pressure on land and underwater. When surrounded by air, ambient pressure = atmospheric pressure = barometric pressure. When surrounded by water, ambient pressure = water pressure.

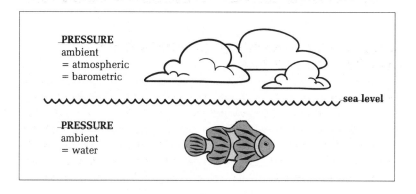

TABLE 1.
VARIOUS UNITS OF MEASUREMENT FOR AMBIENT PRESSURE

(fsw = feet sea water; Hg = mercury)

| | ambient pressure at: | |
	sea level	33 fsw
used in diving		
psi	14.7	29.4
atmospheres	1	2
bar (non-U.S. only)	1.01	2.02
used in other fields*		
cm H_2O	988	1976
inches Hg	29.92	59.84
mm Hg (torr)	760	1520
kilopascal	101.3	202.6

*meteorology, science, medicine

WHAT IS AN "ATMOSPHERE" OF PRESSURE?

One atmosphere (atm.) is the air pressure at sea level and equals 14.7 psi. Note that the term "one atmosphere" is just a measurement; you don't have to *be* at sea level to be surrounded by one atmosphere. You could be in a submarine 330 feet underwater and still be surrounded by one atm. of pressure (though the submarine hull would be surrounded by 10 atm. of water pressure).

Similarly, two atm. is twice the sea level pressure. Two atm. = 29.4 psi, a pressure reached at 33 fsw (Table 1). You could also experience this pressure on land, in a hyperbaric chamber. Conversely, the air pressure at 18,000 feet altitude = 7.35 psi, but this could be experienced at sea level as well, inside a chamber that can simulate altitude.

Don't confuse "atmosphere," which is a unit of measurement, with "atmospheric pressure," which is a general term for the surrounding air pressure. Atmospheric pressure could be any value, e.g., one atm. (sea level pressure), one-half atm. (18,000 feet), zero (outer space), or three atm. (inside a hyperbaric chamber).

Another important unit of measurement is millimeters of mercury, abbreviated mm Hg (Hg is the chemical symbol for mercury). Some texts refer to mm Hg by the term "torr," after the Italian Evangelista Torricelli (1608-1647), a pioneer in the measurement of atmospheric pressure; one mm Hg = one torr. Air pressure at sea level is 760 mm Hg (or 760 torr). In medicine and science, mm Hg is commonly used as the unit for partial pressures of gases.

Note that psi and mm Hg reflect different ways of measuring the same thing. At sea level air *weighs* 14.7 pounds per square inch of earth's surface, so the pressure is 14.7 psi. It is also true that this weight of air will *support* a column of mercury 760 mm high (Figure 6), so the air pressure is also 760 mm Hg.

I also mentioned the weather forecaster's lingo, e.g., "the barometer is 30 inches of mercury and rising." Inches and millimeters are both measurements of length. In the United States, non-scientific measurements remain largely non-metric (many people would like to change that!). In most of the rest of the world the metric system is used for all measurements. Metric lengths are described in millimeters, centimeters, meters and kilometers. Table 2 lists some common units of measurement for average atmospheric pressure, shown for various altitudes.

TABLE 2.
AVERAGE ATMOSPHERIC PRESSURE
AT VARIOUS ALTITUDES

Measured in atmospheres (atm.), pounds per square inch (psi), millimeters mercury (mm Hg) and inches mercury (in. Hg); latter two are rounded to nearest whole digit.

Location	Ht (ft.)	atm.	psi	mm Hg	in. Hg
Sea level	zero	1.00	14.7	760	30
Denver	5280	.75	12.3	640	24
Pike's Peak, Colorado	14410	.63	8.52	550	22
Andes Mtns.	18000	.50	7.35	380	15
Mt. Everest summit	29028	.25	4.12	253	10
Outer space	(50 miles)	0	0	0	0

WHAT IS THE DIFFERENCE BETWEEN ABSOLUTE PRESSURE AND GAUGE PRESSURE?

Sea water weighs about 64 pounds per cu. foot (the exact weight depends on the quantity of dissolved salt, which varies slightly in the world's oceans). Using this value, 33 cu. feet of water weighs 33 x 64 = 2112 pounds. Dive to 33 feet depth, lay horizontal, and you will have 2112 pounds of water over every square foot of your body; this comes to 14.7 pounds per square inch, which is the atmospheric pressure at sea level.

At 33 feet depth a diver is under *two* atmospheres of pressure: one atmosphere from the air above sea level and a second atmosphere from the 33 feet of water. The fact that 33 feet of sea water equals the pressure of the entire atmosphere is important in understanding the term

Figure 6. The weight of air at sea level will support a column of mercury 760 mm high. In a simple experiment shown by this figure, a tube longer than 760 mm, and closed at one end, is filled with liquid mercury. The tube is then inverted so that its open end is submerged in a pan of mercury, at which point mercury in the tube falls to a certain height. The height of the column of mercury in the inverted tube equals the pressure of air over the open pan of mercury. At sea level the column of mercury is 760 mm high, so 760 mm Hg is the pressure of air at sea level.

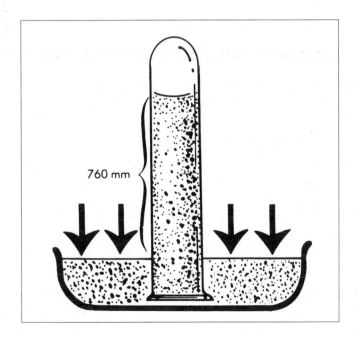

760 mm

"gauge pressure." Gauge pressure, discussed in some diving books, is the water pressure read by gauges that arbitrarily set sea level pressure to zero. Such instruments read the pressure at 33 feet depth as "1 atm. gauge," meaning that the pressure from water *alone* is 1 atm.

However, if the dive commenced at sea level, then at 33 feet the actual, real, absolute pressure on the diver is *two atmospheres*, one from earth's atmosphere (14.7 psi) and another from the water (also 14.7 psi). Unless you have one of these gauges don't be concerned about gauge pressure. You need to know the actual or absolute pressure as you dive. If you commence your dive at sea level the absolute pressure at 33 fsw is two atmospheres; at 66 fsw, three atmospheres; at 99 fsw, four atmospheres; etc.

TEST YOUR UNDERSTANDING

7. What are the gauge and absolute pressures for a scuba diver at a depth of 132 fsw?

8. If you dive in a mountain lake where the atmospheric pressure is 3/4 that at sea level, what is the absolute pressure (in atmospheres) at a depth of 34 feet (equivalent to 33 fsw)?

   a. 1
   b. 1.75
   c. 2
   d. cannot determine from this information

WHAT CAUSES CHANGES IN ATMOSPHERIC PRESSURE?

There are 25.4 millimeters to the inch, so a barometric pressure "30 inches of mercury" is the same as "762 millimeters of mercury." That amount of atmospheric pressure will support a column of mercury 30 inches or 762 mm high. The terms "rising" and "falling" as applied to barometric pressure refer to minor changes in atmospheric pressure with changes in weather. A "high pressure front" is one where the barometric pressure for a mass of air is slightly higher than average. Although "high and low pressure" fronts may have profound consequences for the weather (e.g., a low pressure front portends bad weather), the pressure changes, per se, have little effect on people; the variations are usually too small to be of any significance.

Barometric pressure at a specific location (e.g., the airport at Denver, the beach at Waikiki, the top of the Empire State Building) seldom fluctuates by more than 30 mm Hg (1.2 inches Hg) throughout the year. There is, of course, an average barometric pressure for any given location. At sea level throughout the world this average barometric pressure is 760 mm Hg. Fluctuations in barometric pressure at a specific location, used to predict the weather, are of course different from changes in barometric pressure that come about from changes in altitude or depth.

Changes in pressure with altitude have nothing to do with the weather, but are due to the *change in weight of air above you*. The closer to the earth's surface, the greater the weight of air above you and the greater the air pressure. Similarly, pressure changes in water are solely related to the *change in weight of water above you*; the deeper you dive, the greater the weight of water above you and the greater the water pressure.

TEST YOUR UNDERSTANDING

9. List A shows barometric pressures recorded at four different locations. Match each pressure with a single location in list B where the pressure was most likely recorded.

A		**B**
253 mm Hg	-	Miami
640 mm Hg	-	Denver
747 mm Hg	-	inside hyperbaric chamber during a treatment
1520 mm Hg		for decompression sickness
	-	outer space
	-	1000 feet down in a coal mine
	-	summit of Mt. Everest

WHAT IS THE COMPOSITION OF AIR?

Air is a mixture of gases, mainly oxygen (21% by volume) and nitrogen (78% by volume). The other 1% of air is made up of several other gases such as carbon dioxide (CO_2), argon, krypton and neon. The actual percentage composition of dry air (what scuba divers inhale) is shown in Table 3. For scuba diving purposes it is convenient to consider nitrogen as 79% of the air, since the other inert gases (principally argon) must also be considered in computing decompression schedules. Thus you will find many texts listing nitrogen as "79%" of the air.

In any mixture of gases (e.g., air), the individual gases don't chemically combine with each other. The gases maintain their individual identity and percentage regardless of how much or little pressure the

TABLE 3.
PERCENT COMPOSITION OF DRY AIR

Nitrogen	78.084
Oxygen	20.948
Argon	00.934
Carbon dioxide	00.031
Other gases**	00.003
Total	100.00

** Neon, helium krypton, xenon, hydrogen,
   ozone, nitrous oxide and methane.

mixture is subjected to. The percentages of gases shown in Table 3 are the same throughout the breathable atmosphere. They are also the same inside a tank of compressed air *and* in the air as it emerges from the tank on its way to the diver's lungs, regardless of depth. This fact takes on critical importance as water pressure increases with increasing depth because, although the percentages are un-changed, the total pressure exerted by each gas component increases proportionately. The increases in component gas pressures account for some of the major problems inherent in compressed air diving: nitrogen narcosis, decompression sickness and oxygen toxicity (see Sections G and I).

WHAT ARE THE GAS LAWS AND WHY ARE THEY IMPORTANT TO DIVING?

So far we have discussed pressure as it relates to air in the atmosphere. Scuba divers, of course, are interested in what happens to air *under water*. Air under water obeys the same laws as air in the atmosphere. I will introduce the gas laws in this section and, in Section E, use them to further explain physiology underwater. The four important gas laws are those of the Englishmen Robert Boyle (1627-1691), John Dalton (1766-1844), and William Henry (1774-1790), and the Frenchman Jacques Charles (1746-1823).

The idea is not to belabor laws of physics, but to emphasize relationships that explain what happens when you dive. The four gas laws are useful because they predict changes in air pressure, volume and temperature as compressed air divers descend and ascend.

WHAT IS BOYLE'S LAW?

Boyle's law states:

At constant temperature, the volume of a gas varies *inversely* with the pressure, while the density of a gas varies *directly* with pressure.

Simplified: If temperature is kept constant, as air pressure increases the volume of a gas decreases, and vice versa. Mathematically,

$$PV = K$$

where P and V are the pressure and volume, respectively, and K is a constant. Change P, and V will change in the opposite direction, so that their product is maintained at a constant value. Now let's illustrate this law. Suppose you have a container open on one end that is inverted over water; as the container is lowered in the water the trapped air will be compressed by the water pressure (Figure 7). Assume the container holds one liter of air at sea level pressure (one atmosphere). PV = 1 liter x 1 atm. = 1. Increase the air pressure to 2 atmospheres and Boyle's law predicts the volume of air in the container will be 1/2 liter. Increase pressure to 3 atmospheres and the volume of air falls to 1/3, and so forth (Figure 7).

Note that Boyle's law also relates to gas *density*. Increase the pressure of a fixed volume of gas and the density increases, and vice versa. This

---

TEST YOUR UNDERSTANDING

10. A balloon containing 6 liters of air at sea level is taken to a depth of 165 feet. What will the volume of air be in the balloon at that depth? What will be the change in gas density, compared to sea level?

11. A scuba diver takes an extra tank of compressed air to a depth of 99 fsw, which he does not breathe from. Compared to sea level what are the density and volume of air in the tank? (Assume temperature is constant.)

    a. same
    b. higher
    c. lower

consequence of Boyle's law becomes particularly important on deep dives; it predicts that the inhaled air will become denser the deeper one goes. As a result of increasing air density, deep divers often notice greater difficulty breathing.

Without doubt Boyle's is the most important law in scuba diving (but not the most important *rule*, which is *never hold your breath*). All certification courses stress Boyle's law. Don't leave home without it!

Figure 7. A container open on one end has one liter of air at one atmosphere. The air is compressed by taking it underwater. Boyle's law predicts that at two atmospheres pressure (33 fsw) the volume of air in the container will decrease by one half and the density of air will double; at three atmospheres, volume will decrease to 1/3 and density will triple, etc.

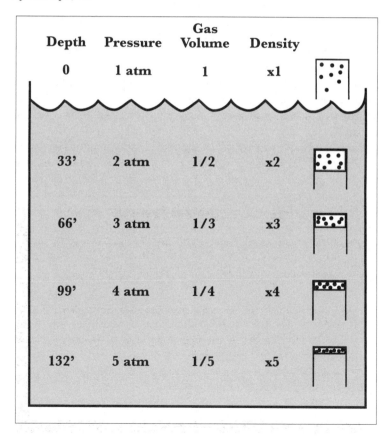

Depth	Pressure	Gas Volume	Density	
0	1 atm	1	x1	
33'	2 atm	1/2	x2	
66'	3 atm	1/3	x3	
99'	4 atm	1/4	x4	
132'	5 atm	1/5	x5	

WHAT IS CHARLES' LAW?

Charles' law states:

At a constant volume, the pressure of gas varies directly with absolute temperature.

Simplified: Given a constant volume of gas, the higher the temperature the higher the gas pressure, and vice versa.

Mathematically:

$$\frac{P_1}{P_2} = \frac{T_1}{T_2}$$

where P_1 and P_1 are the beginning and final pressures, and T_1 and T_2 are the beginning and final temperatures (remember, volume is kept constant).

Compared to Boyle's law, Charles' law is not as important for scuba divers because temperature underwater seldom changes enough to seriously affect air pressure. However, the law is useful to keep in mind when filling air tanks, especially when there is a large difference between air and water temperatures. Suppose you have a steel scuba tank holding 80 cu. ft. of air at a pressure of 3000 psi, filled when the air temperature was 90°F. Now you take the tank into water that is 75°F. Before you take your first breath of that tank's air, Charles' law predicts that the tank pressure will be...what?

Lower than 3000 psi. Since T_2 is less than T_1, the law predicts that P_2 will be less than P_1. (To know how much less you need to convert T_1 and T_2 into absolute temperatures by adding 460 to each fahrenheit temperature.)

Scuba shop proprietors know about Charles' law, which is why they often fill tanks in a water bath where the temperature is about the same as the ocean (or wherever the diving will take place).

12. A tank is filled to 3000 psi when the air temperature is 85°F. A diver takes the tank into the water and, while still on the surface, notices its air pressure is only 2700 psi. Assuming no air has been inhaled from the tank, which one of the following statements is correct?

    a. The tank has less cubic feet of air than when it was filled.
    b. The tank has the same cubic feet of air but the air exerts less pressure than when the tank was filled.
    c. The tank has more air but under lower pressure than out of the water.

WHAT IS DALTON'S LAW?

Dalton's law states:

The total pressure exerted by a mixture of gases is equal to the sum of the pressures that would be exerted by each of the gases if it alone were present and occupied the total volume.

Simplified: The pressure of any gas mixture (e.g., air) is equal to the sum of pressures exerted by the individual gases (e.g., oxygen, nitrogen, and each of the minor gases).

Mathematically:

$$P_{TOTAL} = P_1 + P_2 \ldots + P_{OTHER}$$

where P_{TOTAL} is the total pressure of a gas mixture (e.g., air), and P_1 and P_2 are the *partial* pressures of component gases (e.g., oxygen and nitrogen). The term P_{OTHER} is used to signify partial pressures of all other gases in the mixture.

WHAT IS PARTIAL PRESSURE?

Partial pressure is a very important concept in scuba diving, in part because it aids in understanding Dalton's law. Partial pressure is the pressure exerted by an individual gas, whether that gas is part of a mixture (such as air) or dissolved in a liquid (such as blood) or in any body tissue. Partial pressure of a gas (P_G) is determined by the fraction of the gas in the mixture (F_G) times the total pressure of all the gases (excluding any water vapor present):

$$P_G = F_G \text{ x total gas pressure (excluding water vapor)}$$

In air at sea level, the partial pressures of oxygen and nitrogen are:

PO_2:   .21 x 1 atmosphere = .21 atm.
PN_2:   .79 x 1 atmosphere = .79 atm.

Note that we could have used any of the terms in Table 1 (page D-6) to denote partial pressure. Thus, in mm Hg the partial pressures of oxygen and nitrogen at sea level are (assuming no water vapor):

PO_2:   .21 x 760 mm Hg = 160 mm Hg
PN_2:   .79 x 760 mm Hg = 600 mm Hg

TEST YOUR UNDERSTANDING

13. True or False: The sum of partial pressures of all gases in a gas mixture can never add up to more than the total pressure of the gas mixture.

14. True or False: While scuba diving with compressed air, the partial pressure of inhaled oxygen increases with increasing depth.

15. What is the partial pressure, in atmospheres, of oxygen and nitrogen in the lungs of a scuba diver at 66 fsw?

16. What is the partial pressure of oxygen (in mm Hg) at an altitude of 18,000 feet, where the ambient pressure is 380 mm Hg?

WHAT DOES DALTON'S LAW PREDICT ABOUT CHANGES IN PARTIAL PRESSURE WITH CHANGES IN AMBIENT PRESSURE?

(If you answered questions 13 and 14 correctly you already know the answer to this question.) The percentage of gases making up air is the same throughout the breathable atmosphere. Regardless of altitude, the composition of air is about 21% oxygen, 78% nitrogen, 1% other. Similarly, even though air is compressed in a scuba tank, the percentage of the individual gas components is the same. Given this fact and Dalton's law, we see that as air pressure increases or decreases, the partial pressure of each gas *will do the same*. With increasing altitude, for example, the partial pressure exerted by each gas in the air will decrease. With increasing depth, the partial pressure exerted by each gas in the air we breathe will increase.

The lower partial pressures at altitude reflect the fact that there are less molecules of O_2 and N_2 per volume than at sea level. At the highest point on earth, the summit of Mt. Everest, air still contains 21% oxygen and 78% nitrogen but the *number* of oxygen and nitrogen molecules per volume of air is only about 1/3 that at sea level (Figure 2); thus the partial pressures of oxygen and nitrogen are only 1/3 those of sea level.

People who fly in unpressurized airplanes, or engage in mountain climbing or hot air ballooning, subject themselves to a decrease in air pressure as they ascend, and an increase in air pressure as they descend; the opposite, of course, happens to scuba divers. Since air at altitude contains fewer O_2 molecules, a passenger plane that flies above a certain altitude must pressurize its cabin to the air pressure of a lower altitude than actually flown.

When you fly at 30,000 feet, for example, the cabin is pressurized to an altitude of about 7000-8000 feet. At 7000 feet altitude, but not 30,000 feet, the air contains enough oxygen molecules for comfortable breathing at rest (albeit fewer than at sea level). If the plane suddenly lost its artificial cabin pressure at 30,000 feet and did not descend immediately to a safer altitude, and there was no way to get extra oxygen to the passengers and crew, everyone aboard the plane would soon lose consciousness. If the problem remained uncorrected everyone would eventually succumb to hypoxia.

As a practical matter people can live and work up to about 16000 feet; beyond that altitude hypoxia makes it difficult to breathe for long periods, particularly with any exertion. However, people have actually climbed to the summit of Mt. Everest without breathing extra oxygen, a feat of incredible endurance (some would say incredible foolishness).

Two principal adaptations allow people to function at high altitude: increased blood volume (hemoglobin carries most of the blood oxygen, so the more blood, the more of the scarce oxygen molecules can be taken up from the thin atmosphere); and hyperventilation, which is the medical term for over breathing. Hyperventilation lowers the blood carbon dioxide level and allows the mountain dweller to bring more oxygen molecules into the lungs. Hyperventilation is much more effective in adding oxygen to the blood when the blood is low in oxygen than when it is normally supplied. (While hyperventilation is a positive adaptation for altitude, it can cause problems in divers, both breath-hold and scuba; see Section K.)

WHAT IS HENRY'S LAW?

Henry's law states:

The amount of any gas that will dissolve in a liquid at a given temperature is a function of the partial

pressure of the gas in contact with the liquid and the solubility coefficient of the gas in that particular liquid.

Simplified: As the pressure of any gas increases, more of that gas will dissolve into any solution with which it is in free contact.

Mathematically:

$$\frac{VG}{VL} = aP_g$$

where VG is the volume of a particular gas, VL is the volume of a particular liquid, a is the solubility coefficient for the gas in that liquid, and P_g is the pressure of the gas in contact with the liquid.

Taken together, Henry's and Dalton's laws predict two very important consequences:

1) *When ambient pressure is lowered (as at altitude), the partial pressure of oxygen and nitrogen in the body must fall, and there will be less molecules of each gas dissolved in the blood and tissues.*

2) *When ambient pressure is raised (as when diving), the partial pressure of oxygen and nitrogen in the body must rise, and there will be more molecules of each gas dissolved in the blood and tissues.*

The second statement is the physiologic basis for three important problems associated with compressed air diving: decompression sickness, nitrogen narcosis, and oxygen toxicity. These conditions are discussed in Sections G and I.

TEST YOUR UNDERSTANDING

17. A sample of air is taken at 18,000 feet during a hot air balloon ride, and the partial pressures of oxygen and nitrogen are measured. Similar measurements are taken at sea level, and on air as it is inhaled by a scuba diver at a depth of 99 fsw. Using units of atm., complete the table with partial pressures of oxygen and nitrogen for the three sites.

	99 fsw	sea level	18,000 feet
PO_2			
PN_2			

TEST YOUR UNDERSTANDING

18. Listed below are 12 statements that relate to the entire section. State which are true and which are false.

    a. Air pressure is due to the weight of the air.

    b. Water is much heavier than air and for this reason exerts a much greater pressure.

    c. Partial pressure of a gas is independent of the ambient pressure.

    d. The percent change in ambient pressure between 18000 feet altitude and sea level is the same as that between sea level and 33 feet of sea water.

    e. There are several ways to specify the measurement of air pressure, e.g., psi, mm Hg, inches Hg, and atmosphere (atm.). Average air pressure at sea level = 1 atm. = 760 mm Hg = 14.7 psi.

    f. Gauge pressure and absolute pressure are the same.

    g. Air is a mixture of gases made up of approximately 21% oxygen, 78% nitrogen, and 1% other gases. These percentages are the same regardless of altitude, or of the outside pressure exerted on air.

    h. When breathing compressed air, more oxygen will dissolve in blood at 66 fsw than at 33 fsw.

    i. Boyle's law states that pressure of a gas (at constant temperature) is inversely related to its volume: if pressure increases volume decreases, and vice versa.

    j. For a given tank pressure, the density of inhaled gas is constant during scuba diving.

    k. Henry's law explains why there is increased nitrogen in the tissues at depth when scuba diving.

    l. Charles' law predicts that the pressure of air in a scuba tank will fall if the outside temperature falls.

Answers to TEST YOUR UNDERSTANDING

1. c. Air pressure at sea level is 14.7 psi, which means the total column of air from sea level to outer space one inch square weighs 14.7 lbs. Since a square foot contains 12 x 12 = 144 square inches:
   144 sq. in. x 14.7 lbs./sq. inch = 2116.8 lbs.

2. c. A square yard contains 9 sq. feet, or 9 x 144 sq. inches. Hence the column of air over a sq. yard weighs 9 x 144 x 14.7 = 19,051.2 lbs.

3. True

4. True

5. True

6. False

7. At 132 fsw absolute or total ambient pressure = 5 atm. Gauge pressure (pressure of water alone) = 4 atm.

8. b. 1.75 atm.

9. 253 mm Hg - summit of Mt. Everest
   640 mm Hg - Denver
   747 mm Hg - Miami
   1520 mm Hg - inside hyperbaric chamber

10. Volume at 165 feet = 1 liter; density 6 times as great

11. a. The tank is a rigid structure. The compressed air is unaffected by ambient pressure until it leaves the tank.

12. b.

13. True

14. True

15. At 66 fsw, PO_2 = .63 atm.; PN_2 = 2.37 atm.

16. Partial pressure of oxygen is .21(380), or about 80 mm Hg.
    (This answer assumes dry air; any water vapor in the air will slightly lower the partial pressures of the other gases.)

17.

	99 fsw	sea level	18,000 feet
PO_2	.84	.21	.105
PN_2	2.74	.78	.394

18. c, f, and j are false; the other statements are true.

REFERENCES AND BIBLIOGRAPHY

For the sport diver, the training manuals of NAUI, PADI and SSI provide much useful information on physics and physiology of diving, as well as on all the diving skills. In addition, the following six books are highly recommended reference works for those who wish to read further on dive physics and physiology; the last three are textbooks marketed mainly to physicians and other medical professionals.

Richardson D., Shreeves J.T., van Roekel G., Hornsby A., *Encyclopedia of Recreational Diving*. International PADI, Inc., Santa Ana, CA.; 2nd edition, 1997.

NOAA Diving Manual, 3rd Edition. Best Publishing Co., Box 30100, Flagstaff, AZ; 1996.

U.S. Navy Diving Manual, Vol. 1 (Air Diving) and Vol. 2 (Mixed-Gas Diving), Best Publishing Co., Box 30100, Flagstaff, AZ; 1993.

Bennett P, Elliott D, editors. *The Physiology and Medicine of Diving*. 4th edition. W.B. Saunders Co., Philadelphia; 1993.

Bove AA, Davis JC, editors. *Diving Medicine*. 3rd Ed., W.B .Saunders., Philadelphia; 1997.

Edmonds C, Lowry L, Pennefather J. *Diving and Subaquatic Medicine*. Butterworth Heinemann, Oxford; 1992.

DIVING ODDS N' ENDS

Some Famous Wrecks

Apart from the *Titanic* (see Section A), many other famous wrecks have been discovered or explored in recent years. Listed in alphabetical order are ten wrecks that continue to receive coverage in the popular press and magazines. (fsw = feet sea water; figure shown is deepest depth of vessel).

Andrea Doria - 697-ft. Italian luxury liner, cruising from Genoa to New York; hit by the Swedish passenger liner *Stockholm* on July 25, 1956; sank next morning in Atlantic Ocean, 50 miles south of Nantucket; 52 people died (*Dorea* has since claimed lives of many divers); 240 fsw.

Atocha - Spanish galleon carrying gold to Spain; sank in hurricane 1622, about 7 miles off southern tip of Florida; uncovered over period of 15 years (1970-1985) by Mel Fisher and his company, Treasure Salvors; is considered the world's richest discovered wreck; 132 fsw.

Bismarck - German battleship, one of largest and most powerful of World War II; sunk by the British in the Denmark Strait between Greenland and Iceland, May 27, 1941; discovered June 1989 by Robert D. Ballard, using the same underwater camera vehicle his team used to discover *Titanic*; approx. 15700 fsw.

Central America - Side wheel steamer carrying gold from California to New York; sank in hurricane September 9, 1857, 160 miles off coast of Charleston, South Carolina; 8045 fsw.

Edmund Fitzgerald - Largest Great Lakes ship when built in 1958; over 700 feet long, 75 feet wide; sunk November 10, 1975 in Lake Superior, during a storm; later located broken in two, at depth of 530 feet.

Lusitania - 787-ft. luxury liner of British Cunard Line, largest and fastest liner at time of her launch in 1907; torpedoed by German submarine while sailing from U.S. to England, May 7, 1915; sunk 11 miles off coast of Ireland with loss of 1198 lives (out of 1959 crew and passengers); 320 fsw.

Monitor - Union ironclad warship, famous for its epic standoff with Confederate ironclad *Virginia* (originally named *Merrimack*) in March 1862; on December 31, 1862, while being towed, *Monitor* filled with water and sank, 20 miles southeast of Cape Hatteras, North Carolina; 230 fsw.

Pandora - a British frigate carrying home prisoners who rebelled against Captain Bligh and were involved with the *H.M.S. Bounty* mutiny; *Pandora* struck a reef off coast of Australia in 1792; 110 fsw.

Rhone - British mail carrier traveling from England to St. Thomas, U.S. Virgin Islands; sank in hurricane 1859; off Salt Cay in British Virgin Islands; 90 fsw.

San Diego - World War I U.S. battleship; torpedoed by Germans July 18, 1918 off coast of Long Island, New York, within sight of shore; now Long Island's "most dived wreck;" 75 fsw

Water and the Physical Laws That Affect All Divers

WHAT ARE THE IMPORTANT DIFFERENCES BETWEEN AIR AND WATER?

The gas laws discussed in Section D apply equally well to air at any pressure. The laws are particularly important in understanding what happens to air-containing spaces underwater, particularly the lungs, sinuses, and middle ears. Before discussing air pressure underwater, it will be useful to review important differences between air and water (Table 1).

1) Water is much heavier than air. A cubic foot of air weighs 1/12 pound (lb). A cubic foot of fresh water weighs 62.4 lbs and a cubic foot of sea water weighs 64 lbs. (Figure 1).

2) Water molecules are made up of hydrogen and oxygen, chemical symbol H_2O. Each water molecule contains two atoms of hydrogen and one atom of oxygen. Salt water contains salt (sodium chloride, chemical symbol NaCl) and other minerals in solution (i.e., dissolved into it, not chemically combined with the water). Salt adds to the weight of water, and for this reason sea water has slightly greater weight - and hence pressure - than fresh water (sea water contains approximately 35 pounds of salt for every 1000 pounds of water). It takes a depth of 34 feet of fresh water to equal one atmosphere of pressure, as opposed to 33 feet of sea water.

3) Air is a mixture of gases, principally oxygen (O_2, 21% of the air by volume) and nitrogen (N_2, 78% by volume). Each gas exerts its own independent pressure, the sum of which equals the total air pressure (Dalton's law). Unlike water, air (and any other gas or mixture of gases) is compressible; the greater the pressure exerted, the more tightly packed together are the individual gas molecules. Regardless of the air pressure, however, water molecules are much more tightly packed together than air molecules. Compared to air at sea level pressure (1 atm.), water is about 800 times denser.

4) Just as air has weight and exerts pressure on all sides of an object in the atmosphere, water exerts pressure around any object immersed in it. We can push water out of the way because its weight is distributed on all sides and the molecules can be easily moved. The resistance we feel underwater reflects the extreme density of water (compared to air), and the fact that it takes time for water molecules to move out of the way.

5) Water pressure, like air pressure, is a function of weight; the deeper one goes the greater the surrounding water pressure. The marked increase in water pressure with depth affects every scuba and non-scuba diver, indeed anyone who goes underwater (unless inside a heavy vessel with walls that resist pressure, such as a submarine).

TABLE 1.
SOME DIFFERENCES BETWEEN
AIR AND WATER

	Air	Fresh Water	Sea Water
Description	Mixture of gases	Liquid	Liquid with dissolved minerals
Composition	21% O_2 78% N_2 1% other gases	H_2O molecules	H_2O molecules + dissolved minerals
Weight per cu. ft. (lbs)	1/12 (at sea level)	62.4	64
Maximal weight per volume:	depends on pressure	is same at all depths	is same at all depths
Relative Density	1 (sea level)	800	800
Compressible	Yes	No	No
Freezing point (turns to solid)	-500°F	32°F	24°F

Figure 1. Weight of water vs. air at sea level.

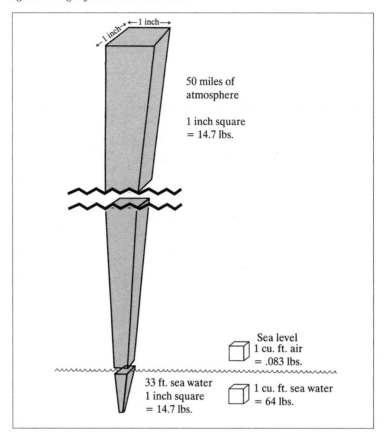

50 miles of
atmosphere

1 inch square
= 14.7 lbs.

Sea level
1 cu. ft. air
= .083 lbs.

33 ft. sea water
1 inch square
= 14.7 lbs.

1 cu. ft. sea water
= 64 lbs.

6) Since water is *not* compressible, unlike air it does not become denser as pressure increases. A cubic foot of water at 130 feet depth has the same weight and density as a cubic foot of water at 33 feet. In contrast, a cubic foot of air at sea level weighs more than a cubic foot of air in the Rocky Mountains or the Himalayas.

7) Differences between air and water, in both weight and density, predict a radical difference in pressure with changes in altitude/depth. Sea water pressure changes one whole atmosphere every 33 feet (every 34 feet for fresh water). Provided they are of the same circumference, a column of sea water 33 feet high weighs the same as a column of earth's entire atmosphere (Figure 1).

8) Water freezes, whereas air does not freeze at any temperature occurring in nature. Sea water freezes at a much lower temperature than fresh water because of the dissolved salt, which slows down the formation of water crystals.

WHAT DOES BOYLE'S LAW PREDICT ABOUT CHANGES IN PRESSURE WITH DEPTH?

It is always convenient to illustrate Boyle's law with balloon models. Balloons are round and easily compressible. By taking an air-filled balloon underwater, Boyle's law can be nicely demonstrated (Figure 2).

Assume a balloon is filled with 12 liters of air at the surface, then taken underwater. Figure 2 shows the changes in density and air volume with depth *as predicted by Boyle's law*. The balloon shrinks and its air becomes denser with increasing depth; this is because the pressure increases with depth and the balloon is compressible. On ascent the opposite happens; the balloon re-expands and the air density returns to baseline.

Figure 2. Change in Balloon Pressure (in atm.), Volume (in liters), and Relative Density of Air, from Sea Level to 132 Feet. (fsw = feet sea water)

depth (fsw)	pressure (atm.)	volume of air in balloon (l)	density of air in balloon	relative size of balloon
Sea level	1	12	1x	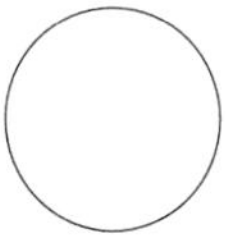
33	2	6	2x	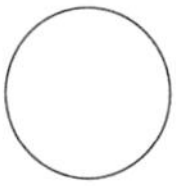
66	3	4	3x	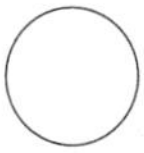
99	4	3	4x	
132	5	2.4	5x	

WHAT DOES BOYLE'S LAW PREDICT ABOUT BREATH-HOLD DIVING?

So much for balloons. What about the body? Underwater, we can view the body as made up of two groups of organs that differ in how they respond to water pressure. One group of organs is compressible by the water pressure, and the other group is non-compressible (Figure 3). Bone, muscle, blood and solid organs such as the kidney, heart, and liver are all non-compressible and therefore unaffected by water pressure; these organs and tissues have the same (or higher) density than water and can withstand intense water pressure without any problem. Were our bodies made up of only non-compressible structures, going underwater would be a lot simpler (though still not hazard-free).

The compressible areas contain some air and include the lungs, middle ears, sinuses, nasal passages, interior of hollow organs (stomach and intestines), and any air pockets you may not know about (e.g., a tooth cavity). If these parts of the body did not contain air they would not be compressible. Conversely, any part of the body that is compressible underwater must contain air or some other gas.

At the moment a diver holds his breath the mass of air in the body is *fixed*; no new air can enter or leave. Given that the mass of air is fixed at that point, Boyle's law predicts that the compressible spaces will be affected by changes in pressure. A fixed mass of gas (the diver's air-containing spaces) subjected to an increase in pressure underwater will compress (shrink in size). But by how much?

Assume a typical breath-hold diver's lungs contain 8 liters of air at full inhalation (one liter equals about one quart). At 33 feet his lungs could theoretically shrink to half the sea level volume, or 4 liters, if they behave just like a balloon. The same percent shrinkage could occur in the sinuses, middle ears, and all other compressible body spaces, if they too behave like balloons.

However, our air-containing spaces don't behave exactly like balloons; they are not as easily and evenly compressible. The lungs are supported by a bony rib cage, the sinuses are embedded in the skull, only part of the middle ear is exposed to water pressure (the tympanic membrane), etc. Also, trained breath-hold divers can transfer some air from the throat to the middle ear (via the eustachian tube), retarding the shrinkage of that small space.

So, on the one hand, our compressible air spaces are much more complex than the simple balloon models used to illustrate Boyle's law. On the other hand, we do have compressible air spaces and Boyle's law predicts that they *must* shrink in size if the outside pressure is greater than the inside pressure. It is just impossible to predict exactly how much they will shrink, or how such shrinkage will affect the individual diver.

If the breath-hold diver goes too deep, the spaces will shrink so much that blood starts leaving the capillaries to fill in the spaces. The result can be lung, sinus or nasal hemorrhage, or a ruptured tympanic mem-

Figure 3. Compressible and non-compressible organs.

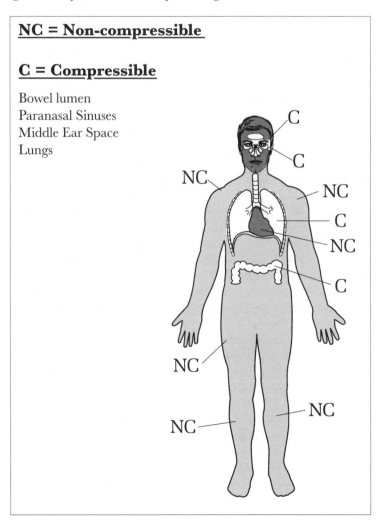

<u>NC = Non-compressible</u>

<u>C = Compressible</u>

Bowel lumen
Paranasal Sinuses
Middle Ear Space
Lungs

brane. With ascent, all the breath-hold diver's shrunken spaces will expand back to their original size. Because there is no over expansion, there is no risk of blowing out a lung or other air space.

Breath-hold diving, practiced for centuries, is still employed for both recreation and commerce (ama divers of Japan and Korea, pearl divers of Hawaii, resort divers of Mexico, sport divers of California). It requires special skills beyond the ability to hold one's breath, such as withstanding the squeeze of descent and quickly accomplishing a goal when the desired depth is reached. Scuba requires none of these skills but others, of a different sort, that are easy to learn. For most people, scuba is much easier to master than breath-hold diving.

TEST YOUR UNDERSTANDING

6. On descent, does the density of air in a breath-hold diver's lungs increase or remain the same?

7. Assume a diver's lungs contain 8 liters at the time he commences a breath-hold dive to 33 fsw. How much air will his lungs contain at that depth?
   a. 8 liters
   b. Less than 8 but more than 4 liters
   c. 4 liters

WHAT DOES BOYLE'S LAW PREDICT FOR THE DIVER BREATHING COMPRESSED AIR?

Water contains oxygen (both dissolved and as part of the water molecule, H_2O). Unlike fish, land animals are not equipped to extract the dissolved or free oxygen and use it for breathing. Like all other mammals (including the aquatic variety such as dolphins, porpoises and whales), humans underwater are cut off from life-supporting oxygen.

For centuries the only underwater option was breath-hold diving, an activity practiced only by the most daring and hardy. For most people even 20 seconds underwater can seem like eternity. The advent of scuba made it possible for just about anyone with healthy lungs and heart to stay underwater for long periods. (This advance has not come without a price. Compressed air diving presents two physiologic problems breath-hold divers don't worry much about: decompression sickness and air embolism.)

Boyle's law predicts that the compressible spaces of a breath-hold diver will compress because the amount of air in these spaces (i.e., the total number of air molecules) is fixed at the point of breath-hold; hence, as pressure increases the *volume* occupied by the air must decrease.

Does Boyle's law also apply for scuba divers? Absolutely; after all, a law is a law. But the consequences are different because scuba divers breathe compressed air underwater. First, the *amount of air* (the number of air molecules) in each of the scuba diver's compressible spaces *increases* along with the water pressure. Second, the *volume* of each compressible space remains fairly constant throughout the dive.

Thus, even though a space is compressible it should not be compressed during scuba diving. While diving, the extra molecules of air that enter these spaces (lungs, sinuses, middle ears) allows them to maintain the *same pressure* as the surrounding water pressure. At a given depth, though the ambient pressure is increased the volume in any compressible space remains constant because the gas density increases.

Compressible body spaces while scuba diving (compared to sea level) have:

- Same volume (size)
- Increased number of gas molecules
- Increased gas density

HOW MUCH AIR IS IN A SCUBA TANK?

Scuba divers can remain underwater because they carry a supply of air. The amount of air carried in a tank depends on its size and filling pressure. Most tanks used for recreational diving are designed to carry anywhere from about 60 to 100 cu. ft. of air; the typical tank found in most resorts carries 80 cubic feet (cu. ft.) when filled to 3000 psi. If the tank is filled to a lower pressure, the volume of air it contains will be less.

Eighty cu. ft. is the volume inside a box 5 ft. x 4 ft. x 4 ft., or the volume of a telephone booth 7 ft. x 3.3 ft. x 3.3 ft. (Figure 4). Since a cubic foot of air weighs 1/12 lb, the air in an 80 cu. ft. tank filled to capacity weighs about 6.7 lbs. This weight is in addition to the much heavier weight of the tank itself.

HOW DOES AIR PRESSURE CHANGE FROM THE SCUBA TANK TO THE DIVER'S LUNGS?

Sea level pressure is 14.7 psi. An 80 cu. ft. tank at 3000 psi contains 80 cu. ft. of air that has been compressed 204 times (3000 psi/14.7 psi) higher than sea level pressure. If you tried to breathe air at 3000 psi, it would blow you away; you couldn't do it. The scuba diver is able to breathe tank air by virtue of a two-stage regulator system that 1) steps the pressure down to a level slightly above ambient, and then 2) delivers the air at ambient pressure. Table 3 shows examples of regulator and airway pressures for various depths.

The *first stage regulator* brings the pressure down to ambient + a pre-determined pressure. The pre-determined pressure is set by the regulator's design, but is generally 120-140 psi. Thus, the pressure in the hose between first and second stages is 120 to 140 psi higher than the ambient pressure.

The *second stage regulator* contains a demand valve that requires only a slight inspiratory effort to open; when the diver inhales on the mouth-

Figure 4. An 80 cu. ft. capacity scuba tank can hold as much air as would fill a telephone booth 7 ft. x 3.3 ft. x 3.3 ft. at sea level.

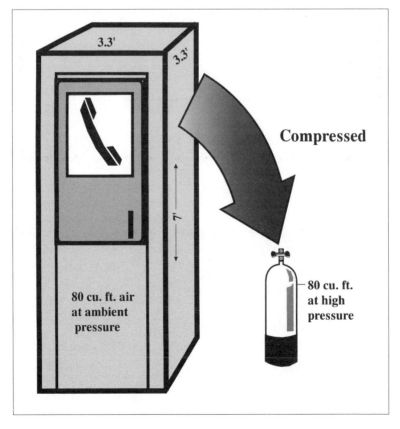

TABLE 3.
Ambient and Tank Pressures for Various Depths.

Shown are pressures for: surrounding water (ambient), air in scuba tank, air leaving 1st and 2nd stage regulators, and air in the lungs. Ambient pressure is determined solely by depth, and is the pressure inside the diver's lungs when breathing with scuba equipment. Tank pressures for a given depth will vary depending on the rate of air consumption and duration of the dive; at each depth in this table a tank psi of 1500 is shown as example. The first stage regulator lowers tank pressure to ambient plus some intermediate pressure determined by the regulator's design, in these examples 140 psi. The second stage regulator lowers the ambient + intermediate pressure to the ambient pressure only, which is the pressure inhaled by the diver. (atm. = atmospheres; psi = pounds per square inch.)

depth (fsw)	ambient (atm.)	ambient (psi)	air in hose after tank (psi)	air on exiting 1st stage (psi)	in the 2nd stage (psi)	lungs (psi)
0	1	14.7	1500	154.7	14.7	14.7
33	2	29.4	1500	169.4	29.4	29.4
66	3	44.1	1500	184.1	44.1	44.1
99	4	58.8	1500	198.8	58.8	58.8
132	5	73.5	1500	213.5	73.5	73.5
165	6	88.2	1500	228.2	88.2	88.2

piece attached to the second stage, the demand valve opens and air enters the lungs at ambient pressure. Note that the air is at the predetermined pressure immediately upon leaving the second stage (i.e., 120-140 psi), but it rapidly reaches ambient by the time it is inhaled (Figure 5). The second stage regulator is also designed so that air flow ceases when the diver exhales. (When air flow doesn't cease on exhalation it is said to "free-flow," a problem that can usually be corrected by adjusting the regulator or briefly occluding the mouthpiece.)

Recreational divers use "open circuit" scuba, which means all exhaled air enters the surrounding water; none is re-breathed. The value of 1500 psi for tank pressure in Table 3, for each depth, is shown as example only. Obviously, as the dive progresses the amount and pressure of air in the tank will decrease. The rate at which the tank's air volume and pressure decrease is a function of the diver's ventilation rate

Figure 5. Scuba diver at 66 fsw (3 atm. or 44 psi). The pressure in the hose connecting the first stage and second stage regulators is the ambient pressure + 140 psi or 184.1 psi. The air pressure leaving her second stage regulator is at ambient pressure (44 psi). The pressure in the tank (on her back, not shown) does not affect the regulator pressures (as long as the tank pressure is above some minimum value, usually the ambient pressure).

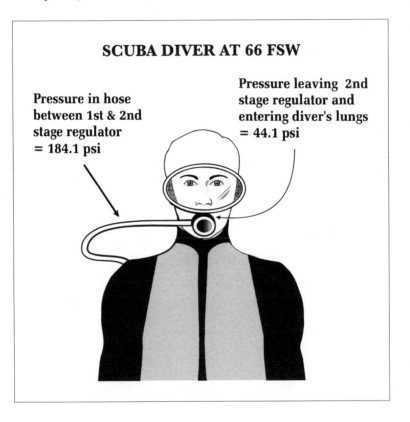

SCUBA DIVER AT 66 FSW

Pressure in hose between 1st & 2nd stage regulator = 184.1 psi

Pressure leaving 2nd stage regulator and entering diver's lungs = 44.1 psi

---

TEST YOUR UNDERSTANDING

8. If ambient pressure is higher than tank pressure, air flow will:
    a. cease
    b. slow down
    c. remain unchanged

9. What effect does an increase in ambient pressure have on air pressure inside the tank?

(how much air is breathed per minute), depth, and length of time underwater. Note that regardless of the tank's psi, as long as it is above some minimum value the first and second stage regulators will deliver air at the ambient pressure. (Not all regulators work the same at very low tank pressures.)

WHAT IS BUOYANCY?

Buoyancy refers to the tendency of objects immersed in water to float or sink. Objects that are positively buoyant float on top of water; objects that are negatively buoyant sink; and objects that are neutrally buoyant neither float nor sink, but stay where you place them (Figure 6). This principle was first stated by Archimedes (Greek mathematician and engineer, lived about 287 B.C. to 212 B.C.). He observed that an object immersed in water sinks or floats depending on the *weight of water it displaces*. If the weight of water displaced is less than the object's weight, it sinks; if the displaced water weighs more, the object floats; and if the displaced water is the same the object is neutrally buoyant.

Figure 6. Objects that float are positively buoyant and those that sink are negatively buoyant. Objects that stay where placed are neutrally buoyant.

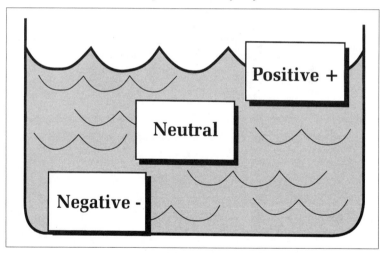

For example, a cubic foot of solid wood weighing 63 lbs. would float in sea water (cu. ft. = 64 lbs) and sink in fresh water (cu. ft. = 62.4 lbs.). A cubic foot of solid steel weighs much more than 64 lbs., and so will sink in any body of water, whereas a cubic foot of styrofoam will always float. The steel displaces much less than its weight of water, the styrofoam much more.

WHAT IS BUOYANCY CONTROL?

"Buoyancy" also refers to an all important scuba diving skill, perhaps the one most difficult to master. A diver who has learned to control buoyancy has learned: the proper amount of lead weight to carry for each dive; how to use natural breathing to inflate or deflate the lungs to control vertical position; how to position equipment in order to stay horizontal; when (and when not) to put air in the BC; and how to ascend at a slow and steady rate.

Good buoyancy control is perhaps the single skill that most distinguishes experienced from novice divers. For most divers it does not come easily or quickly. Consider the many factors that can affect a diver's buoyancy:

- Innate buoyancy differs among individuals, and depends on the amount and distribution of body fat, bone and muscle; as a result, some people naturally float and some sink. Fat tissue has a lower density than bone or muscle, so people with a lot of fat are more likely to float (i.e., displace an amount of water weighing more than their body), whereas lean, muscular folks are more likely to sink (i.e., displace an amount of water weighing less than their body).
- The amount of air in the lungs affects buoyancy. If you establish neutral buoyancy during quiet breathing, a full inhalation will make you rise (become positively buoyant), whereas a full exhalation will make you sink (negatively buoyant).
- A wet suit will be positively buoyant on the surface but will change to neutrally or negatively buoyant at depth.
- A typical 80 cu. ft. aluminum scuba tank filled with air is negatively buoyant by 2-3 lbs., but when near empty the same tank will be 2-3 lbs. positively buoyant. (80 cu. ft. or air weighs about 6 lbs.)
- The typical buoyancy compensator is positively buoyant without any air, and becomes more so as it is inflated.
- Most ancillary equipment carried on a dive, such as a light, knife, or camera, tends to sink and therefore adds to negative buoyancy.
- Some fins are positively buoyant, some negatively buoyant.
- Finally, salt water weighs more than fresh water (64 lbs. vs. 62.4 lbs. per cu. ft.), so divers are more buoyant in salt than in fresh water.

Because most people have slight positive buoyancy naturally, and because the BC and wet suit add to positive buoyancy on the surface, it is usually necessary to carry lead weights while diving. Weights tip the scale to negative buoyancy and allow the diver to sink easily below the surface. Depending on body makeup and type of equipment carried or worn, warm water divers need anywhere from 4 to about 12 pounds of lead weight. The single item most affecting the amount of weight required is the wetsuit (the thicker the suit, the more weight needed to establish negative buoyancy).

As the dive progresses buoyancy is constantly changing. Consider:

- Pressure compresses air cells in the wet suit, so the positive buoyancy contributed by the suit on the surface decreases significantly at depth.
- As air is used up, the tank's buoyancy changes from negative to neutral to positive (steel tanks remain negative buoyant throughout the dive).
- Any air in the BC at depth will expand as the diver rises, increasing buoyancy steadily with ascent; the higher the diver ascends the greater the increase in positive buoyancy.
- Any change in the breathing pattern during the dive (e.g., a tendency to hyperventilation) may alter the diver's average lung volume, and thus affect buoyancy.

For the novice diver the net result of all the factors affecting buoyancy can be confusion and a bad dive. Consider two typical scenarios.

Novice A goes to 60 feet with a group of other divers. He has trouble emptying his BC of air and kicks hard to stay at depth and with the group; no matter how hard he tries to stay down he keeps rising. He looks in vain for something to hold on to. His depth gauge shows 40 feet...then 30...then 20. He simply cannot dump any air out of his BC and a few seconds later breaks through the surface of the water.

Novice B claims trouble sinking on her dives. She enters the warm Caribbean water with 16 pounds of lead, even though the dive master warns "it is too much." At 50 fsw she has difficulty staying off the bottom and puts some air in her BC. She then starts to rise, so she dumps some air. All the while she notices herself kicking hard to stay level and with her buddy. About 20 minutes into the dive she alerts her buddy that her tank has only 800 psi; her buddy still has 1800 psi. Together they begin an ascent to the safety stop line.

Diver A's problem was a BC with residual air that he could not properly vent. The closer he came to the surface the quicker he rose, as air in his BC expanded further. Fortunately he did not hold his breath and suffered no barotrauma from the rapid ascent.

10. A scuba diver rests prone a few inches from the sandy bottom, motionless. He takes in a full breath and rises about 2 feet; on full exhalation he falls back toward the bottom. He is:

    a. Positively buoyant
    b. Negatively buoyant
    c. Neutrally buoyant

11. A diver, with scuba equipment, weighs 192 pounds and displaces three cubic feet of sea water. On the surface of the ocean he is:

    a. Positively buoyant
    b. Negatively buoyant
    c. Neutrally buoyant

12. A diver, with scuba equipment, weighs 192 pounds and displaces three cubic feet of fresh water. On the surface of a fresh water lake he is:

    a. Positively buoyant
    b. Negatively buoyant
    c. Neutrally buoyant

Diver B's problem was carrying too much weight; this caused her to work extra hard underwater just to stay level. As a result, she used up air much faster than her buddy. As with Diver A, she had a less than optimal dive because of poor buoyancy control.

(Both divers encountered a stressful situation and reacted suboptimally. The concept and handling of stress are discussed in Section K.)

WHAT CAUSES WEIGHTLESSNESS UNDERWATER?

To "float" as if defying gravity - a feeling of weightlessness - is one of the many thrills of diving. The feeling comes from establishing neutral-buoyancy underwater. At that point the gravity force pulling your body down is equal to the water pressure pushing it up, and you neither sink nor rise.

The sensation is reportedly similar to what is experienced in outer space, which is why astronauts train with scuba gear before some space missions. However, the mechanisms are different. In outer space the astronaut is far enough away from earth to escape the effects of gravity, and it is gravity which makes us have (and feel) weight.

On the surface or underwater, gravity still exerts an effect, but it can be nullified by establishing neutral or positive buoyancy. In outer space lead weights will float just like the astronaut because they are also free of earth's gravity. When a diver is neutrally buoyant, his weight belt, if detached, will quickly drop because it is negatively buoyant and subject to earth's gravity.

HOW DOES ONE LEARN TO ACQUIRE PROPER BUOYANCY?

First, understand that buoyancy is not a static phenomenon, but one that changes constantly in the water, even if you stay at a level depth (because the quantity of tank air is constantly decreasing, and also because breathing affects buoyancy). Appreciating buoyancy as a constantly changing factor during every dive is the first step to mastering it.

Second, understand the role of the BC. As a rule, one should not have to rely on the BC for buoyancy control. For novice divers this piece of advice may seem paradoxical; a BC is, after all, a *buoyancy compensator* (sometimes also referred to as a *buoyancy control* device). No matter. Experienced divers learn how to use their lungs to fine tune buoyancy, and reserve the BC for an occasional adjustment, mainly to compensate for the decrease in wet suit buoyancy with depth.

Ideally, inflating the BC should only be necessary on the surface (for flotation), for wet suit compensation, and for emergency ascents. However, because wet suit compression will alter buoyancy at depth, it is often necessary to add a little air to compensate and re-establish neutral buoyancy. From that point of the dive, buoyancy should be controlled mainly by breathing. (It will also be necessary toward the end of the dive to dump out any air added to the BC, in order to prevent too rapid an ascent.)

Third, one can take a formal buoyancy control course, offered in many resorts around the world. These courses teach the nuances of buoyancy control, including how to position equipment on your body so weight is evenly distributed.

Finally, gain experience. There is no substitute for experience, which means making many dives. Some divers find that learning good buoyancy control takes perhaps 100 or more dives. It also helps to practice such basic open water skills as the fin pivot. (In this skill the diver establishes neutral buoyancy with only his fins touching the bottom; using his fins as the fulcrum, he can then rise up with each deep inhalation, and fall back toward the bottom with each exhalation.) Only with many dives can one experiment with equipment, weights, wet suits and breathing techniques, and learn to master buoyancy control.

Answers to TEST YOUR UNDERSTANDING

1. Both a and b are correct. A square-foot column of sea water 33 ft. deep weighs 33 ft. x 64 lbs./ft. = 2112 lbs. This is equivalent to the weight of a column of air one foot square extending from sea level to outer space.

2. c. Since air at sea level weighs only 1/12 lb. per cubic foot, it would require 64 x 12 = 768 cu. ft. of air to equal the weight of one cu. ft. of sea water.

3. No.

4. At 6 atm. (165 fsw) the balloon would be compressed to 1/6 its original volume, or 2 liters.

5. Ans. 8 liters. From 99 fsw to 33 fsw the volume will double to 4 liters; it will double again from 33 fsw to the surface.

6. Increase, as explained by Boyle's law

7. b. The new volume would be four liters if lungs behaved like balloons. Because of the bony rib cage and other anatomic features, lungs don't behave exactly like balloons, so the final lung volume would be somewhat greater than four liters.

8. a. cease

9. None. The tank, usually made of steel or aluminum, is strong enough to withstand pressures much greater than those encountered while diving. Consequently, air pressure within the tank is unaffected by the ambient pressure. Once air leaves the tank and enters the lungs its pressure will be the same as ambient.

10. c. Neutrally buoyant.

11. c. Neutrally buoyant. The volume of sea water displaced has the same weight (192 lbs.) as the diver + equipment.

12. b. Negatively buoyant. The volume of fresh water displaced weighs 187.2 lbs., which is less than the weight of diver + equipment (192 lbs.), so the diver will sink.

REFERENCES AND BIBLIOGRAPHY

For the sport diver, the training manuals of NAUI, PADI and SSI provide much useful information on physics and physiology of diving, as well as on all the diving skills. In addition, the following six books are highly recommended reference works for those who wish to read further on dive physics and physiology; the last three are textbooks marketed mainly to physicians and other medical professionals.

Richardson D., Shreeves J.T., Van Roekel G., Hornsby A. *Encyclopedia of Recreational Diving*. International PADI, Inc., Santa Ana, CA.; 2nd edition, 1997.

NOAA Diving Manual, 3rd Edition. Best Publishing Co., Box 30100, Flagstaff, AZ; 1996.

U.S. Navy Diving Manual, Vol. 1 (Air Diving) and Vol 2 (Mixed-Gas Diving), Best Publishing Co., Box 30100, Flagstaff, AZ; 1996.

Bennett P, Elliott D, editors. *The Physiology and Medicine of Diving*. 4th edition. W.B. Saunders Co., Philadelphia; 1993.

Bove AA, Davis JC, editors. *Diving Medicine*. 3rd Ed., W.B. Saunders, Philadelphia; 1997.

Edmonds C, Lowry L, Pennefather J. *Diving and Subaquatic Medicine*. Butterworth Heinemann, Oxford; 1992.

DIVING ODDS N' ENDS

Selected Non-documentary Movies with Diving Themes /Scenes (of which there are few, and most of them woefully short on plot or acting, or both); listed in order of release.

Beneath the 12-mile Reef; **1953.** Entertaining film centered around sponge divers off the Florida coast.

20,000 Leagues Under the Sea; **1954.** Disney version of the classic Jules Verne novel about Captain Nemo and his submarine Nautilus. This is the best of three movies with the same title; the other two appeared in 1916 (a silent film) and 1972.

The Silent Enemy; **1958.** World War II adventure has frogmen fighting it out in Gibraltar Harbor. Movie highlights underwater photography (in black and white).

Thunderball; **1965.** An early James Bond thriller starring Sean Connery; underwater scenes filmed off Nassau.

Around the World Under the Sea; **1966.** Early underwater movie starring Lloyd Bridges of *Sea Hunt* fame in scuba gear.

The Deep; **1977.** An action-adventure film about recovering treasure from a wreck off Bermuda. One of the better stories in films of this genre.

Airport 77; **1977.** Typical Hollywood melodrama. Story about a Boeing 747 that crashes intact into the ocean, trapping its passengers. Film contains scene of Navy divers working to raise the plane. (Predictable outcome; excellent use of lift bags).

Raise the Titanic; **1980.** About a plot to raise the world's most famous wreck in order to recover rare cargo of radioactive material.

For Your Eyes Only; **1981.** A second James Bond thriller with underwater scenes, this time starring Roger Moore as 007.

Never Say Never Again; **1983.** Yet another James Bond movie with underwater action; a remake of the popular *Thunderball* (1963).

The Big Blue; **1988.** Loosely based on the life of world champion free diver Jacque Mayol.

The Abyss; **1988.** The best of the underwater genre films, an engrossing story about aliens whose ship rests on the bottom of the ocean. Includes scenes on liquid breathing and the high pressure nervous syndrome.

Leviathan; **1988.** A poor remake of *Alien*. Entire action except for last, brief scene takes place three miles underwater.

Deep Star Six; **1988.** Drama centering on top-secret navy base on ocean floor; of 'B' or 'turkey' movie status.

Lords of the Deep; **1988.** Another underwater thriller 'B' movie; this one at 10,000 fsw.

DIVING ODDS N' ENDS

The Great White Shark

The great white shark, *Carcharodon carcharias*, is the most feared fish in the sea. The 1975 movie Jaws, based on the Peter Benchly novel about a people-eating great white, actually caused a slump in the scuba industry. After seeing the great shark monster do its thing, many people simply would not go near salt water.

The great white is found in tropical and subtropical waters, but is especially numerous in Australian waters. Richard Ellis, who has written extensively on sharks, believes the great white has much more to fear from people than vice versa. His 1991 book, *Great White Shark* (co-authored with J.E. McCosker), includes a complete listing of great white attacks on humans from 1926 through 1990; several attacks are described in detail.

According to the U.S. Navy Manual, the shark can grow up to 25 feet long. *Guinness Book of Records* states that the largest great white accurately measured was 20 ft. 4 in. long and weighed 5000 lbs.; it was found in the Azores in 1978.

DIVING ODDS N' ENDS

Earth's Most Venomous Creature

According to an 1994 article in National Geographic (Hamner WM), the distinction goes to Australia's box jellyfish, *Chironex fleckeri*. This species of jellyfish inhabits Australia's north coast from the Queensland town of Rockhampton on the eastern shore all the way to the middle of Western Australia. It stays close to shore and affects swimmers in this huge coastal region. Fortunately the jellyfish is not found on the Great Barrier Reef.

At maturity the box jellyfish has a body as big as a basketball (and is square or box like), with up to 60 tentacles each 15 feet long. Skin contact with the tentacles can kill a human in four minutes, and 65 people have died from its sting this century. The Australians have developed a potent anti-venom to the box jellyfish which is credited with saving lives.

<u>NOTES</u>

Effects of Unequal Air Pressures While Scuba Diving: Ear Squeeze, Sinus Squeeze, Air Embolism and Other Forms of Barotrauma

WHAT DOES BOYLE'S LAW PREDICT ABOUT UNEQUAL PRESSURES?

Once again we come to all-important Boyle's law: for a given mass of gas at a constant temperature, the product of pressure (P) and volume (V) is constant (K):

$$P \times V = K.$$

We have already seen how, for the breath-hold diver, Boyle's law predicts that compressible air spaces will shrink on descent and re-expand on ascent, and that the situation is different for scuba divers because compressed air is continuously inhaled. Even if the scuba and breath-hold diver go to the same depth and spend the same amount of time underwater (e.g., one minute), the effects of water pressure are radically different on the two divers. Because tank air is inhaled at the ambient pressure, the scuba diver's lungs and other compressible air spaces *do not* shrink.

Consider that all the body's air-containing spaces are in contact with inhaled air. At the same time, there is a natural tendency for air anywhere in the body - in the lungs, middle ears, sinuses and other spaces - to diffuse into the blood. As air is absorbed into the blood, it is replenished by fresh air inhaled from the scuba tank.

If the absorbed air was not replenished, the air spaces would, over time, shrink and close. (This in fact happens in some lung diseases. Any part of a lung that becomes plugged, such as from mucus or a tumor, will shrink completely until it becomes airless.) Shrinkage and closure of an air space will not happen as long as it is in contact with a fresh supply of air. Does Boyle's law still apply to such spaces? Unequivocally, yes. When fresh air enters the diver's lungs it is at the *same pressure* as the surrounding water pressure. This pressure, of course, is higher than at sea level and so the air is *correspondingly denser.*

As long as the diver continuously breathes from the scuba tank, the density of inhaled air will change with ascent and descent. For this reason the "given mass of air" stipulated in Boyle's law, which is really the number of air molecules, changes as the depth changes. On descent the "given mass" increases as the inhaled air becomes denser; on ascent the "given mass" decreases as the inhaled air becomes less dense. Stated another way, when breathing compressed air underwater, *the actual number of air molecules*, in the lungs and all other air spaces, increases on descent and decreases on ascent.

Assume two people dive from a boat to a depth of 99 feet; one diver holds his breath and the other diver uses compressed air (scuba). Also assume that the lungs of each diver contain 10 billion air molecules and the lungs behave like balloons. Table 1 shows the physical changes in air in the lungs of each diver at 33, 66 and 99 fsw. (Actually, the breath-hold diver's lungs, being tethered by a rib cage, don't behave exactly like balloons. Also, some gas exchange takes place even with breath holding, since oxygen is taken up from air in the lungs while a smaller amount of CO_2 is added to that air; as a result, the number of molecules does not remain exactly the same.)

TABLE 1.

Change in mass of gas, lung volume and air density with depth: breath-hold vs. scuba. Mol. = no. of air molecules in lungs (billions); vol. = volume of air in lungs (liters); den. = relative density of air in the lungs. See text for discussion.

depth (ft.)	breath-hold diver			scuba diver		
	mol.	vol.	den.	mol.	vol.	den.
sea level	10	8	1	10	8	1
33	10	4	2x	20	8	2x
66	10	3	3x	30	8	3x
99	10	2	4x	40	8	4x

For the breath-hold diver, the mass of gas (the number of molecules) in the air spaces remains about the same during the dive, so as water pressure increases the lungs must shrink (Boyle's law). For the scuba diver, however, the mass of gas (number of molecules) *increases* along with the increase in water pressure, so the lungs do not shrink.

Thus the lungs (and other air spaces) of a scuba diver at 33 fsw contain *twice as many* air molecules as at sea level, and also *twice as many* air molecules as a breath-hold diver at the same depth (allowing for slight variation due to absorption of oxygen into the blood). Since the volume of air in the scuba diver's lungs doesn't change, the *density of air* (how close the molecules are to one another) must be greater (see Table 1).

At 99 fsw the *breath-hold diver's* lungs contain about the same number of molecules as on the surface, but in only 1/4 the volume; hence the air, being compressed by the increased pressure, is four times denser than on the surface. At 99 fsw the *scuba diver's* lungs are filled with air just as dense, but since there are four times the number of molecules as on the surface the lung volume is preserved (Table 1). As long as there is good communication with inhaled air, the scuba diver's compressible air spaces will fill up with extra molecules and *will not shrink.*

TEST YOUR UNDERSTANDING

1. Based on the sea level values provided in Table 1, what would be the number of molecules and volume of air in a scuba diver's lungs at 132 fsw?

2. Using Boyle's law, describe what would happen to each of the following if a scuba diver holds her breath at 66 fsw and attempts ascent to the surface.

   a. number of molecules in the lungs
   b. density of air in the lungs
   c. volume of air in the lungs

Everything described so far fits with Boyle's law. 'Pressure times volume' is a constant value when the mass of gas (number of gas molecules) is fixed; it is not constant if the gas density changes, as occurs with changes in depth, because then the mass of gas in any space also changes.

The most critical result of Boyle's law occurs when the mass of gas is fixed, as would occur in the lungs of a scuba diver if breath is held. If the scuba diver was to breath-hold *and* ascend, the fixed mass of gas at the time of breath-hold would inexorably expand in volume (as predicted by Boyle's law) *until the diver exhaled or the lungs ruptured.* This, of course, is why a breath-hold ascent from any scuba dive is so dangerous.

WHAT IS THE DIFFERENCE BETWEEN SCUBA DIVING WITH THE GLOTTIS CLOSED AND OPEN?

The glottis is the voice box, located just under your chin inside the neck. Also called the larynx, it leads directly into the trachea (the "windpipe") which then leads to the lungs (see Section C). We "close" the glottis when we hold our breath, which is why you can't speak and hold your breath at the same time. (The universal sign of someone choking on food is fingers to the throat and inability to speak.)

What happens when the glottis is open or closed relates directly to the difference between compressible and non-compressible structures, as was discussed in Section E. Non-compressible structures include the blood, bones and all solid organs; compressible structures include the lungs, sinuses, middle ear, and the hollow organs such as the stomach and intestines. Figure 1 shows effects on the lungs from increased ambient pressure when the glottis is closed ("Closed"), and when air is replenished from scuba apparatus ("Scuba").

A scuba dive with breath held (glottis closed) is tantamount to a breath-hold dive (Table 1); the lungs will be squeezed by the increased ambient pressure. An initial volume of 6 liters (e.g., after taking in a regular breath) could theoretically shrink to only 1.2 liters at a depth of 132 feet. However, the scuba diver has the option (which should always be exercised) to continuously breathe compressed air, in which case lung volume will stay the same at all depths (allowing for slight variation with regular breathing). In both situations (glottis closed and breathing compressed air) the density of air in the lungs will increase with increasing depth.

Air in the tank is highly pressurized, approximately 3000 psi (equivalent to 204 atmospheres) for an 80 cu. ft. tank filled to capacity. The two-stage regulator allows compressed air to be inhaled at the ambient pressure, so the scuba diver can maintain normal lung volume at all depths. (The increased density of the inspired air at depth is seldom great enough to impair work of breathing during recreational diving.)

Tank pressure should be at least 500 psi before beginning any ascent (ideally, one should arrive at the safety stop with no less than 500 psi). Five hundred psi are equivalent to 34 atmospheres. Since the maximum RSD depth of 130 feet equals only about five atmospheres, there should always be a large gradient for air to flow from the tank to the diver's lungs.

WHAT IS BAROTRAUMA?

'Baro' refers to pressure (e.g., a *baro*meter is an instrument for measuring pressure). Barotrauma is physical damage to any part of the body

Figure 1. Effects on lungs with glottis open and closed.

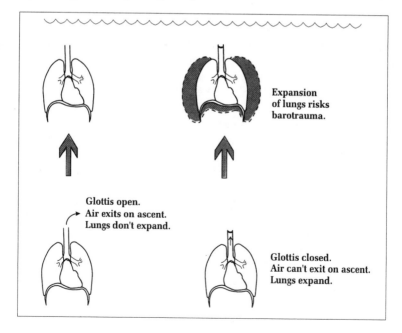

Expansion
of lungs risks
barotrauma.

Glottis open.
Air exits on ascent.
Lungs don't expand.

Glottis closed.
Air can't exit on ascent.
Lungs expand.

as a result of unequal air pressures; it is from either compression or expansion of a body part. The tissues may rupture, blood supply may be compromised, or swelling may occur. All conditions discussed in this chapter are forms of barotrauma.

In the case of diving, the unequal pressures are between some cavity of the body (the middle ear, the sinuses, the lungs, etc.) and the ambient air pressure. The consequences of barotrauma may range from mild discomfort in the affected area (e.g., ears or sinuses), to various levels of pain, to rupture of an organ, such as the ear's tympanic membrane or a part of the lung. Rupture of an organ while diving is particularly hazardous because of the risk of drowning.

Barotrauma is one of three pressure-related problems encountered in scuba diving; the other two are decompression sickness and nitrogen narcosis (Table 2). Barotrauma problems (including the most severe, arterial gas embolism), are physiologically explainable by Boyle's law. Non-barotrauma, pressure-related problems are physiologically explainable by the laws of Dalton and Henry, as will be discussed later.

WHAT BAROTRAUMA PROBLEMS CAN OCCUR ON DESCENT?

Most problems on descent relate to inadequate communication between the upper airway and the middle ears and sinuses. The most frequently en-countered problem on descent is middle ear "squeeze," an ear discomfort or pain from shrinkage of the middle ear space (Figure 2). This problem may begin at only a few feet depth. The earliest symptoms are similar to the "ear stuffiness" we sometimes feel when a plane rapidly descends. Unchecked during a dive, the feeling can rapidly progress to actual pain and ear damage.

The pathologic result of continued squeeze in any space is engorgement of the mucosal lining, swelling, fluid buildup and finally hemorrhage into the space. In unchecked middle ear squeeze, the tympanic membrane or round window can collapse inward and burst, leading to extreme dizziness (vertigo) and an emergency situation. In a compilation of 1001 disorders referred to an otolaryngology (ear, nose, throat) diving specialist, the middle ear accounted for 399 (40%); 314 of the total (31%) were manifested by pain on descent (Roydhouse 1985).

WHAT IS THE CAUSE OF MIDDLE-EAR SQUEEZE AND HOW CAN IT BE PREVENTED?

Squeeze on the middle ear is prevented by making sure inhaled compressed air travels from the back of the nose (nasopharynx) into the middle ear spaces. The only route of passage into the middle ear is through a tiny, compressible canal called the eustachian tube (after its discoverer, the Italian Bartolommeo Eustachi, 1524-74). Anatomically, this is a soft and flexible canal that functions as a one-way flutter valve; it easily opens up when pressure in the middle ear is higher than in the nasopharynx, but tends to close shut when pressure in the nasopharynx is higher than in the middle ear. As a result, gas flow is passive from the middle ear to the nasopharynx on ascent (you don't have to think about it), but "active" on descent (you have to make it happen).

TABLE 2.
PRESSURE-RELATED PROBLEMS IN DIVING

1) Barotrauma (explainable by Boyle's Law)

On descent
Ear/sinus squeeze
Tympanic membrane rupture
Alternobaric vertigo
Barodontalgia

On ascent
Reverse ear/sinus squeeze (usually associated with inflammation in
    upper airway)
Alternobaric vertigo
Pulmonary barotrauma and sequelae, e.g., pneumothorax,
    pneumomediastinum, air embolism (see text for discussion)
Miscellaneous: barodontalgia; gastrointestinal expansion distress

2) Non-barotrauma (explainable by Dalton's and Henry's Laws)

Nitrogen narcosis ("martini effect")
Decompression sickness (DCS)
    Principal manifestations of DCS:

TYPE I	cutaneous
	musculoskeletal (the "bends")
TYPE II	pulmonary (the "chokes")
	vestibular
	neurologic
	cardiovascular

Figure 2. Middle ear squeeze. The external ear canal leads to the flexible tympanic membrane or eardrum, which is exposed to the ambient pressure. Behind the ear drum is the middle ear air space, which will be compressed at depth unless pressure is equalized, via the eustachian tube, with inhaled air. If the eustachian tube is blocked - as may happen without equalization after descending just a few feet - fresh air cannot enter the middle ear space and the ear drum will bulge inward, causing pain. If the diver descends too quickly without equalization, the tympanic membrane can rupture. If the diver continues to descend slowly without equalization, blood and fluid from surrounding tissue will be forced into the middle ear space.

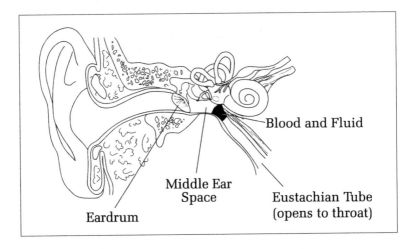

Thus the diver has to consciously work to keep the eustachian tube open on descent, or else it will seal shunt and prevent compressed air from reaching the middle ear. This is done by one of several maneuvers, including blowing against a closed mouth and nose, swallowing, yawning, or the Valsalva or Frenzel maneuvers. (The Valsalva is a forced exhalation with nose pinched, lips closed against mouthpiece, glottis open. The Frenzel is accomplished with nose pinched and lips closed against the mouthpiece; the back of tongue is thrust against soft palate, gently pushing air through the eustachian tubes.)

Whichever method is used, it must be done frequently on descent because at some point no maneuver will work; this is the situation when the pressure keeping the tube shut is too great. If the pressure gradient across the tube (nasopharynx to middle ear) exceeds 90 mm Hg - a gradient reached at only about 4 feet depth - none of the maneuvers will open the eustachian tube and the diver *must* ascend to relieve the pressure. Scuba divers are universally taught to prevent middle ear squeeze by forcing air through the eustachian tubes *before* symptoms occur, just before or at the beginning of descent and then every few feet. "Equalize early and often" is the universal advice.

WHAT IS THE TREATMENT OF MIDDLE EAR SQUEEZE?

Treatment of middle ear squeeze depends on its severity. Mild cases often to respond to decongestants. Antibiotics may be indicated if there is tympanic membrane rupture, but such a problem should be referred to an otolaryngologist. In all cases, diving should be avoided until the ear has returned to normal.

WHAT OTHER FORMS OF BAROTRAUMA OCCUR ON DESCENT?

The inner ear can also be affected, with rupture of the round or oval windows, cochlear damage and permanent hearing loss. Tinnitus, vertigo, and deafness after a dive are the classic symptoms of inner ear barotrauma. In such cases, antibiotics and bed rest are indicated, with surgical repair if there is no improvement (Neblett 1985; Davis & Kizer 1989).

External ear squeeze may occur if the ear canal is blocked with ear wax or ear plugs; divers should never wear ear plugs for this reason. Another common cause of external ear squeeze is a tight-fitting wetsuit hood.

The sinuses have no natural one-way valve by which to vent expanding air, but as long as there is no sinus blockage the diver can avoid "sinus squeeze." Sinus squeeze is accompanied by a painful feeling behind the cheekbones, between the eyes, in the upper teeth area, or over the forehead.

A blockage from outside the sinuses (as from nasal polyps) may produce sinus squeeze on descent, as air cannot enter the sinuses and equalize the pressures. In severe cases, the diver can experience sinus hemorrhage and a bloody nose. Decongestants and analgesics are used for mild cases of sinus squeeze. Antibiotics may be needed if there is evidence of fluid or blood in the sinus cavities. Diagnosis of this problem may require a CT scan of the sinuses.

WHAT BAROTRAUMA PROBLEMS CAN OCCUR ON ASCENT?

Closed air spaces pose a serious threat on ascent from a dive. Boyle's law predicts that closed air spaces will expand as the ambient pressure decreases on ascent. As long as the eustachian tube and sinus passages are not blocked, the middle ears and sinuses will vent expanding air into the nose, from where it will be exhaled along with expanding air from the lungs.

"Reverse squeeze" can occur if the eustachian tube and nasal passages are blocked on ascent. This is much less common than squeeze on descent, for if compressed air can get into these spaces it usually can get out. However, sometimes with an infection divers can get air into the spaces but then the air is blocked coming out. The sinus and/or middle ear spaces attempt to expand as the air in their spaces expands; the result is pain on ascent. In a worst-case scenario, middle ear expansion without adequate venting could lead to rupture of the tympanic membrane *outward*, resulting in severe pain, vertigo, and drowning. For these reasons people with upper respiratory infection, sinus or nasal congestion, or middle ear infection should not dive until the problem is resolved.

Alternobaric or "pressure" vertigo is a feeling of disorientation and spinning caused by a sudden, and unilateral, pressure difference between the middle and inner ear (Farmer 1990). It usually occurs during or immediately after an attempt to equalize middle ear pressure by the Valsalva maneuver. Alternobaric vertigo has been described on both ascent and descent, but is more common on ascent. If symptoms persist on the surface treatment is with decongestants, although surgery (a myringotomy - placing an opening in the tympanic membrane) may be necessary.

Any unvented space can cause discomfort or pain on ascent. Gastric discomfort is rare because of the ease of venting the stomach and

---

TEST YOUR UNDERSTANDING

4. Ear pain on descent cannot be cleared without ascending because (choose all that may apply)

   a. The eustachian tube will not respond to any maneuver.
   b. Any forceful attempt might rupture the ear drum.
   c. You could develop vertigo.
   d. The air pressure is too dense.

5. The best time to begin clearing your ears is:

   a. Before you enter the water.
   b. When you begin your descent.
   c. At 5 feet depth.
   d. At any point within the first 10 feet.

intestines but does occur (Weeth 1965; Edmonds 1976). Barodontalgia (tooth pain), usually from an improperly or incompletely filled tooth, can occur on ascent when air in the cavity expands.

WHAT IS PULMONARY BAROTRAUMA?

Pulmonary barotrauma is any damage to the lungs from unequal air pressures. The greatest danger to the diver on ascent is from pulmonary barotrauma, a risk greatly increased if breath is held. The consequence can be serious, even fatal. The potential for pulmonary barotrauma is why the first rule of scuba diving is *never hold your breath.*

Continuous breathing allows the lungs and communicating spaces to maintain equilibrium with the increased ambient pressure. If breath is held on ascent, air in the lungs will try to expand against an essentially fixed chest volume; depending on the vertical distance of a breath-hold ascent, the result can be anywhere from simple over inflation to lung rupture and passage of air into the blood stream.

A maximum safe rate of ascent in RSD is considered to be 60 feet a minute (the slower the better); at all times the diver should *continuously breathe.* Should a diver run out of air and have to make an emergency ascent, proper technique requires continuous exhalation underwater (by saying "Ahh...") in order to vent the expanding lung volume. This maneuver keeps the glottis open and allows continuous exhalation of expanding air, so the lung volume does not increase.

For an equivalent change in depth the risk of expansion barotrauma is greatest near the surface, a fact explainable by Boyle's law. A breath-holding scuba diver rising from 33-feet depth to the surface experiences a change in ambient pressure from two to one atmospheres absolute; if the lungs fully expand within the chest cavity, lung volume will try to *double.* By contrast, a 33-foot rise from 99 to 66 feet depth (i.e., from 4 to 3 atmospheres) would maximally increase a breath-holder's lung volume only 33 percent, posing much less risk of barotrauma (Figure 3).

The Greatest Risk of Expansion Barotrauma is Near the Surface.

Figure 3. Ambient pressure and percentage change in lung volume with equivalent depth change (33 feet). In each instance the diver is breathing compressed air at the point of breath-hold.

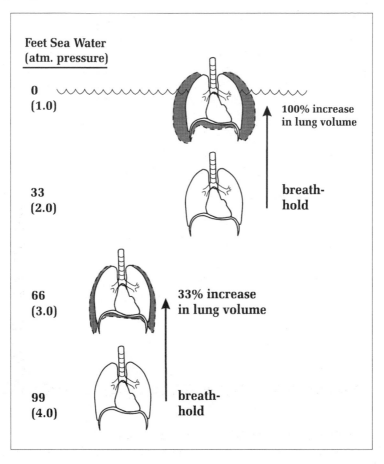

Barotrauma correlates with both increase in pressure in the lungs and 'over stretching' of the lung tissue. Experiments in dogs undergoing rapid ascent in a chamber showed that the lungs can withstand much higher pressures (before barotrauma occurs) if the chest cavity is bound and 'over stretching' is prevented (Schaefer 1958).

Although both over stretching of lung tissue and the pressure of expanding air are factors favoring lung trauma, pressure seems to be the major one. The pressure difference across the lungs (from inside to outside) that is the threshold for experimental barotrauma is about 80 mm Hg; this can occur with *a breath-hold ascent from only four feet!* The pressure difference (and risk of barotrauma) is obviously much greater with breath-hold from greater depths. During a breath-hold ascent from 33 feet the lung volume would try to double, almost guaranteeing barotrauma if breath were held at or near the diver's total lung capacity (Figure 3). If the lungs could not vent expanding air, they would be subjected to a distending pressure of nine times the barotrauma threshold!

Pulmonary barotrauma usually manifests immediately after ascent but may be delayed for several hours. It may also recur after an initial period of improvement (Krzyzak 1987). People suffering pulmonary barotrauma should be treated with a high inspired oxygen concentration, 100% if available. Oxygen "denitrogenates" the blood and hastens absorption of bubbles (see Section H).

TEST YOUR UNDERSTANDING

6. With scuba, pulmonary barotrauma is most likely to occur (choose one):
   a. With a rapid drop in a vertical current from 60 fsw to 80 fsw.
   b. By breathing from a free-flowing regulator at a depth of 60 feet.
   c. By rapid up and down motion below the surface and near the shore, from heavy wave action.
   d. From coughing at a depth of 60 feet.

7. All of the following except one can result from pulmonary barotrauma:
   a. pneumothorax
   b. air in the mediastinum
   c. middle ear squeeze
   d. air around the heart

HOW DOES PULMONARY BAROTRAUMA OCCUR?

The presumed mechanism of pulmonary barotrauma is as follows. With ascent, if the expanding air cannot be properly vented, the lungs (or some portion of them) expand in response to the increase in pressure; if they expand too much, individual alveoli are prone to rupture. If the lungs are structurally normal, i.e., there are no blebs, bullae, or areas of abnormal tissue (which are more prone to rupture), barotrauma should not occur until a transpulmonary pressure of around 80 mm Hg is reached (Schaefer 1958). Above 80 mm Hg the alveoli are prone to tear and vent air into the surrounding space (called the interstitial space). This transpulmonary pressure should not occur in healthy lungs unless breath is held on ascent.

From the interstitial space, escaped air can take one of three paths (Figure 4): between the two lungs (mediastinal air), around one of the lungs (pneumothorax), or into the blood stream (air embolism) (Macklin 1944).

1) Escaped air can dissect along tissue layers into the area known as the mediastinum, the large space between the two lungs. Once in the mediastinum, the air can go into spaces around the heart (but not in it), into the neck, and into spaces around the abdominal organs.

2) Escaped air can rupture through the visceral pleura (thin membrane that lines the lungs), resulting in a *pneumothorax*, which is an abnormal air collection between the chest wall and the lung. This air collection can compress or collapse the lung.

Figure 4. Three pathways air can take once there is a rupture of lung tissue.

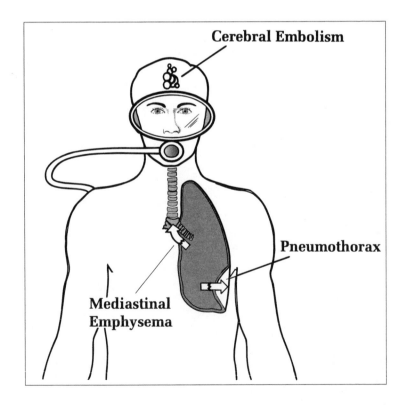

3) Escaped air can enter the pulmonary veins, from where it can travel to the arterial circulation as an *air embolism* (traveling air bubbles). This is by far the most serious complication of a ruptured lung, since the air embolism can block blood vessels to the brain or heart and be fatal.

WHY DOES PULMONARY BAROTRAUMA OCCUR?

There is no doubt that pulmonary barotrauma results from unequal air pressures across the lung. But why does it occur in some people and not others? Is it always from a breath-hold ascent?

Although breath-hold ascents account for some cases, there are also cases of barotrauma where the divers are certain they never held their breath. There are two explanations for this latter group. First, some divers probably have abnormal lungs and don't know it. Such changes as subpleural blebs and bullae (abnormal air pockets in the lungs) can often be demonstrated by chest CT scanning or even a plain chest x-ray in people with no respiratory symptoms or problems. After one diver suffered major barotrauma, a chest x-ray that was done before the dive was reviewed; it showed a large bulla, or abnormal air space with thin walls. Probably a certain percentage of people have such "weak lungs" (for want of a better term); these weak lungs may cause them no difficulty except when exposed to slight pressure changes that would not affect normal lungs.

Still, there are apparently other divers with completely normal lungs, who are confident breath was not held, yet who still suffered pulmonary baro-trauma. These events are difficult to explain, and are fortunately rare (as is pulmonary barotrauma in general). Pulmonary baro-trauma remains a definite, albeit small, risk of scuba diving.

A hyperbaric chamber is not used for pulmonary barotrauma unless there is suspicion of air embolism (discussed below). Chest tube placement for pneumothorax follows the same guidelines as without diving. Pneumothorax is particularly dangerous if the patient is to be transported by air or receive hyperbaric therapy (which might be needed for decompression sickness or air embolism, not the pneumothorax). The decreased barometric pressure of altitude, as well as the decompression phase of hyperbaric therapy, will further expand the pneumothorax space and increase the risk of compressing the lung (and, if very severe, the heart).

WHAT IS ARTERIAL GAS EMBOLISM?

Arterial Gas Embolism (AGE) is the most serious medical problem related to pulmonary expansion barotrauma. It is a major cause of sport diving deaths (Arthur 1987; Kizer 1987). AGE accounts for about 40% of the case load at active dive accident treatment centers in the U.S. (Kizer 1987).

AGE is thought to occur when alveoli rupture and air enters the pul-monary veins, from where it travels through the left heart chambers and into the arterial circulation. Despite this presumed mechanism AGE victims usually do not usually show obvious evidence of lung rupture when their chest x-rays are examined (Kizer 1987; Gorman 1989; Williams 1990).

AGE characteristically manifests within minutes of surfacing. In cases of AGE reported to the national Divers Alert Network in 1988, 78% had their first symptoms within five minutes and 88% within 10 minutes (DAN 1988). The early onset of symptoms is in contrast to decompression sickness (discussed in Section G). Decompression sickness is caused by a different type of bubbles (pure nitrogen) and causes symptoms that come on more gradually than AGE.

The brain is the most commonly affected major organ in AGE, although air emboli can also block coronary arteries and lead to heart attack (Kizer 1987). Cerebral air embolism can present with sudden unconsciousness or acute neurologic deficit (stroke). Other neurologic symptoms include severe headache, difficulty speaking, and visual loss (Dick 1985). The major alternative diagnosis to AGE is decompression sickness but treatment is the same for both conditions: recompression in a hyperbaric chamber.

TEST YOUR UNDERSTANDING

8. Arterial gas embolism can occur from conditions explained by:
   a. Boyle's law
   b. Boyle's and Dalton's laws
   c. Boyle's, Dalton's and Henry's laws
   d. None of the gas laws

9. For arterial gas embolism to occur there must be (choose all that apply):
   a. a greater pressure inside the lungs than outside the body
   b. a stretching of the lung tissue
   c. weak or diseased lungs
   d. breath-hold on ascent

WHAT IS TREATMENT OF AGE?

First aid treatment of suspected AGE requires putting the patient in comfortable position; usually this will be supine and flat. The head-lower-than-the-body position (so-called Trendelenburg position) was once thought to prevent embolism to the brain, but this has not been substantiated and is no longer recommended (Butler 1988).

Other first aid includes administering a high concentration of oxygen (see Section H) and plenty of fluids. Arrangements should be made to transport the victim to the appropriate medical facility (See Section R). Although symptoms of AGE may improve after first aid, recompression in a chamber is still considered mandatory (Kindwall 1983; Kizer 1987; Green 1987), for two reasons. First, patients with AGE can relapse after initial improvement. Second, AGE may be accompanied by decompression sickness, a condition more insidious in onset and which also responds to recompression therapy. One review found a 12% prevalence of both conditions in seriously ill patients referred for recompression therapy (Green 1987). Once AGE is suspected, the patient should be referred to a hyperbaric chamber.

TEST YOUR UNDERSTANDING

10. True or False: in theory, the gas composition of the bubbles in arterial gas embolism and decompression sickness is essentially the same.

11. The mechanism(s) leading to arterial gas embolism and decompression sickness are essentially the same, and they are treated the same.

12. Which of the following conditions should be treated with recompression (hyperbaric) therapy?

    a. ruptured tympanic membrane
    b. severe sinus squeeze with nose bleeds
    c. arterial gas embolism
    d. pneumothorax
    e. decompression sickness
    f. nitrogen narcosis

Answers to TEST YOUR UNDERSTANDING

1. 50 billion molecules; volume of 8 liters.

2. Number of molecules would stay about the same; density would decrease with ascent; volume of air would increase with ascent.

3. d. Her lungs would attempt to expand to three times their initial volume, to 18 liters; this is an impossibly large lung volume so there would be lung rupture become she reached the surface.

4. a, b, c

5. a or b

6. c. Rapid up and down motion increases risk of pulmonary barotrauma if breath is held, which it might be in a stressful situation. If breath is not held, mild, non-sustained coughing should not lead to barotrauma.

7. c

8. a. Boyle's law. The other laws have nothing to do with the pulmonary barotrauma that leads to arterial gas embolism.

9. a and b. Note that the lungs do not have to be weak or diseased for arterial gas embolism to occur. If breath is held on ascent, normal lungs can rupture and lead to air embolism. At the same time breath does not have to be held for embolism to occur; under some conditions weak or diseased lungs (as from asthma or blebs) can spontaneously rupture.

10. False. Arterial gas embolism is due to bubbles of air; decompression sickness is due to bubbles made up, at least initially, of almost pure nitrogen.

11. False. They may be treated the same (with recompression in a hyperbaric chamber), but the causes are different.

12. c and e. The other conditions are not accompanied by bubbles in the blood and tissues, and would not respond to recompression therapy.

REFERENCES AND BIBLIOGRAPHY

SECTION F. Effects of Unequal Air Pressure Underwater: Ear Squeeze, Sinus Squeeze, Air Embolism and Other Forms of Barotrauma

See references at the end of Section G.

DIVING ODDS N' ENDS

Top 10 Diving Destinations

According to polls in various magazines, the top 10 diving destinations for Americans are:

1. Florida Keys
2. Bahamas
3. Cozumel
4. Cayman Islands
5. Hawaii
6. U.S. Virgin Islands
7. East coast of Florida, off Broward and Dade Counties
8. British Virgin Islands
9. Bonaire
10. Turks & Caicos

DIVING ODDS N' ENDS

Diving the Bikini Atoll

In 1946 the U.S. Military Governor of the Marshall Islands informed the 167 residents of Bikini - a tiny atoll in the Micronesian Pacific halfway between Hawaii and Australia - that they would have to move. The U.S. had selected remote Bikini atoll as *the* site of post-war atom bomb testing. On July 1, 1946 a B-29 dropped the world's fourth atomic bomb over a fleet of 95 ships anchored in Bikini Lagoon, sinking them all. Declared uninhabitable until recently, Bikini may become the next dive mecca. Several travel companies are negotiating with native Bikinians (who have received millions of dollars from the U.S. government in compensation for their forced displacement) to allow diving over the wrecks of Bikini. (Davis, NYT, 1994)

<u>NOTES</u>

Effects of Increased Dissolved Nitrogen From Scuba Diving: Decompression Sickness

WHAT HAPPENS TO INHALED AIR AT DEPTH?

Dalton's Law states that the total pressure of a gas is equal to the sum of pressures of its individual components. In the case of air:

$$P(t) = PO_2 + PN_2 + P(x)$$

where $P(t)$ is the total air pressure, PO_2 and PN_2 are partial pressure of oxygen and nitrogen, respectively, and $P(x)$ is the partial pressure of remaining gases (less than 1% of air).

For example, at sea level the total air pressure is 1 atm. or 760 mm Hg. Of this total air pressure, 21% (or .21) is from oxygen, 78% (.78) from nitrogen, and 1% (.01) from other gases. The percentage of an individual gas times the total air pressure gives the pressure of that component gas. Thus, at sea level:

		in mm Hg	in atm.
$760(.21) = PO_2$	=	159.6 mm Hg	.21 atm.
$760(.78) = PN_2$	=	592.8 mm Hg	.78 atm.
$760(.01) = P_{other}$	=	7.6 mm Hg	.01 atm.
Total		760.0 mm Hg	1.0 atm.

Dalton's law states that the individual gases of any gas mixture will have the *same pressure* alone or as part of the mixture. Thus, at sea level, the oxygen component of air will support a mercury column 159.6 mm high, and the nitrogen component will support a mercury column 592.8 mm high.

At depth all pressures increase, for both air as a mixture and for its component gases. For example, a doubling of ambient air pressure, which occurs at just 33 fsw, will double the partial pressure of oxygen, nitrogen, and other component gases. At 66 fsw, the ambient pressure is tripled, along with the partial pressure of oxygen, nitrogen and other gases inhaled at that depth.

TEST YOUR UNDERSTANDING

1. Air contains 21% oxygen and at sea level has a pressure of one atm. Relative to sea level, what is the percentage of oxygen, the oxygen pressure, and the number of oxygen molecules inhaled at a depth of 33 ft? At 66 ft?

2. What is the pressure, in mm Hg, of inspired oxygen at 33 fsw when breathing compressed air? At 66 fsw?

3. What is the pressure, in mm Hg *and* atm., of inspired nitrogen at 33 fsw when breathing compressed air? At 66 fsw?

4. If 1% of the tank air is a gas contaminant, what will be the percentage and the pressure of that contaminant when tank air is inhaled at 66 fsw?

HOW DOES THE INCREASED PRESSURE AT DEPTH AFFECT GAS IN THE BODY?

The increased pressure of each gas component at depth means that *more* of each gas will dissolve into the blood and body tissues at depth, a physical effect predicted by Henry's Law. To review, Henry's law states that the amount of gas dissolving into any liquid or tissue with which it is in contact is proportional to the partial pressure of that gas (see Section D). Inhaled gases are in close contact with blood entering the lungs. Hence, the greater the partial pressure of any inhaled gas, the more that gas will diffuse into the blood. Literally, if the partial pressure of an inhaled gas increases, more molecules of that gas enter the blood.

Taken together, Boyle's and Henry's laws explain why, as a diver descends while breathing compressed air:

1) inhaled PO_2 and PN_2 increase (Figure 1); and

2) the amount of nitrogen and oxygen entering the blood and tissues also increase.

Figure 1. Henry's and Dalton's laws predict that, with descent, inhaled PO_2 and PN_2 will increase and cause an increased amount of nitrogen and oxygen to enter the blood and tissues. The opposite occurs on ascent: inhaled PO_2 and PN_2 decrease, and allow the excess nitrogen and oxygen to leave the blood and tissues. At sea level there is no net movement of nitrogen in and out of the body.

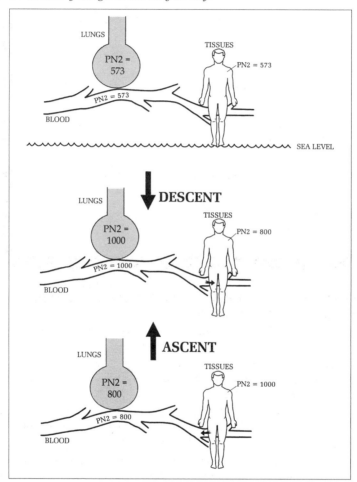

IS THERE RISK OF OXYGEN TOXICITY IN DIVING?

Since the pressure of all inhaled gases increases with increasing depth, there is risk of inhaling too much oxygen and developing oxygen toxicity. However, this is unlikely to occur in recreational diving because the depth limit (130 feet) effectively limits length of exposure to high oxygen concentrations. The recreational diver *is* exposed to high oxygen pressures, but not long enough to risk oxygen toxicity. The problem is a potential hazard at greater depths, or when breathing mixtures containing more than 21% oxygen (e.g., nitrox). Oxygen toxicity is discussed further in Section I.

HOW DOES NITROGEN DIFFER FROM OXYGEN AND CO_2?

Unlike oxygen and carbon dioxide, nitrogen (N_2) is inert; it is not metabolized by the body. At sea level the amount of N_2 inhaled and exhaled is the same. This is not the case for O_2 and CO_2, which are not inert gases but instead participate in metabolism; as a result less O_2 is exhaled than inhaled, and more CO_2 is exhaled than inhaled.

When breathing compressed air at depth, more gas molecules of air are inhaled because the air is at a higher pressure, and hence denser, than at sea level. Both the pressure and amount of inhaled nitrogen and oxygen are greater at depth than at sea level. Most of the extra oxygen is metabolized and doesn't pose any problem at recreational depths. But what about nitrogen, which is inert? The extra nitrogen that is inhaled has nowhere to go but into the blood and tissues, where it stays in the gas phase ("dissolved") at the higher pressure, until the ambient pressure is reduced; then it starts to dissolve back out, and is excreted in the exhaled air.

Two important problems relate to the increased quantity and pressure of nitrogen from inhaling compressed air: *nitrogen narcosis* and *decompression sickness*. Although both problems are related to too much nitrogen, they are distinct.

Nitrogen narcosis is a function of the increased pressure of the gas and is only a problem as long as that pressure remains elevated. Thus nitrogen narcosis is solely a function of depth (see Section I). For some divers narcosis begins to manifest in the 80-130 fsw range, for others much deeper. Because the problem is related only to depth, it can be cured by ascent. Although divers have succumbed from nitrogen narcosis, deaths appear to be due to drowning or failing to ascend (due to confusion), or to running out of air. Those who ascend escape the effects of nitrogen narcosis and recover completely.

Decompression sickness (DCS) is not due to the pressure of nitrogen at depth per se, but instead to the formation of bubbles as dissolved nitrogen comes out of the tissues with ascent. Since bubble formation is in part related to the total amount of nitrogen in the tissues, the dive time is important (the longer the dive, the more nitrogen enters the tissues, up to a point). Thus DCS is a function of depth *and duration* of the dive and, at least among recreational divers, is a far more common problem than nitrogen narcosis. Unlike nitrogen narcosis, DCS can lead to permanent physical impairment.

WHAT IS THE HISTORY OF DECOMPRESSION SICKNESS?

Decompression sickness was appreciated as early as the mid-19th century, among bridge-building caisson workers. A caisson is a huge enclosed space sunk to the bottom of a lake or river, and pressurized with air to keep out water. Its use dates from the early 19th century. Men work inside a caisson while excavating for bridge foundations. By the mid-19th century it was observed that length of exposure to the increased air pressure in the caisson, and the worker's speed of ascent, correlated with development of joint pains after surfacing - then called "the bends." Afflicted men reminded some of the posture affected by fashionable women of the time, the 'Grecian Bend.' These women, with their bustles and full-length skirts, walked slightly stooped or 'bent over.' Of course the caisson workers were not just posturing; they were in real pain. The bends was a well recognized problem during construction of the Brooklyn Bridge in the 1870s.

In 1878 Paul Bert, an eminent French physiologist, published his classic work *Le Pression Barometrique,* in which he recommended slow ascent in order to prevent the bends (Bert 1878). Over the next decade "Caisson Disease" became a recognized malady, and slow ascent from the caisson's high pressure was accepted as the method of prevention. In his 1892 edition of *The Principles and Practice of Medicine,* an important medical textbook of the era, Dr. William Osler devoted a full page to 'Caisson Disease'. Osler's clinical description cannot be improved upon today. He wrote:

> This remarkable affection, found in divers and in workers in caissons, is characterized by a paraplegia, more rarely a general palsy, which supervenes on returning from the compressed atmosphere to the surface...
>
> The symptoms are especially apt to come on if the change from the high to the ordinary atmospheric pressure is quickly made. They may supervene immediately on leaving the caisson, or they may be delayed for several hours. In the mildest form there are simply pains about the knees and in the legs, often of great severity, and occurring in paroxysms. Abdominal pain and vomiting are not uncommon. The legs may be tender to the touch, and the patient may walk with a stiff gait. Dizziness and headache may accompany these neuralgic symptoms, or may occur alone. More commonly in the severe form there is paralysis both of motion and sensation, usually a paraplegia but it may be general, involving the trunk and arms...In the most extreme instances the attacks resemble apoplexy, and the patient rapidly becomes comatose and death occurs in a few hours. In the cases of paraplegia [paralysis below the trunk] the outlook is usually good, and the paralysis may pass off in a day, or may continue for several weeks or even for months. Identical features are met with in the deep-sea divers.

> The explanation of this condition is by no means satisfactory... It has been suggested that the symptoms are due to the liberation in the spinal cord of bubbles of nitrogen which have been absorbed by the blood under the high pressure...
>
> A large majority of the cases recover. The severe neuralgic pains often require morphia [morphine]. Inhalations of oxygen and the use of compressed air have been advised. When paraplegia develops the treatment is similar to that of other forms. In all caisson work care should be exercised that the time in passing through the lock from the high to the ordinary pressure be sufficiently prolonged.

Early in this century the British physiologist John Scott Haldane and colleagues, in experiments with goats and humans, worked out safe decompression tables for divers (Boycott 1908; see Sections A and J). Their calculations, based on half-times for nitrogen in various parts of the body, formed the basis for navy dive tables still in use today.

WHAT CAUSES DECOMPRESSION SICKNESS?

Henry's and Dalton's Laws predict that, as the diver descends, excess nitrogen will enter the blood and all body tissues. These laws also predict that, on ascent (as ambient pressure decreases) the extra nitrogen that accumulated will diffuse out of the tissues and into the circulation.

Decompression sickness (DCS) arises when excess nitrogen leaving tissue forms bubbles large enough to cause symptoms. Size of bubbles is important, since small bubbles can often be found in divers with no symptoms (detection of bubbles is with Doppler ultrasound). DCS arises when the pressure gradient for nitrogen leaving the tissues is so great that large bubbles form, probably by coalescence of many smaller bubbles. Large bubbles within tissues and the circulation cause the symptoms and signs of decompression sickness.

When nitrogen bubbles leave the tissues they first enter capillaries and then the veins. Veins (venous circulation) leave the tissues and return to the heart and lungs in order to pick up fresh oxygen. Once going through the lungs, the blood enters the arterial circulation (see Section C).

Nitrogen bubbles travel in the venous circulation to the lungs, but then (in people with normal anatomy) are trapped in the lung capillaries because the bubbles are larger than the tiny diameter of the capillaries. Once trapped, the bubbles break up and the nitrogen gas is exhaled. As a result of being trapped and exhaled, the bubbles do not enter the arterial circulation. However, DCS bubbles *can* bypass the lungs through an *abnormal* opening in the heart, called a patent foramen ovale (PFO; discussed later in this chapter). PFO, a relatively new area of investigation, may explain why some people with DCS apparently have nitrogen bubbles in the arterial circulation.

Because any of the body's tissues can be affected by nitrogen bubbles, DCS symptoms are wide-ranging: from skin mottling to mild tingling in the hands or feet to shock and death. Blockage of blood flow to joints by the bubbles causes pain, which is "the bends." Blockage of blood flow to nervous tissue can cause paralysis or stroke.

There are several theories as to why bubbles form in the first place. In a pure, static fluid such as blood in a beaker that undergoes sudden decompression, bubbles don't form. Why they form in people (and animals) may have something to do with excess nitrogen entering "gas nuclei," sub-microscopic pockets of gas that are said to exist naturally. There are other theories, all too complex to bother with here. Whatever the exact mechanism of bubble formation, the following statements reflect current understanding of decompression sickness.

- Decompression causes excess nitrogen to leave tissues and enter the blood stream, from where it travels to the lungs and is exhaled. Nitrogen leaves the tissues either dissolved in the blood or in bubbles. The dissolved state is harmless whereas nitrogen bubbles, because they are space-occupying, can compress nerves and/or block the circulation of blood. Bubbles can also cause some chemical reactions in the blood which are harmful to the body.

- The larger and more numerous the nitrogen bubbles, the more likely they will cause symptoms of DCS.

- For a given individual, DCS is unpredictable. Its occurrence depends in large part on the recent diving history (i.e., profiles of the preceding dive(s), including rate(s) of ascent), and also on individual host factors, including age, amount of body fat, state of hydration, and individual susceptibility in ways that cannot be quantified.

DCS is sometimes divided into Type I, which encompasses the bends and skin manifestations, and Type II, which includes pulmonary, central nervous system and cardiovascular problems, i.e., the more serious manifestations of DCS (see Section F, Table 2). This division is more useful for retrospective analysis and is less helpful for determining outcome, since many patients with DCS present with a range of symptoms (Green 1987). Also, in some patients Type I symptoms may later progress to Type II symptoms.

Neurologic symptoms are particularly common because nitrogen is highly soluble in fat (five times more than in blood), and dissolves readily in the fatty myelin sheaths that surround nerves. As the diver ascends nitrogen comes out of these nerve sheaths; if too much nitrogen is in these nerve sheaths at the beginning of ascent, bubbles may form and compress nerves even before they enter the venous circulation.

Apart from compressing nerves and blocking circulation, bubbles can also set off certain chemical reactions, collectively called an "inflammatory response." An inflammatory response is marked by release of certain protein compounds that can damage the blood vessels and affect blood clotting (Green 1987). Although this process is poorly understood in decompression sickness, it is important to note that chemical changes do occur in the blood of DCS patients, and that some symptoms are not simply the result of nerve compression or circulation blockage (Bove 1982, Catron 1982, Smith 1994).

IS "THE BENDS" THE SAME THING AS DCS?

No. Strictly speaking, "the bends" is a slang or popular term for the "pain only" manifestations of DCS, a Type I DCS. The pain is usually in the joints, typically in the shoulders or elbows first, but can occur virtually anywhere in the body. Other manifestations of DCS, including skin mottling and itching (also Type I), and all Type II problems (paralysis, lung edema, shock, etc.) are not "the bends."

Less strictly speaking, the term "bends" is sometimes used as a synonym for any manifestation of DCS, or for all DCS-related problems. Thus, the phrase "He got bent" may refer to a diver who developed pain only, who developed pain followed by paralysis, or who died. This is not medical terminology, and physicians reporting on the patient would use more precise language. However, in everyday conversation "bends" and "bent" usually serve to indicate some problem arising from DCS.

WHAT ARE THE DIFFERENCES BETWEEN DCS AND AGE?

In contrast to air embolism, DCS commonly presents gradually, starting as tingling and numbness (Table 1). The median time of onset for the first symptoms of DCS is about 20 minutes after surfacing; for the next symptom, 2 hours. By contrast, arterial gas embolism almost always presents within the first 10 minutes after surfacing from a dive (DAN 1988).

Potential neurologic complications of DCS include stroke and spinal cord paralysis, the latter most likely from occlusion of the blood vessels surrounding the spinal cord. Of 117 symptomatic divers in one study,

TABLE 1.
Comparison of Arterial Gas Embolism (AGE) and Decompression Sickness (DCS)

CHARACTERISTIC	AGE	DCS
Cause	Pulmonary expansion barotrauma	Excess nitrogen leaving tissues too quickly
Risks	Breath-hold ascent; non-communicating air spaces	Exceeding prescribed limits for depth and time underwater
Location and nature of bubbles	Air bubbles in arterial circulation	Nitrogen bubbles in tissues and venous circulation
Onset of symptoms	Within a few minutes of surfacing	Ranges from a few minutes to 48 hour after surfacing, but usually within 6 hours
Clinical syndrome	Unconsciousness; discrete neurologic injury; or a cardiac event	Variable. Usually pain or paresthesias initially; can progress to paralysis, shock. May mimic AGE.
Effect of first aid, including oxygen	Symptoms may improve or go away altogether	Variable, often no effect
Definitive treatment	Recompression in a hyperbaric chamber	Recompression in a hyperbaric chamber

70 were judged to have neurologic decompression sickness and 39 air embolism (Dick 1985). After paresthesia (skin tingling), the most common neurologic decompression symptoms were limb paralysis, vertigo, unsteady gait, mild headache, and blurred vision. Of 133 patients treated for DCS in England over a 20 year period, 81% presented with spinal cord injury, 27% with cerebral injury, and 10.5% with inner ear symptoms (Green 1987).

Shortness of breath from DCS, usually referred to as the "chokes," is much less common than musculoskeletal and neurologic complaints (Dewey 1962; Green 1987). Symptoms of chokes include pain under the breast bone, cough and shortness of breath. The pain is often intensified with a deep breath, and may seem worse when taking in a breath. The cough is generally non-productive but on occasion the patient may cough up some blood.

Chokes is due to movement of many nitrogen bubbles from the venous system to the lungs. Although a small number of bubbles will be trapped and exhaled, a large number can overwhelm the lung circulation, and lead to respiratory distress. Symptoms can occur up to 12 hours after the dive and may persist for 12-48 hours. In severe cases pulmonary edema (fluid in the alveolar spaces) can result from the chokes (Strauss 1979).

WHAT IS THE TREATMENT FOR DCS?

The only effective treatment for DCS (and AGE) is recompression in a hyperbaric chamber, the sooner the better. All manifestations of DCS are potentially reversible if the victim can be quickly recompressed in a chamber. Recompression squeezes the nitrogen bubbles to a smaller size and allows a slower and safer egress of nitrogen from the tissues. Delay in hyperbaric therapy may result in permanent paralysis. Treatment is recommended even if symptoms abate or clear before the patient reaches the chamber. This is because bubbles may still be present in the circulation, and could lead to a more devastating problem later on.

Hyperbaric chambers can be found in or near most large U.S. cities (see Section R). Although altitude can worsen decompression sickness by lowering ambient pressure and increasing nitrogen egress from the tissues, time saved by flying to a chamber generally outweighs the risk. Ideally the transport aircraft should be pressurized to sea level, or else fly as close to the surface as feasible (less than 1000 feet altitude if possible). In many cases the most costly aspect of treating decompression sickness is transporting the victim to a hyperbaric chamber.

A hyperbaric treatment table for DCS is shown in Figure 2. Whether or not to use this particular table, and how often, is always up to the physician evaluating the stricken diver. Also, any complications during treatment (such as oxygen toxicity) could lead to modifications of the schedule.

Some physicians also recommend corticosteroids in DCS to decrease inflammation, but their use is largely anecdotal and efficacy is unproven (Catron 1982). Various other drugs, such as heparin, diazepam, aspirin, and vasodilators, have been studied or used in this condition (Catron 1982); none can be routinely recommended as effective. Except for oxygen, which can be considered a drug, no particular drug is helpful for DCS.

Figure 2. U.S. Navy Table 6 for Treatment of DCS. Light-shaded areas represent periods of 100% O₂, dark-shaded areas periods of air breathing.

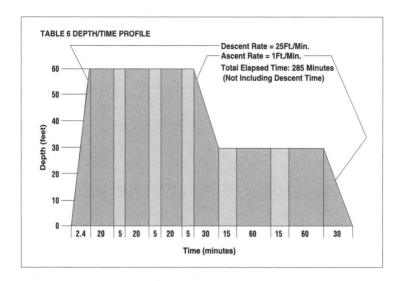

Recompression treatment is usually effective if begun early but the major emphasis, of course, should be on prevention: using common sense and staying well within established limits for each dive.

WHAT IS DECOMPRESSION ILLNESS?

Admittedly, doctors have a way of confusing things at times. Because DCS and AGE are treated basically the same way (by recompression in a hyperbaric chamber), and their root cause is the same (gas bubbles in some part of the body), many hyperbaric physicians feel there is little point in trying to distinguish between the two conditions; they prefer to call *all* bubble disease in divers by one name. I agree with this preference. Unfortunately, the name chosen to cover both forms of bubble disease is "decompression illness."

I say unfortunate because the term is too close to "decompression sickness," which specifically means nitrogen bubble disease from too rapid decompression and *not* AGE, which is from barotrauma. Why choose a name almost identical to one type of bubble disease (DCS), to refer to *all* bubble disease (DCS + AGE)? Well, I didn't choose the name, and I hope someone changes it. A better name would be diver's bubble disease (DBD), or some other general term to encompass both conditions.

I mention all this because some authors now use the term DCI without clearly explaining that they mean *both* DCS *and* AGE. One textbook, otherwise excellent in its explanations, mistakenly calls DCI a "unique condition" characterized by "AGE followed by DCS." It is even conceivable that someone will use the term DCI to mean only DCS (after all, 'illness' and 'sickness' are synonyms). Well, you get the (confusing) picture.

After decades of using 'decompression sickness' to denote nitrogen bubble disease only, the term 'decompression illness' for the entire gamut of bubble problems is bound to be confusing. Keep in mind that although the clinical manifestations and treatment of DCS and AGE are similar, the underlying mechanisms are different. At the very least, all authors should clearly define whatever term they do use.

WHAT IS A PATENT FORAMEN OVALE AND WHAT IS ITS SIGNIFICANCE IN SCUBA DIVING?

The foramen ovale is an opening between the right and left atria of the heart that normally closes shortly after birth. Although the right and left atria share a common wall, after birth there is no direct communication between them. Oxygen-depleted (venous) blood from the entire body enters the right atrium and then goes to the adjacent right ventricle (see Section C). From the right ventricle blood goes to the lungs, where O_2 is taken up and CO_2 given off. The oxygen-rich blood then travels to the left atrium and left ventricle, from where it is pumped out to the arterial circulation and all the body's organs.

In a certain percentage of people the foramen ovale does not close completely at birth, but stays open. Using a variety of methods, some opening can be demonstrated in 20-30% of adults; this situation is called a patent foramen ovale or PFO. A PFO generally causes no problems, as it is small and little or no blood actually passes through the opening. Sometimes an opening is only demonstrated with a transient increase in right atrial pressure, such as during a Valsalva maneuver (or when a diver clears her ears). Thus, in most people with a PFO, the normal flow of blood is still maintained. In a small percentage of people with a PFO, however, the opening is large and a significant amount of blood is "shunted" from the right to the left atrium, thus bypassing the lungs.

Any opening through the heart that lets venous blood bypass the lungs could cause problems. Since Doppler studies have demonstrated venous gas bubbles on ascent from most dives, we infer that the lungs are vital to filtering out these "silent bubbles"; the bubbles break up in the pulmonary capillaries so the nitrogen dissolves harmlessly into the

Figure 3: Foramen Ovale. When closed (normal), venous bubbles go from right atrium to right ventricle of the heart and then into lungs where they are trapped by the lung capillaries and do not enter the arterial circulation. When open (patent), venous bubbles go from right atrium through the patent foramen directly into the left atrium; from there, they enter the left ventricle and the arterial circulation, where they may cause symptoms similar to AGE.

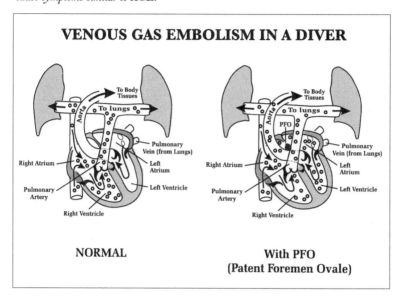

VENOUS GAS EMBOLISM IN A DIVER

NORMAL

With PFO (Patent Foremen Ovale)

blood. Thus, the lungs help prevent small venous bubbles incurred in diving from entering the arterial circulation.

A large patent foramen ovale allows nitrogen bubbles to pass from the right to the left atrium, thus bypassing the lungs and entering the arterial circulation (Figure 3). If these shunted bubbles are in sufficient size and/or number, they can cause organ damage.

This is the theory, and only in recent years has evidence accumulated about the risks from a PFO when scuba diving. Like most situations in diving, however, the risk is a matter of degree; the larger the PFO, and the more bubbles that exist in the venous circulation, the more likely will bubbles bypass the lungs and enter the arterial circulation.

One study, using bubble contrast echocardiography, demonstrated shunting through a PFO in 11 of 30 divers (26 recreational, 4 professional) treated for DCS (Moon 1989); this percentage was statistically higher than the prevalence of PFO in a control group, suggesting PFO can be a risk factor for symptomatic DCS. Eighteen of the patients had serious signs and symptoms, defined as motor weakness, dizziness, or cognitive impairment (confusion, impairment of consciousness); presumably these symptoms arose from venous bubbles traveling to the brain instead of being trapped by the lungs. Another nine patients had only sensory abnormalities, with or without musculoskeletal pain, and 3 had only pain.

Another study, in the British Medical Journal, reported MRI brain scanning in 87 volunteer recreational divers (minimum 160 dives each) and *without symptoms*. The study showed multiple brain "lesions" when there was a large PFO (Knauth 1997). The size of the PFO was defined by the degree of blood shunting through the atrial opening. A brain lesion was defined as a hyper-intense "bright" spot seen on the MRI scan. Several sport divers with a large shunt through their PFO had many more MRI bright spots than did divers without a shunt. Unlike the divers in the paper by Moon, et.al., however, this group had no history of DCS and no symptoms, so the clinical significance of the bright spots is unknown. However, the implication of the MRI findings is clear: venous bubbles at some point did pass through the PFO shunt to directly enter the arterial circulation.

TEST YOUR UNDERSTANDING

5. Below are three case scenarios. State whether the origin of the problem is most likely DCS or AGE.
   a. A 35-year-old man climbs back on the boat following a dive to 60 fsw that lasted for 40 minutes. A minute later he collapses on the deck and appears unconscious.
   b. A 27-year-old woman complains of numbness and tingling a half hour after her third dive of the day. An hour later she cannot move her legs.
   c. A 40-year-old man has weakness and fatigue an hour after his second dive of the day. Two minutes later he develops sudden numbness and paralysis over the left side of his body.

6. Which one of the following pathways correctly describes the route of DCS nitrogen bubbles through a patent foramen ovale?
   T=tissues; V=venous circulation; R=right atrium;
   L=left atrium; A=arterial circulation.
   a. T —> V —> R —> L —> A
   b. T —> V —> L —> R —> A
   c. T —> A —> L —> R —> V
   d. T —> A —> R —> L —> V

From this and other reports (Wilmshurst 1989; Cross 1989; Cross 1992; Wilmshurst 1992; Johnston 1996; Wilmshurst 1996; Wilmshurst 1997) it is now apparent that:

- in a significant percentage of scuba divers (as in the general population) a PFO can be demonstrated;
- if the PFO is large, venous nitrogen bubbles can traverse it and cause brain lesions as seen on an MRI brain scan;
- the scenario of venous nitrogen bubbles passing through a patent PFO is responsible for at least some cases of decompression sickness.

The potential for damage from venous bubbles in the arterial circulation is the same as from air bubbles of arterial gas embolism. Thus the two types of bubbles have different origins (nitrogen egress for DCS, barotrauma for AGE), but the appearance of the patient can be quite similar. This fact highlights the importance of a unified approach to any bubble problem. While the information outlined in Table 1 is correct in principle, many diving accidents caused by bubbles cannot be diagnosed as definitively DCS or AGE.

SHOULD DIVERS BE CHECKED FOR A PATENT FORAMEN OVALE? SHOULD DIVERS WITH A PATENT FORAMEN OVALE NOT SCUBA DIVE?

Patent foramen ovale is something that might be looked for after a diving accident when there are neurologic symptoms (e.g., Type II DCS), to explain the possible mechanism; this is particularly important if the injured diver stayed within acceptable depth and time limits. However, at present there is no general recommendation that all sport divers have a test for patent foramen ovale. The technique to demonstrate it is costly and, more importantly, finding a small PFO does not prove the diver is at any increased risk for a decompression problem.

There are millions of recreational scuba divers. If a PFO can be found in 25% of scuba divers when carefully looked for, and there are only a few hundred cases of DCS reported yearly, it seems highly unlikely that demonstration of PFO would indicate any special risk for DCS. Furthermore, in the study by Knauth, et. al., the significant brain lesions occurred only in *some* of the divers with PFO and a large shunt. Finally, none of the divers with brain lesions had a history of DCS.

Like many other issues in diving, this one is unsettled and somewhat controversial (Wilmshurst 1992; Cross 1992; Wilmshurst 1997). As Wilmshurst pointed out in an editorial accompanying the MRI article:
Decompression illness is a spectrum. It may be so mild that divers do not seek treatment...The fact that the illness can be mild adds plausibility to studies showing an increased prevalence of subclinical lesions in divers with a large shunt but also cautions against accepting data uncritically from studies in which subjects were self selected...Further investigation into the possibility that diving per se causes brain damage is

required, but we must not forget that evidence of pathological change is not proof of functional deficit. (Wilmshurst 1997)

If a diver is known to have a PFO with a large right to left shunt, current knowledge suggests it would probably be prudent to refrain from diving until the opening is repaired (Wilmshurst 1996). At the least, the diver should consult a cardiologist knowledgeable about scuba diving. PFO and diving is an evolving area of research, and anyone interested in the subject should stay tuned for new studies that will surely be done on this important subject.

TEST YOUR UNDERSTANDING

7. State whether each of the following statements is True or False.
   a. Decompression sickness can only occur if the tissue nitrogen pressure is higher than the ambient nitrogen pressure.
   b. DCI and DCS are the same condition.
   c. "The bends" encompasses problems related to arterial gas embolism.
   d. Hyperbaric chamber recompression is usually not considered necessary if DCS symptoms completely disappear with 100% oxygen.

WHY IS IT UNSAFE TO FLY SOON AFTER DIVING?

It is 1 p.m. and Anne has just completed her sixth Caribbean dive over a 3-day period. She boards her plane home at 7 p.m. the same day. Twenty minutes into the flight Anne begins to have severe pain in both elbows and feels achy all over. She thinks she's coming down with the flu, and is thankful it didn't happen while she was diving. She takes two aspirin but the elbow pain persists. Two hours later, on landing, she feels much better, and attributes improvement to the aspirin.

Anne actually suffered a classic episode of type I DCS ("bends") while flying. Had she not boarded the plane so soon after diving she would have developed no elbow pain or flu-like ache.

Dive tables are designed to help prevent episodes of DCS. Unless specifically designed for altitude diving, the tables assume the diver will surface at or close to sea level. The tables assume the diver will experience a controlled decompression from some water depth *to sea level*, so the excess nitrogen can be safely unloaded. If the diver instead goes to an ambient pressure significantly *less* than sea level, the tables are no longer valid.

Flying always presents an ambient pressure less than sea level. Flying in effect represents a *second decompression*, this time between sea level and the cabin altitude. The airplane cabin, although pressurized, is still at a much lower pressure than sea level. At 30,000 feet altitude, the airplane cabin on commercial airliners is usually pressurized to between 7000 and 8000 feet. In fact *everyone* in the plane experiences some decompression, but the amount of nitrogen lost by people who haven't been diving is trivial and causes no symptoms. (Jet fighter pilots who very rapidly ascend from sea level to high altitude can get the bends for the same reason as divers: too rapid ascent causing nitrogen bubbles to form in the tissues and blood.)

Fly too soon after surfacing from a dive and the further reduction in ambient pressure can result in excess nitrogen forming bubbles large or plentiful enough to cause DCS. It is universally recommended that you wait some time after diving before flying.

HOW LONG SHOULD A DIVER WAIT BEFORE FLYING?

The answer to this question is both simple and complex. The simple answer is to wait until the excess nitrogen has off-loaded enough so that you won't develop the bends at altitude. *That* length of time will depend on how many dives have been made over what period of time, the dive profiles, and how many hours have elapsed since the last dive; all this information makes the answer complex, and, ultimately, unique to the individual diver.

DAN and other organizations have, over the years, made general recommendations applicable to various diving activities, e.g., repetitive recreational dives, single recreational dives, decompression dives, etc. DAN's recommendations for recreational divers include the following (as printed in Alert Diver, May/June 1994):

1. Divers making single dives per diving day, should have a minimum surface interval of 12 hours before ascending to altitude. This includes going to altitude by aircraft, automobile or any other means.

2. Divers who make multiple dives per day or over many days, or divers that require obligated decompression stops should take special precautions and wait for an extended surface interval beyond 12 hours before ascending to altitude. Extended surface intervals allow for additional denitrogenation and may reduce the likelihood of developing symptoms. For those diving heavily during an extended vacation, it may not be a bad idea to take a day off at midweek, or save the last day to buy those last-minute souvenirs.

As a general rule, 24 hours after multiple dives is a safe waiting period. A dive computer will also display a time considered safe to fly after repetitive diving, and this may be less than 24 hours. However, in the event of computer failure at any point, always revert to the DAN guidelines. When in doubt, it seems prudent to wait a full 24 hours before flying.

TEST YOUR UNDERSTANDING

8. A 27 year-old woman went diving for a week in the Caribbean. She did 15 dives, averaging a maximum depth of 70 feet; there were no problems during the dives. Twenty-four hours after her last dive she boarded a jet home; the four-hour flight was uneventful. Five days later she noted numbness and tingling of her right hand, with no paralysis. She had never had this symptom before. What is your diagnosis?

Answers to TEST YOUR UNDERSTANDING

1. When air is compressed the percentage of each individual gas remains the same; hence the percentage of oxygen in compressed air is always .21 (21%) regardless of depth. The *partial pressure* of inhaled oxygen (PO_2) does increase with an increase in ambient pressure; at 33 fsw PO_2 will be .42 atm. O_2; at 66 fsw PO_2 will be .63 atm. O_2, etc. Because the gas is compressed the *number of gas molecules* inhaled will increase as well.

2. At sea level the partial pressure of oxygen is .21 x 760 mm Hg = 159.6 mm Hg. Since 33 fsw = 2 atm. total pressure, the PO_2 of inspired air at this depth is 2 x 159.6, or 319.2 mm Hg. At 66 fsw the PO_2 of inspired air is 3 x 159.6, or 478.8 mm Hg.

3. At sea level the partial pressure of nitrogen is .78 x 760 mm Hg = 592.8 mm Hg; this is also .78 atm. N_2. At 33 fsw the PN_2 is 2 x 592.8 = 1185.6 mm Hg, or 1.56 atm. N_2. At 66 fsw the PN_2 is 3 x 592.8 =1778.4 mm Hg, or 2.34 atm. N_2.

4. If a certain percentage of tank air is a gas contaminant (e.g., 1%), *that percentage* will be unchanged at whatever depth the air is inhaled. However, the *pressure* of the contaminant, just like the component

gases of air, will equal the surrounding or ambient pressure, which at 66 fsw is 3x atmospheric. Since 1% of sea level air pressure is 7.6 mm Hg, the contaminant will have a pressure of 3 x 7.6 mm Hg, or 23.8 mm Hg.

5. a. AGE
   b. DCS
   c. Most likely DCS

6. a. T —-> V —-> R —-> L —-> A

7. a. True
   b. False
   c. False
   d. False

8. Many times diagnosis will depend on the details of the dive profile and post-dive history. Two aspects of this real case history argue against DCS as the diagnosis. First, there were no symptoms on the plane. Since high altitude expands any bubbles in the body, the lack of symptoms during flight suggests no significant amount of bubbles were remaining at the time (i.e., that she adequately decompressed by waiting 24 hours). Second, five days after the last dive is well outside the time for presentation of DCS.

   The same symptom appearing hours after her last dive would have been highly suggestive of DCS, and may have lead to chamber recompression. Presenting as it did, however, the chance of DCS being the cause was very remote. She was referred to her family physician and the problem resolved spontaneously.

REFERENCES AND BIBLIOGRAPHY

The following articles are quoted in Section G and F.

Arthur DC, Margulies RA. A short course in diving medicine. Annals Emerg Med 1987; 16:689-701.

Boettger ML. Scuba diving emergencies: pulmonary overpressure accidents and decompression sickness. Annals Emerg Med 1983;12:563-567.

Boycott AE, Damant GCC, Haldane JS. The prevention of compressed-air illness. J Hyg Camb 1908;8:342-443.

Bove AA. The basis for drug therapy in decompression sickness. Undersea Biomed Res 1982;9:91-111.

Butler BD, Laine GA, Leiman BC, et al. Effect of the Trendelenburg position on the distribution of arterial air emboli in dogs. Annals Thor Surg 1988;45:198-202.

Catron PW, Flynn Et, Jr. Adjuvant drug therapy for decompression sickness: a review. Undersea Biomed Res 1982;9:161-74.

Cross SJ, Thomson LF, Jennings KP, Shields TG. Right-to-left shunt and neurological decompression sickness in divers. (Letter). Lancet 1989;ii;568.

Cross SJ, Evans, SA, Thomson LF, et. al. Safety of subaqua diving with a patent foramen ovale. BMJ 1992;304:481-2.

Cross SJ, Lee HS, Thomson LF, Jennings K. Patent foramen ovale and subaqua diving (letter). BMJ 1992;304:1312.

Colebatch HJH, Smith MM, Ng CKY. Increased elastic recoil as a determinant of pulmonary barotrauma in divers. Resp Physiol 1976;26:55-64.

Davis JC, Kizer KW. Diving Medicine. In: Auerbach PS, Geehr EC, editors. *Management of Wilderness and Environmental Emergencies*, 2nd edition. The C.V. Mosby Co., St. Louis, 1989.

Dewey AW, Jr. Decompression sickness, an emerging recreational hazard. N Engl J Med 1962: 267:759-65; 812-20.

Dick APK, Massey EW. Neurologic presentation of decompression sickness and air embolism in sport divers. Neurology 1985; 35:667-671.

Edmonds C. Barotrauma. In Strauss R., editor. *Diving Medicine*. New York, Grune & Stratton, 1976.

Green RD, Leitch DR. Twenty years of treating decompression sickness. Aviat Space Environ Med 1987;58:362-6.

Gorman DF. Decompression sickness and arterial gas embolism in sports scuba divers. Sports Medicine 1989;8:32-42.

Johnston RP, Broome JR, Hunt PD, et. al. Patent foramen ovale and decompression illness in divers (letter). The Lancet 1996; 348: 1515.

Kindwall EP. Diving emergencies. In: Kravis TC, editor. *Emergency Medicine*; Aspen Systems Corporation, Rockville, Maryland, 1983.

Kizer KW. Dysbaric cerebral air embolism in Hawaii. Ann Emerg Med 1987;16:535-41.

Knauth M, Ries S, Pohimann S, et. al. Cohort study of multiple brain lesions in sport divers: role of a patent foramen ovale. BMJ 1997; 314:701-703.

Krzyzak J. A case of delayed-onset pulmonary barotrauma in a scuba diver. Undersea Biomed Res 1987;14:553-61.

Macklin MT, Macklin CC. Malignant interstitial emphysema of the lungs and mediastinum as an imporant occult complication in many respiratory diseases and other conditions: An interpretation of the clinical literature in the light of laboratory experiment. Medicine 1944;23:281-358.

Mebane GY, Dick AP. *DAN Underwater Diving Accident Manual.* Divers Alert Network, Duke Univesity, 1985.

Moon RE, Camporesi EM, Kisslo JA. Patent foramen ovale and decompression sickness in divers. Lancet 1989;1:513-514.

Neblett LM. Otolaryngology and sport scuba diving. Update and guidelines. Annals Otology, Rhin and Laryng. Supplement 1985; 115:1-12.

Orr D. Know When to Say When. Judging your risks before flying after diving is your own informed decision. Alert Diver, May/ June, 1994; p. 13.

Osler W. *The Principles and Practice of Medicine,* D. Appleton and Co., New York; 1892. Page 827.

Roydhouse N. 1001 disorders of the ear, nose and sinuses in scuba divers. Can J Appl Spt Sci 1985;10:99-103.

Schaefer KE, McNulty WP Jr., Carey C, Liebow AA. Mechanisms in development of interstitial emphysema and air embolism on decompression from depth. J Appl Physiol 1958;13:15-29.

Strauss RH. Diving Medicine: State of the Art. Amer Rev Resp Dis 1979;119:1001-1023.

Weeth JB. Management of underwater accidents. JAMA 1965; 192: 215-219.

Wilmshurst P, Byrne JC, Webb-Peploe MM. Relation between interatrial shunts and decompression sickness in divers. Lancet 1989;II;1302-1306.

Wilmshurst. Patent formen ovale and subaqua diving (letter). BMJ 1992;1312.

Wilmshurst P. Transcatheter occlusion of foramen ovale with a button device after neurological decompression illness in professional divers. The Lancet 1996;348:752-753.

Wilmshurst P. Brain damage in divers (editorial). BMJ 1997; 314: 689-690.

DIVING ODDS N' ENDS

Why Don't Whales Get The Bends?

Whales can dive very deep and stay underwater a long time before surfacing for air. How long? A bottlenose whale can stay submerged for up to two hours. Whales are able to stay under by efficient use of oxygen, plus the ability to carry a relatively large amount of oxygen on myoglobin (a muscle protein similar to hemoglobin).

How deep can they go? A pilot whale can dive to 1500 feet, a sperm whale to 3000 feet. According to *Guinness Book of Records*, the record belongs to the sperm whale, with a recorded depth of 8202 ft.

Whales don't get the bends from such deep dives because they don't breathe compressed air. Although they stay down far longer than any human breath-holder, the whale's relatively small lung volume (compared to body size) doesn't contain enough nitrogen to saturate much of its enormous body mass. Thus on ascent there is very little "extra" nitrogen to come out of the whale's tissues. (Humans have a much larger ratio of lung volume to body size, and some deep breath-hold divers have developed symptoms of the bends.)

Now if the whale dove with compressed air...

DIVING ODDS N' ENDS

Lloyd Bridges

Bridges starred as Mike Nelson in the popular TV adventure series *Sea Hunt*, which aired weekly from 1957 through 1961. An avid diver himself, his show is generally credited with interesting many thousands of people in undersea life and diving.

Bridges also appeared in several undersea feature films, including *16 Fathoms Deep, Around the World Under the Sea,* and *Daring Game*. His non-diving movies include *Airplane, Airplane II, The Rainmaker* and *Hot Shots*.

Less well known is that Bridges was co-author of an early dive training book, *Mask and Flippers*, published in 1960.

DIVING ODDS N' ENDS

The BIGGEST Animals in the Sea...

The biggest fish is the whale shark, scientific name *Rhincodon typus. R. typus* is pure shark but *as big as* a whale; adult whale sharks can grow up to 40 feet in length and weigh over 15 tons. Unlike most other sharks, the whale shark eats only plankton.

The biggest animal, of course, is a mammal - the whale. And the biggest of these is the blue or sulphur-bottom whale, *Balaenoptera musculus*. This animal can grow up to 110 feet in over-all length and weigh over 200 tons. Some dinosaurs may have been as long but none was as heavy. The blue whale is the largest animal that has ever lived on earth.

DIVING ODDS N' ENDS

There Has To Be a Better Ending (*The Big Blue*)

Toward the end of the movie *The Big Blue*, Jacque Mayol's girlfriend is seen walking down a narrow street to his apartment. It is bright morning, and Mayol has had nightmares about his friend Enzo's death from free diving the previous day. His girlfriend enters the apartment and gasps at the site: Mayol laying in bed, dazed, his nose and ears all bloody. No explanation as to how he got that way. End of scene.

In the next frame Mayol is running out of the apartment, toward the dock and his free-diving apparatus (a sled that allows competitors to descend to record depths). His girlfriend gives chase, begging him not to dive. Mayol's bloody face is unchanged from the previous scene; girlfriend also looks the same. In fact everything is the same except...it is now *night time*. Clearly, in the context of the scene only a few minutes have elapsed since she entered Mayol's apartment. But the sun has long set and it is hours later! Minor editing glitch, you say. OK, OK, but the next (and last) scene makes Free Willy look like a sophisticated flic. Mayol's girlfriend, seeing that he is compelled to dive, has a change of heart and helps launch the sled. He goes deep, meets his friend the dolphin, then surfaces and cavorts with other dolphins. End of movie.

The Big Blue is muddled like this all the way through, but it is worth viewing for anyone addicted to diving lore. Just don't expect a true-to-life or true-to-the-facts film biography. Mayol himself has disavowed this film as a less than faithful biography.

Oxygen Therapy For Diving Accidents: At Atmospheric and Hyperbaric Pressure

WHAT IS OXYGEN THERAPY?

Oxygen, of course, is part of the air we breathe. Oxygen is also the most widely prescribed "drug" in hospitals; about a quarter of all patients in an acute care hospital receive inhaled oxygen at some point in their stay. Since air already contains 21% oxygen, what doctors prescribe is more accurately known as *supplemental* oxygen, i.e., an inhaled oxygen concentration greater than the 21% in surrounding air. Sometimes the gas mixture prescribed is called "enriched" air, to distinguish it from "ordinary" air.

In hospitals, 100% oxygen is piped into each patient's room, ready for delivery at whatever concentration needed. The actual percentage of oxygen delivered is determined by the type of appliance used to bring the pure oxygen from the wall source to the patient's face, e.g., nasal prongs or various types of face mask. These appliances serve to mix the 100% oxygen from the wall source with the 21% oxygen from ordinary air; depending on the appliance used, the percentage of oxygen delivered to the patient can range between just above 21% to over 90%.

The oxygen percentage a doctor orders depends on the clinical condition of the patient. Generally, the lower the patient's oxygen level, the higher the O_2 concentration needed. Pure or undiluted (100%) oxygen is only used rarely, and then only in an intensive care unit. To minimize the risk of oxygen toxicity physicians try to keep the inhaled oxygen concentration at 40% or lower.

WHAT IS OXYGEN TOXICITY?

Oxygen toxicity is damage to some part of the body from inhaling too much oxygen. It is impossible to get oxygen toxicity by inhaling air (21% oxygen) at sea level or lower pressures. A significantly higher percentage of oxygen than the normal 21%, or inhalation at a significantly higher ambient pressure than sea level, can cause oxygen toxicity. As used in hospitals, outside of a hyperbaric chamber, the main risk is lung damage. Under water, inhaling too much oxygen (usually a result of the higher ambient pressures), the main risk is seizures. The specific parameters determining oxygen toxicity - the amount inhaled, the pressure, the duration, etc. - are discussed in Section I.

WHAT IS THE DIFFERENCE BETWEEN OXYGEN THERAPY FOR BUBBLE DISEASE AND OTHER MEDICAL CONDITIONS?

Supplemental oxygen is widely employed to improve a patient's low oxygen level. Virtually any condition affecting the lungs can lead to a low oxygen level: asthma, bronchitis, emphysema, pneumonia, heart failure, etc. Apart from patients with "bubble disease" - DCS or AGE - if the oxygen level is not reduced there is usually no need to prescribe oxygen therapy.

By contrast, oxygen is used in DCS and AGE to shrink bubbles that have formed in the blood and tissues. It is usually *not* given to improve a low oxygen level. A low blood oxygen level is *not* the problem in DCS or AGE (unless the lungs are clogged with bubbles, or there is some other direct effect on the lungs, e.g., aspiration from near drowning). In any case, the initial blood oxygen level doesn't matter. For all cases of DCS or AGE the first aid goal is to administer 100% inhaled oxygen.

Table 1 summarizes some important differences in oxygen therapy for DCS/AGE (of any cause) and for all other medical conditions. Note that, compared to the universe of patients receiving oxygen, the number treated for DCS or AGE is minuscule. Outside of compressed gas diving, DCS and AGE are rarely encountered, which is one reason why most hospitals don't have a hyperbaric chamber. Scuba diving, however, is very popular, and the role of supplemental oxygen in treating the rare case of DCS or AGE should be understood by all divers.

Once extra oxygen is inhaled the gas does not accumulate for later use; it is metabolized right away. The fact that oxygen is not stored by the body is why people die quickly when air is cut off; all available oxygen at that point is completely exhausted in about four minutes. This is also the reason why, if a patient with pneumonia is low on oxygen, it does no good to prescribe "30 minutes of oxygen twice a day." Intermittent dosing may be appropriate for most other drugs, because they stay in the body for some time, but not for supplemental oxygen. To be effective for patients whose blood is low in oxygen, supplemental oxygen has to be supplied and inhaled *continuously*, until the underlying problem is corrected. (Football players who come off the field for a few whiffs of oxygen on the sidelines are not really benefitted in any physiologic sense; by the time they get back in the game the supplemental oxygen they inhaled has been completely used up.)

TABLE 1.
Differences in Using Supplemental Oxygen for Bubble Disease (AGE and/or DCS) and All Other Medical Conditions.

	AGE and/or DCS	All Other Conditions
No. patients treated per year	hundreds*	millions
O$_2$ concentration used	100% (alternating with periods of air breathing)	24% to 100%, continuous, until patient is no longer hypoxic without it
Ambient pressure at which O$_2$ is given	at atmospheric until a hyperbaric chamber is available; then above atmospheric	atmospheric**
Blood test required to determine proper O$_2$ concentration?	no	yes***
Goal of O$_2$ therapy	shrink gas bubbles in blood and tissues	raise a low blood oxygen level
Risk of oxygen toxicity	100% O$_2$ may cause seizures during hyperbaric therapy, or cause lung disease at atmospheric pressure	100% O$_2$, over hours to days, may cause lung disease; no seizures expected when 100% O$_2$ is given at atmospheric pressure

----
* Rough estimate, based on DAN statistics for reported dive accidents.
** Except for a few specific and uncommon conditions, such as severe carbon monoxide poisoning and gangrene, which might be treated in a hyperbaric chamber in some hospitals.
*** Measurement of oxygen saturation with pulse oximetry, or arterial blood gas analysis for measuring PO$_2$.

WHY IS 100% OXYGEN RECOMMENDED FOR ALL VICTIMS OF A SCUBA DIVING ACCIDENT?

Scuba accident victims may be low on oxygen, especially if they have aspirated water or developed some other lung complication, but the main reason for 100% oxygen therapy is to shrink any gas bubbles formed during ascent. Treatment of gas bubbles requires 100% oxygen regardless of the blood oxygen level, and for as long as is practical; just how long is governed by the risk of oxygen toxicity.

(Note. Examination of the patient is not a reliable guide to the blood oxygen level. A patient can be in distress with a normal oxygen level, or appear calm and peaceful while succumbing from hypoxia. Neither respiratory rate nor the skin color are reliable guides to hypoxia. Hospitals can measure the patient's oxygen level in various ways. It is unlikely that any test for blood oxygen will be available at the site of a diving accident but, for reasons stated, none is really needed.)

Unlike the typical patient with a low oxygen level (from pneumonia, heart failure, asthma, etc.), the victim of bubbles from diving should benefit from even a short period of 100% oxygen. One hundred percent oxygen may prevent existing bubbles from expanding, or even shrink them enough to provide symptomatic relief. *The main reason to have supplemental oxygen available at the site of any scuba dive is to treat DCS or AGE*, two of the most serious dive-related problems. For either problem hyperbaric oxygen therapy is optimal, but until transport can be arranged to a hyperbaric chamber, the victim should receive 100% oxygen at atmospheric pressure, via a face mask.

The secondary reason to have supplemental oxygen available is to treat hypoxia (low oxygen level), such as is found in victims of near-drowning accidents. Oxygen can be very helpful for any hypoxic victim, but that is not the primary reason for having oxygen available when diving. Some might argue that this is quibbling over reasons, but nonetheless there are two very different indications for supplemental oxygen in dive accidents. It is primarily as treatment for DCS/AGE that oxygen is recommended at every dive site.

REASONS TO HAVE OXYGEN
AT EVERY DIVE SITE

Primary: To treat DCS/AGE

Secondary: To treat hypoxia (e.g., near-drowning, shock)

No matter what the indications, when oxygen is used as part of first aid for a diving victim it is always given at atmospheric pressure (i.e., not under hyperbaric conditions).

HOW IS OXYGEN USED AT ATMOSPHERIC PRESSURE?

On land, outside of a hyperbaric chamber, oxygen is always delivered at the ambient (atmospheric) pressure. The oxygen concentration administered can vary from just over 21% up to the maximum, 100%. At sea level the ambient pressure is 760 mm Hg, also known as "one atmosphere" (1 atm.; 14.7 psi). At an altitude of 18,000 feet the ambient pressure is half that at sea level, and so equals 0.5 atm (7.35 psi).

It should be apparent that the most oxygen a patient can receive on land, outside of a hyperbaric chamber, is 100% given at sea level pressure; this is one atmosphere of oxygen and is abbreviated "1 atm. O_2". (You could get a slightly higher oxygen pressure if you administer 100% oxygen on land below sea level. The few habitable areas below sea level are so close to sea level that their ambient pressure can be considered 1 atm.)

In Denver, where the average atmospheric pressure is about 85% of sea level, 100% inspired oxygen equals .85 atmosphere of oxygen (.85 atm O_2). One hundred per cent oxygen delivered at 18,000 feet, where the ambient pressure is 0.5 atmosphere, is 0.5 atm. O_2, etc.

As pointed out in Section D, it is important to keep the different pressure terms clear. There are several terms in common use that mean the same thing; the box below reviews some definitions discussed earlier.

- when surrounded by air: ambient pressure = atmospheric pressure = barometric pressure

- 1 atmosphere = the average air pressure at sea level
  = 760 mm Hg = 14.7 psi;
  0.5 atmosphere = 1/2 the average air pressure at sea level =
  380 mm Hg = 7.35 psi; etc.

- when surrounded by water: ambient pressure = water pressure + atmospheric pressure above the water = atmospheres of air pressure at that depth (e.g., a depth of 66 fsw is 3 atmospheres, 99 fsw is 4 atmospheres, etc.)

WHAT ARE ATMOSPHERES OF OXYGEN?

Atmospheres of oxygen are based on the O_2 concentration in the inspired gas mixture and the ambient pressure. One atm. O_2 is 100% oxygen delivered at one atmosphere of pressure; other combinations of concentration and pressure can also equal one atm. O_2. Study the following relationships for one, two and three atm. O_2 to solidify the concept of atm. O_2 (fsw = feet sea water). Then study Figure 1, which shows the rise in atmospheres of oxygen with depth, while breathing compressed air.

1 atm. O_2 =

100%	O_2 inhaled at sea level pressure (1 atmosphere)
50%	O_2 at 2 atmospheres of pressure (reached at 33 fsw)
25%	O_2 at 4 atmospheres of pressure (99 fsw)
21%	O_2 at 4.76 atmospheres of pressure (124 fsw)
5%	O_2 at 20 atmospheres of pressure (627 fsw)

2 atm. O_2 =

100%	O_2 at 2 atmospheres of pressure (33 fsw)
50%	O_2 at 4 atmospheres of pressure (99 fsw)
25%	O_2 at 8 atmospheres of pressure (231 fsw)
21%	O_2 at 9.52 atmospheres of pressure (282 fsw)
5%	O_2 at 40 atmospheres of pressure (1287 fsw)

TEST YOUR UNDERSTANDING

1. A diver is at 66 fsw breathing compressed air.

    a. What is the pressure at that depth in atmospheres?
    b. How many atm. O_2 is she inhaling?
    c. How many atm. N_2 is she inhaling?

2. A mountain climber is at 18,000 feet altitude.

    a. What is the ambient pressure in atmospheres? In psi?
    b. When breathing mountain air, what atm. O_2 is he inhaling?
    c. When breathing 100% O_2 via a face mask, what atm. O_2 is he inhaling?

3. A diver decompresses at 11 fsw while breathing 100% O_2.

    a. How many atm. O_2 is he inhaling?
    b. How would you gauge his relative risk of oxygen toxicity?
    c. How deep would he have to go to inhale 2 atm. O_2?

3 atm. $O_2 =$

100%	O_2 at 3 atmospheres of pressure (66 fsw)
50%	O_2 at 4 atmospheres of pressure (99 fsw)
25%	O_2 at 12 atmospheres of pressure (363 fsw)
21%	O_2 at 14.28 atmospheres of pressure (439 fsw)
5%	O_2 at 60 atmospheres of pressure (1947 fsw)

HOW IS OXYGEN USED AT THE DIVE SITE?

Standard resuscitation and treatment protocols, including CPR when necessary, should be followed in any life-threatening situation. The information provided herein is intended only as a general discussion of the rationale and use of oxygen therapy for suspected bubble disease. Medical and first aid texts, several of which are listed in the bibliography, can be consulted for more detailed information on how to provide oxygen, transport the patient, etc.

Oxygen toxicity should not be a concern when giving oxygen as part of first aid. If possible, always give 100% oxygen via a positive pressure (tight fitting) mask; this concentration of O_2 is part of first aid for any scuba diving accident. At the same time, arrange to transport the victim to an appropriate medical facility. Do not worry about oxygen toxicity unless 100% oxygen is administered continuously for more than two hours. At that point, if an appropriate medical facility has not been reached and supplemental oxygen is still available, an air break of 15-30 minutes should begin, followed by continuation of 100% oxygen.

If the diver's symptoms abate during treatment, 100% O_2 is still recommended if either DCS or AGE is suspected; bubbles could reform and symptoms could recur. However, don't insist on a tight fitting mask if the diver finds it very uncomfortable or is vomiting; you can alternate with a loose fitting oxygen mask. In first aid for a diving accident, it is always more important to give some oxygen than none at all.

Since 1991 DAN has sponsored half-day courses on oxygen therapy for certified divers. The DAN Oxygen First Aid in Dive Accidents Course, usually held at a local dive shop, uses both lecture and hands on experience to teach three important aspects of first-aid oxygen therapy: 1) how to make oxygen available at any dive site; 2) how to use the recommended equipment; 3) the advantages of oxygen therapy for dive accident victims.

1) OXYGEN AVAILABILITY. For field use oxygen comes in small green tanks (typical capacity about 40 cu. ft. at 1500 psi) that look like small scuba tanks, but contain 100% oxygen instead of compressed air (Figure 2). Tanks of oxygen are always painted green,

Figure 1. Atmospheres of O_2 (vertical axis) while breathing compressed air at various depths (horizontal axis). (fsw = feet sea water; sl = sea level)

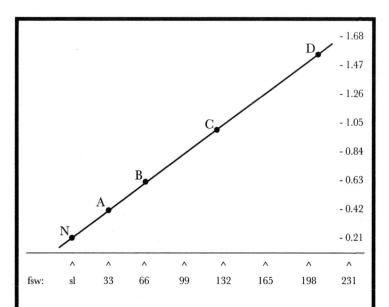

N = normal, or .21 atm. O_2. Note that at sea level the atm. O_2 is .21 whether breathing compressed or non-compressed (room) air.

A = 0.42 atm. O_2, equal to breathing compressed air at 33 fsw or 42% O_2 at sea level; this amount of oxygen is routinely given to patients for long periods, without apparent toxicity.

B = .63 atm O_2, equal to breathing compressed air at 66 fsw or 63% O_2 at sea level; this amount of oxygen would risk mild pulmonary oxygen toxicity after more than 24 hours. Maximum RSD bottom time on first dive to this depth is less than one hour, so oxygen toxicity is not a consideration.

C = 1.00 atm O_2, equal to breathing compressed air at 130 fsw or 100% O_2 at sea level; this amount of oxygen would cause chest discomfort after a few hours, and risk serious oxygen toxicity after 24 hours. Maximum RSD bottom time on first dive to this depth is approximately 10 minutes, so oxygen toxicity is not a consideration.

D = 1.5 atm. O_2; this amount of oxygen cannot be given at sea level outside of a hyperbaric chamber. 1.5 atm. O_2 poses serious risk for oxygen toxicity, the first manifestation of which may be seizures. As shown, it can be reached breathing compressed air at a depth of approximately 200 feet.

Figure 2. DAN oxygen tank and equipment for field use. (Courtesy Diver's Alert Network)

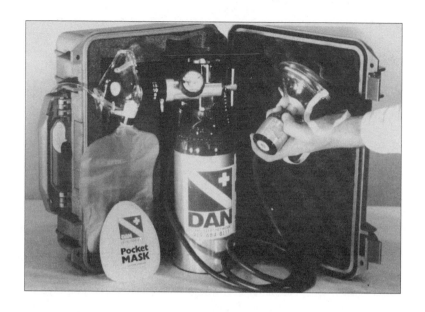

either the entire tank (if made of steel) or the top portion (if aluminum).

DAN recommends, and good practice mandates, that all dive boats and dive facilities carry a readily accessible tank of oxygen, an oxygen regulator and appropriate face masks for first aid use. In fact, it is recommended that one should avoid diving from a boat that does not have oxygen on board. Each year more and more dive boats are carrying oxygen

2) HOW TO USE. A principal focus of the DAN Oxygen Course is on how to use the equipment. It does no good for the distressed diver if the boat contains a tank of oxygen that no one knows how to use. (Note: This section is for informational purposes only. Formal training in both CPR and use of oxygen equipment should be obtained from qualified instructors in a hands-on situation.)

As with any tank of compressed air, a regulator is required to lower the pressure so it can be safely delivered to the diver. Scuba air tank regulators *cannot* be used for this purpose. You need a special O_2-tank regulator. A green plastic tube delivers oxygen from the regulator to the mask, which fits over the diver's mouth and nose.

(Advantages of oxygen therapy are discussed later in this chapter.)

WHAT ARE THE TYPES OF OXYGEN MASKS AVAILABLE FOR DIVE ACCIDENT VICTIMS?

Three types of oxygen delivery masks are available in the DAN oxygen kit: a demand-valve-with-mask, a pocket mask, and a non-rebreathing mask (Table 2, Figures 3 and 4). The first two masks can deliver close to 100% oxygen to the diver; the last one can deliver about 70-80% oxygen.

The demand-valve-with-mask is similar to the demand valve found in all second stage scuba regulators; with each inhalation, it delivers compressed gas (100% oxygen) to the diver's mouth and nose under a slight positive pressure. As with a second stage regulator, the diver must first initiate a breath for the gas to be delivered; thus the demand-valve-with-mask cannot be used on the non-breathing victim. To assure close

---

TABLE 2.

Three types of face masks recommend by DAN for oxygen delivery at the site of a diving accident.

Mask Type	Concentration O_2 delivered	Principal Use	Comment
demand-valve-with-mask-	Close to 100%	Victim is breathing, not vomiting; victim initiates each breath, which is delivered under positive pressure	Tight mask-face seal mandatory
pocket mask	Close to 100%	Victim is not breathing; rescuer provides all breaths	Tight mask-face seal mandatory
non-re breathing mask	70%-80%	Victim is breathing	Loose fitting mask; uses large amount of oxygen

---

to 100% oxygen, the mask must make a tight seal with the diver's face (i.e., no air leaks around the mask).

The positive pressure given by the demand-valve-with-mask is only *slightly higher than atmospheric*. If atmospheric pressure is 760 mm Hg, the pressure inside this mask on inhalation may be 770 mm Hg, or only about .01% higher. This is obviously not hyperbaric therapy, which is two or more *times* atmospheric pressure (i.e., 1520 mm Hg or greater). The extra pressure inside the mask helps facilitate entry of pure oxygen into the diver's lungs.

For the victim who is not breathing (apneic), the pocket mask can be used; it is so-called because the mask easily folds and fits into one's pocket (Figure 4). The pocket mask is designed to fit snugly over the victim's mouth and nose. As long as the mask-face seal is airtight, the victim can

Figure 3. DAN's 'mini' charter boat oxygen unit, showing oxygen regulators (lower right), demand valve with mask, lower left, and non-rebreather face mask (attached to box cover); oxygen tank is not shown. (Courtesy Diver's Alert Network)

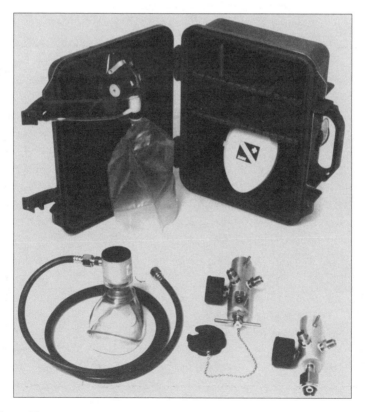

be ventilated through a port on the mask *by the rescuer* using artificial respiration-but *without mouth-to-mouth contact.*

The pocket mask technique of resuscitation is a variation of standard mouth-to-mouth breathing taught in basic CPR. (Obviously, if the victim is also pulseless cardiac compressions must be delivered at the same time.) A plastic tube connects the oxygen regulator to the mask, so that each breath delivered by the rescuer should provide a high concentration of oxygen. A one-way valve diverts the victim's exhaled air away from the rescuer.

The third type of mask is called a non-rebreather (Figure 3) because it does not allow the victim to rebreathe any of his own exhaled air; the flow of oxygen-enriched air through the mask is great enough to quickly wash away exhaled air. It is an excellent backup mask to the first two types, and can deliver somewhere around 70-80% oxygen. The non-rebreather is useful for the victim who can't tolerate the positive pressure mask, or who is vomiting. Also, if there are two dive accident victims, the non-rebreather can be used for one while the demand-valve-with-mask is used for the other (both masks are fed from a single tank of oxygen and single regulator). One disadvantage of the non-rebreather is that it delivers oxygen continuously instead of only on demand, and so is relatively wasteful of the gas.

Figure 4. Pocket mask for oxygen administration. (Courtesy Diver's Alert Network.)

DAN markets all the necessary oxygen therapy equipment (regulator, masks) in one convenient kit, available to oxygen course instructors and dive shop/boat operators. DAN will also supply the oxygen tank and a training mannikin, as well as a special carrying case for boats (see Section R for DAN's address).

WHAT ARE THE ADVANTAGES OF SUPPLEMENTAL OXYGEN THERAPY FOR DIVE ACCIDENT VICTIMS?

The overall goals of supplemental oxygen therapy are to hasten recovery, preserve organ function, save a life. Behind these goals are two basic reasons for using 100% oxygen when bubble disease (AGE or DCS) is suspected:

- If the victim is hypoxic (low in oxygen), the extra oxygen might raise the blood oxygen level enough to provide more (and sufficient) oxygen for the brain, heart and other vital organs.
- The extra oxygen will help shrink existing nitrogen or air bubbles and prevent others from forming, and so provide important first aid while the victim is transported to a hyperbaric chamber. The victim may experience symptomatic relief with just 100% oxygen delivered at atmospheric pressure.

WHAT IS THE PHYSIOLOGIC BASIS FOR OXYGEN THERAPY?

The two stated reasons for oxygen therapy can be better understood by reference to blood oxygen pressures. Oxygen pressure in the blood is called the PaO_2: partial pressure (P) of oxygen (O_2) in the arterial blood (a). At sea level and breathing air (21% O_2), normal PaO_2 is about 80 to 100 mm Hg. This means that the oxygen pressure in the blood, by itself, will support a column of mercury 80 to 100 mm high. Because air pressure falls with altitude, the normal PaO_2 also falls with altitude. In Denver, for example, the normal PaO_2 is only 65 to 85 mm Hg. On the summit of Mt. Everest PaO_2 has been estimated in air-breathing climbers to be only about 30 mm Hg! (Any lower and the climbers would not have lived to report the ascent.)

If a healthy person inhales 100% oxygen at sea level, nitrogen in the lungs and tissues is replaced by the pure oxygen. This "washout" of nitrogen by 100% oxygen is reflected in a much higher PaO_2, about 600 mm Hg at sea level. (During the washout with 100% O_2 at sea level, the blood *nitrogen* pressure actually falls from about 573 mm Hg to almost zero.)

While PaO_2 goes up markedly with 100% oxygen, the actual number of oxygen molecules in the blood goes up only slightly. A PaO_2 of 600 mm Hg puts only about 7% more oxygen molecules into the blood than a PaO_2 of 100 mm Hg, even though the oxygen pressure is six times higher.

WHY DOES A PaO_2 SIX TIMES NORMAL PROVIDE ONLY 7% MORE OXYGEN IN THE BLOOD?

The point made in the last paragraph may be confusing and it bears some elaboration. The reason a given percentage increase in PaO_2 does not translate into the same percentage increase in oxygen molecules (oxygen content) is because the blood hemoglobin is almost fully saturated with oxygen at a PaO_2 of 100 mm Hg.

In the normal situation, 98% of all oxygen in the blood is carried by hemoglobin; the other 2% is dissolved in the plasma. Oxygen pressures above 100 mm Hg add only *dissolved* oxygen to the blood; at an ambient pressure of one atmosphere (sea level), this extra dissolved oxygen is a small amount when compared to the hemoglobin-bound oxygen, and not enough to make a big difference to patients with lung or heart disease.

Table 3 shows a range of PaO_2 values that can be achieved by varying the O_2 concentration inhaled at one atmosphere. Note that oxygen content increases significantly until PaO_2 is in the normal range; beyond 100 mm Hg, only about 0.3 volumes% of oxygen are added for every 100 mm Hg increase in PaO_2. When the PaO_2 is six times normal the blood contains just 7.5% more oxygen molecules.

Thus, there is a major distinction between oxygen *pressure* and oxygen *content* in the blood. Oxygen pressure directly reflects the pressure of inhaled oxygen, and is due solely to the unbound (dissolved) fraction of oxygen in the blood; it is the same value regardless of the hemoglobin content. Oxygen content, on the other hand, reflects the actual number of oxygen molecules in the blood, both bound to hemoglobin and unbound (dissolved). A low hemoglobin value will not affect a diver's oxygen pressure, but will have a direct effect in reducing oxygen content. Table 3 shows these differences.

Inhaling 100% oxygen at one atmosphere of pressure (sea level) adds greatly to oxygen pressure, but very little to the oxygen content. That is why, when the goal is to improve a low PaO_2 (the situation in virtually all non-diving-accident patients who receive oxygen therapy), there is no reason to exceed the normal PaO_2 range of 80-100 mm Hg, especially as it may add some risk of oxygen toxicity.

The goal is different for victims of AGE or DCS, where the principal rationale for oxygen therapy is to shrink gas bubbles in the tissues and circulation. The higher the oxygen *pressure* in the blood, the faster nitrogen is kicked out of the bubbles and the quicker they will shrink. The limiting factor in maintaining high oxygen pressures in victims of DCS/AGE is *oxygen toxicity*.

TABLE 3.

PaO_2 and oxygen content when various oxygen concentrations are inhaled at one atmosphere pressure (sea level). Note that above a PaO_2 of 100 mm Hg, very little extra oxygen is added to the blood.
SL = sea level. fsw = feet sea water.

Concentration (%) of inhaled O_2	Atm. O_2 inhaled	PaO_2 mm Hg*	O_2 Content Vol. %**	Eq. alt. or depth+
8	.08	27	10	20,000
10.5	.105	36	12	18,000
12	.12	40	15	16,000
15	.15	50	18	14,000
21	.21	80***	19.90	SL
21	.21	90***	19.97	SL
21	.21	100***	20	SL
35	.35	200	20.3	28 fsw
50	.50	300	20.6	40 fsw
65	.65	400	20.9	68 fsw
85	.85	500	21.2	100 fsw
100	1.00	600	21.5	132 fsw

* PaO_2 values assume normal lungs.
** O_2 content reflects actual number of oxygen molecules; values shown assume a normal hemoglobin content.
*** Within the range of normal values at sea level, breathing air; 80 mm Hg is low normal PaO_2, 100 mm Hg is high normal.
   + Equivalent altitude or depth in feet, breathing air. For example, inhaling 8% oxygen at sea level is equivalent to inhaling air at an altitude of 20,000 ft.; inhaling 100% oxygen at sea level is equivalent to inhaling air at a depth of 132 feet.

TEST YOUR UNDERSTANDING

4. A diver is inhaling one atm. O_2. Based on this information alone, she could be inhaling any of the following amounts of oxygen, except *one*.

   a. 25% oxygen at 99 fsw
   b. 50% oxygen at 33 fsw
   c. 100% oxygen at sea level
   d. 150% oxygen at 18,000 feet altitude
   e. Compressed air at 132 fsw

5. Below are five terms, each used to express an oxygen level in the blood. Which one of these terms correlates with the actual number of oxygen molecules carried in the blood?

   a. oxygen pressure, in mm Hg
   b. oxygen pressure, in atmospheres
   c. oxygen saturation of hemoglobin
   d. oxygen content
   e. amount of oxygen dissolved in the plasma

WHY DOES REPLACING NITROGEN WITH OXYGEN SHRINK BUBBLES?

Nitrogen and oxygen are handled very differently in the body. Nitrogen is inert; it is not metabolized by the tissues. It is just *there*. Under ordinary (non-diving) conditions, the pressure of nitrogen in our blood and tissues is the same as in our lungs and in the atmosphere (Figure 5).

Diving upsets this equilibrium because it subjects you to changing ambient pressures. As you descend breathing compressed air, the pressure of inhaled air (and its individual components) changes with surrounding water pressure. The pressure of inhaled nitrogen and oxygen increase, and so more nitrogen and oxygen molecules enter the blood and tissues (according to Henry's Law). Figure 5 also shows that on descent there is a nitrogen pressure gradient from inhaled air and lungs (highest) to blood (intermediate) to tissues (lowest).

Nitrogen, being inert, accumulates in the body *with every dive*. Oxygen, by contrast, is metabolized and doesn't accumulate in the tissues to any great extent. (Oxygen toxicity comes from high inspired oxygen pressures, not from any accumulation of oxygen molecules in the body).

The extra nitrogen that accumulates on descent begins to leave on ascent (Figure 5). As the ambient pressure decreases the nitrogen pressure gradient reverses, so that nitrogen pressure is highest in the tissues, intermediate in the blood and lowest in the lungs. Without this reverse gradient divers would never remove the excess nitrogen accumulated on any dive. DCS occurs when the nitrogen that accumulated in the tissues on descent comes out *too fast* on ascent; instead of dissolving harmlessly in the blood, from where it can be exhaled, it forms nitrogen bubbles large enough to inflict pain or cause blockage of blood flow.

Figure 5. Relative pressures of nitrogen in air and blood. When not diving there is no gradient (A). Nitrogen pressure increases with each dive. Because it takes time for nitrogen to equilibrate, there is a gradient from lungs to tissues with descent (B), and from tissues to lungs with ascent (C).

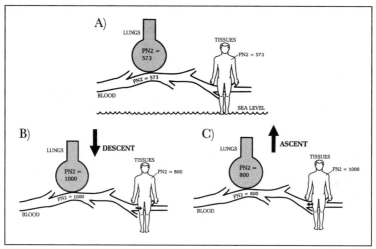

The origin and composition of bubbles differ between AGE and DCS, but the principle of treatment is the same for both: exchanging nitrogen in the bubbles for oxygen. Both types of gas bubbles contain a high nitrogen content. In AGE bubbles it is 78% (same as ordinary air), and in DCS bubbles it is near 100%.

Since nitrogen concentration in AGE bubbles is the same as in the blood and air (78%), there is no gradient for nitrogen to leave the bubbles. Eventually some oxygen from inspired air finds its way into the bubbles and they do shrink, but that is a slow process, "too little, too late" for the victim. Treating AGE (and DCS) requires hastening shrinkage of bubbles, and there are only two ways to accomplish this: compress the bubbles by increasing the ambient pressure, or speed up nitrogen's exit from the bubbles.

Increasing the ambient pressure requires a hyperbaric chamber. (In theory, sending the diver back down in the water would also work, but this is a tricky form of therapy and impossibly dangerous for any seriously ill diver. Although in-water recompression is a routine practice in some remote commercial dive operations, it is never recommended for the recreational diver. Without a full face mask for the diver, and professional support personnel both below the water and on the surface, sending an ill recreational diver back down is an invitation for disaster.) In lieu of a hyperbaric chamber, supplemental oxygen is used to hasten nitrogen's exit from the bubbles. If effect, 100% inspired oxygen is used to *de-nitrogenate the blood* and shrink any gas bubbles.

As the victim inhales 100% oxygen, nitrogen in the blood is "kicked out" by the oxygen and is exhaled by the lungs. Initially, the bubbles still contain a high nitrogen pressure. However, as nitrogen leaves the blood (replaced by oxygen), a large nitrogen gradient forms between the inside of the bubble and the surrounding blood; this fosters nitrogen's exit from the bubble (Figure 6). At the *same time* that nitrogen exits, some oxygen enters the bubble. However, because this O_2 is given up to the tissues for metabolism, there remains a net loss of gas molecules from the bubble and the bubble shrinks.

In summary, the purpose in giving 100% O_2 to anyone with suspected bubble disease is to rid the blood of nitrogen, so that a large nitrogen gradient forms between inside and outside the bubble. In this manner nitrogen flows *out* of the bubbles and into the blood, from where it can be excreted by the lungs. This principle of therapy requires only a high inspired oxygen concentration; it does not require a hyperbaric chamber. Pure oxygen is the preferred washout gas because it contains

Figure 6. Nitrogen in bubbles with supplemental oxygen.

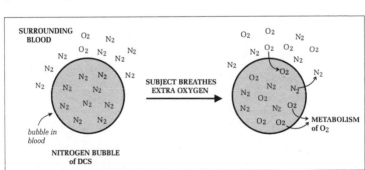

no nitrogen, and the extra oxygen does not accumulate in the body. The risk of oxygen toxicity can be reduced by decreasing the concentration of inhaled oxygen (e.g., a mixture of 50% O_2 + 50% N_2), but this reduces the gradient for nitrogen diffusion out of the bubble.

Fortunately, it is not difficult to get oxygen into the bubbles. Under normal circumstances there is always a positive pressure gradient for oxygen between air sacs in the lungs and the blood bathing them; otherwise, no oxygen would enter the blood and be delivered to the tissues. Likewise, there is a positive pressure gradient between oxygen in the blood and inside the bubbles; and a positive gradient between oxygen in the bubbles and the tissues. Thus, when supplemental O_2 is given, oxygen will flow:

- from the lungs into the blood, then
- from blood into any bubbles in the blood, and
- from the bubbles into the surrounding tissues, where it is metabolized

A bubble containing air will shrink slowly, as it contains 78% non-metabolizable nitrogen (which moves nowhere) and only 21% oxygen. A bubble containing pure nitrogen (as found in DCS) will shrink even more slowly; that it shrinks at all is due to the fact that some oxygen eventually finds its way into the bubble, replacing nitrogen.

HOW IS OXYGEN THERAPY USED AT HYPERBARIC PRESSURES?

Unless trained in hyperbaric medicine, you will never be called upon to administer this type of therapy. Even so, all divers should be aware of the role of hyperbaric chambers in treating bubble disease. Hyperbaric chambers are heavy, rigid structures that can hold one or more people in an environment of high ambient pressure. Every hyperbaric chamber treatment is like a compressed air dive, only there is no water and the limits of compression are rigorously controlled by the hyperbaric operator.

In the U.S. there are about 300 operating hyperbaric chambers; about 68% of them are the monoplace type (Figure 7). Monoplace means that only one person can fit inside the chamber at a time. Multiplace chambers can accommodate two or more people, depending on their size. In addition to treating more than one patient at a time, multiplace chambers offer a great deal more flexibility than monoplace chambers:

- A hyperbaric tender (nurse or other medical assistant) can accompany the patient inside the multiplace chamber and

Figure 7. (Top) Monoplace hyperbaric chamber. (Below) A multiplace chamber.

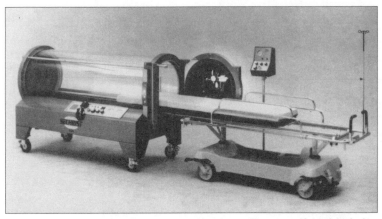

Photo courtsey of Sechrist Industries, Inc.

administer to his or her needs. Tenders can rotate in and out of the chamber while the patient continues to receive treatment.

- Any ancillary equipment needed can be easily entered into the chamber, including a mechanical ventilator.
- The patient can receive 100% oxygen through a head tent or face mask, while the tender is breathing compressed air.

Hyperbaric therapy can be administered with any percentage of oxygen from 21% (ordinary air) to 100%. Either way, hyperbaric therapy will increase the oxygen *pressure* in the patient's blood. (Two atm. O_2 can be achieved at 33 fsw breathing 100% O_2, or at 282 fsw breathing compressed air). Two fundamental principles of hyperbaric therapy hold regardless of the type of chamber used, the concentration of oxygen inhaled, the ambient pressure achieved, or the duration of therapy:

1) **The higher the ambient pressure, the greater the shrinkage of bubbles.** Whereas 100% oxygen at atmospheric pressure can only denitrogenate the blood and hasten nitrogen out of the bubbles, hyperbaric pressures will actually compress the bubbles. The higher ambient pressure inside the chamber increases the gas pressure in the blood, which in turn compresses the bubble according to Boyle's law. Even with minimal compression the victim may find immediate pain relief. When the hyperbaric pressure is removed (equivalent to an ascent) the bubble can re-expand; however, it does not re-expand to the same pre-compression size, because its nitrogen content is also reduced during compression. This is where oxygen plays a vital role in hyperbaric therapy.

2) **The higher the blood oxygen pressure, the faster the gas bubbles will shrink.** Hyperbaric oxygen therapy greatly increases oxygen pressure in the blood, driving oxygen into the bubbles and hastening nitrogen's exit. This is the same mechanism as when 100% O_2 is given under atmospheric pressure, but greatly accelerated. Thus there are two reasons for bubble shrinkage from 100% O_2 inhaled under pressure:

   * denitrogenation of the blood creates a favorable nitrogen gradient (N_2 out);
   * the high blood oxygen pressure creates a favorable oxygen gradient (O_2 in).

If oxygen was not metabolized, merely replacing nitrogen with oxygen would not decrease the bubble's size; however, oxygen, once inside the bubble, then enters the tissues, where it is metabolized. Thus, the bubble shrinks.

Hyperbaric oxygen therapy (HBO) goes one giant step further than is possible with 100% oxygen at atmospheric pressure. Whereas one atm. O_2 is achievable without a hyperbaric chamber, with a chamber the patient can receive two, three or any number of O_2 atmospheres.

Because hyperbaric therapy with air actually puts more nitrogen into the patient's blood (albeit while shrinking the bubbles), most hyperbaric physicians prefer using short periods of 100% hyperbaric oxygen in treating bubble disease rather than just hyperbaric air.

TABLE 4.

Oxygen atmospheres, PaO_2, and blood oxygen content when 100% oxygen is inhaled at sea level and hyperbaric pressures (in person with normal lungs).

Chamber pressure atm.	O₂ atm. inhaled*	PaO₂**	O₂ Content vol.%***	Equivalent depth (fsw)****
1	1	600	21.5	sea level
2	2	1200	23.3	33
3	3	1800	25.1	66
4	4	2400	26.9	99
5	5	3000	28.7	132
6	6	3600	30.5	165

*	One O_2 atm. = 100% oxygen inhaled at sea level pressure.
**	PaO_2 values are approximate; the actual PaO_2 achieved may be lower if the patient has any impairment of ventilation or perfusion to the lungs.
***	Values shown assume patient has a normal hemoglobin content.
****	Breathing 100% O_2

Table 4 shows expected changes in the blood of subjects undergoing hyperbaric therapy with 100% oxygen (data in this table assumes the patient has normal lungs). Although patients may respond differently at each level of therapy, keep in mind the principles stated above.

WHAT ELSE IS HYPERBARIC THERAPY USED FOR?

Diving accidents are just one of several conditions handled by most hospital hyperbaric centers. There is much controversy about hyperbaric therapy in some diseases. The Undersea and Hyperbaric Medical Society (10531 Metropolitan Ave., Kensington, MD 20895) has developed a list of approved conditions that are generally reimbursable by third party payers. This list includes:

- Gas gangrene (infection with *Clostridium perfringens* bacteria)
- Other severe, acute wound infections
- Chronic refractory osteomyelitis (bone infection)
- Vascular insufficiency to an extremity
- Severe carbon monoxide poisoning

- Life-threatening anemia when the patient refuses blood transfusion or blood is unavailable

For non-diving conditions, hyperbaric therapy aims to raise blood oxygen pressure much higher than achievable by 100% O_2 at one atmosphere *in order to put more oxygen into the blood.* For DCS and AGE, on the other hand, the goal is *to replace any nitrogen in the gas bubbles with oxygen, so the bubbles will shrink faster.*

Note that with HBO therapy the extra dissolved oxygen in the blood can appreciably increase the blood's total oxygen content (Table 4). One hundred percent oxygen at three atmospheres can add an extra 5 vol.% to the blood, about a quarter of the normal value. In extremely anemic patients this extra dissolved oxygen can be important therapeutically, and in some cases sustain a life that might otherwise be lost because of low oxygen content. In bubble disease, however, HBO is given primarily to shrink the bubbles, not to increase the dissolved oxygen content.

WHAT IS A HYPERBARIC TREATMENT TABLE?

The U.S. Navy has treatment tables for DCS and AGE. An example of the DCS table was shown in Figure 2, Section G. Note that these tables are always amenable to modification by the physician treating the patient. However, all treatment tables alternate a high concentration of oxygen (usually 100%) with periods of breathing air. The reason, of course, is to prevent oxygen toxicity, a potential hazard of hyperbaric oxygen therapy.

The specific treatment table chosen, and the number of times it is administered, will depend on the clinical course of the patient and assessment of the hyperbaric physician. Following is a case history.

About 30 minutes after J.W. surfaced from his second dive of the morning he felt numbness and tingling in his legs. This dive, 60 feet for 40 minutes, followed a first dive to 110 feet for 10 minutes. However, he admitted to diving "for just a few seconds" to 120 feet on his first dive, to chase a large grouper.

On the boat J.W. received 100% O_2 by positive pressure face mask. The boat captain radioed ahead for an ambulance to meet at the dock. When the boat docked 30 minutes later, J.W. could not walk; he had near total paralysis of both legs but was mentally alert. He was carried off the boat and into the waiting ambulance.

The closest hyperbaric facility was one hour away, in a local hospital. The ambulance attendant called ahead to have the chamber ready. J.W. continued to receive 100% oxygen en route. In the emergency room he was quickly examined by the hyperbaric physician on duty. Diagnosis: Type II DCS, bubble damage to the spinal cord. A catheter was inserted into J.W.'s bladder so he could urinate, and an intravenous line was started for fluids.

Approximately 15 minutes after arrival to the hospital J.W. entered the multiplace chamber with a nurse tender; treatment was begun on U.S. Navy Table 6. At the end of treatment he felt considerably better and could move his legs a little, but still felt some numbness.

He stayed in the hospital and over the next week received five more hyperbaric treatments. By the end of the week he could walk unassisted. He was discharged at that time, with only some residual decrease in sensation, which improved over time.

J.W. believes he became "bent" solely because he exceeded the diving tables. He plans to dive again and pay much more attention to his depth and bottom time. His physician cautioned him to be very conservative and to dive well within the dive tables.

J.W. was fortunate. The dive boat carried oxygen, a chamber was in the area, he never developed cerebral symptoms (mental confusion, stroke, etc.), and his paralysis cleared with hyperbaric therapy.

TEST YOUR UNDERSTANDING

State whether each of the following statements is true or false.

6. To minimize risk of oxygen toxicity a patient is given 50% oxygen at 3 atm; this amount equals 1.5 atm. O_2.

7. The principle risk of treating a patient with a high oxygen concentration outside of a hyperbaric chamber is seizures.

8. A diver experiences tingling and pain in his legs shortly after surfacing. The main reason for providing oxygen is relief of hypoxia.

9. The principal condition treated by most hospital hyperbaric chambers is decompression illness (divers' bubble disease).

10. Hyperbaric oxygen therapy increases *both* the pressure and the actual number of oxygen molecules in the patient's blood.

11. Treatment tables for decompression problems always alternate a high concentration of oxygen with periods of breathing air.

Answers to TEST YOUR UNDERSTANDING

1. a. 3 atm.
   b. .63 atm. O_2 (three times sea level PO_2)
   c. 2.34 atm. N_2 (three times sea level PN_2)

2. a. .5 atm.; 7.35 psi
   b. .105 or .11 atm. O_2 (sea level is .21 atm. O_2)
   c. .5 atm. O_2

3. a. 1.33 atm. O_2
   b. he is at the threshold of risking oxygen toxicity
   c. 33 fsw

4. d. The maximum oxygen concentration is 100%. The other answers represent one atm. of inhaled oxygen.

5. d. Only oxygen content correlates with the number of oxygen molecules in the blood.

6. true   8. false   10. true
7. false   9. false   11. true

REFERENCES AND BIBLIOGRAPHY

See References for Sections B-E, plus the following:

DAN Oxygen Provider Course Manual. Divers Alert Network, Durham, NC. Updated frequently.

DAN Underwater Diving Accident Manual including Oxygen First Aid Manual. Divers Alert Network, Durham, NC. Updated frequently.

Hendrick W, Thompson B. *Oxygen and The Scuba Diver.* Best Publishing Co., Flagstaff, AZ, 1993.

Lippmann J. *Oxygen First Aid for Divers.* Divers Alert Network, 1993.

Martin L. *Pulmonary Physiology in Clinical Practice.* C.V. Mosby Co., St. Louis, 1987.

Wright SE, Jenkinson SG. Clinical use of hyperbaric oxygen. Clinical Pulmonary Medicine 1994;1:237-249.

DIVING ODDS N' ENDS

Are Divers Hurting Reefs?

Dozens of articles over the years have pointed out how careless divers harm the reefs, mainly by touching, grabbing, bumping and kicking them. However, Jean-Michel Cousteau was quoted in the Wall Street Journal (Sterba 1993) as saying that diver damage, while serious, is "insignificant" compared with other harmful factors such as soil runoff, chemical dumping, over fishing and boat anchoring.

Unfortunately many divers do hurt reefs. While this is both tragic and preventable, other human (and non-diving) activities hurt them far more.

DIVING ODDS N' ENDS

There Has To Be A Better Ending (The Abyss)

At the end of *The Abyss* (my favorite movie of this genre), the characters are at a depth of 12,000 feet, but not in a submarine; they are in an alien space ship and have been there a while. Having arrived breathing some type of exotic gas mixture at the ambient pressure, their decompression time is probably measured in years. How are they gonna get back to the surface (and end this movie)? No problem. The friendly aliens bring them right up to the surface. *In seconds.* Wow.

Dive buffs are scratching their heads. Don't those aliens know about the bends? Are they secretly trying to kill the earthlings? The producers know they have a problem here. How to fix it so the scuba crowd doesn't belittle this film? Easy. On reaching the surface one character exclaims, "And we didn't even have to decompress!" Alien Magic? End of movie.

DIVING ODDS N' ENDS

Homo Aquaticus Revisited

"The imperative need now is to place swimmers underwater for very long periods, to really learn about the sea. I think there will be a conscious evolution of *Homo Aquaticus*, spurred by human intelligence rather than the slow blind natural adaptation of species. We are now moving toward an alteration of human anatomy to give man almost unlimited freedom underwater."

Jacques Yves Cousteau, speaking at the World Congress on Underwater Activities, 1962 (as quoted in Madsen 1986).

■■■■■■■■■■■■■■

Pacific Vortex, a novel by Clive Cussler (1982)

Aboard a ship in the north Pacific, Pitt (the novel's hero) and Boland (the captain) are looking for a missing U.S. Navy submarine, plus the solution to many other unexplained ship disappearances. A sonar man sees

"a school of fish about a hundred yards off the starboard beam...by rough count, over two hundred of them swimming at three fathoms."
"Size man. Size!" Boland snaps.
"Somewhere between five and seven feet in length."
Pitt's eyes shifted from the speaker to Boland.
"Those aren't fish. They're men."
The underwater pirates board the ship. They are humans who carry no breathing apparatus, only weapons of war...
...The only difference [Pitt's] eyes could detect, a difference he hadn't had time to notice before, was a small plastic box that seemed to be adhered to each man's chest under their armpits..It was now easy to see how these strange men from the sea, under concealment of the fog, had silently dispatched almost a hundred ships and thousands of their crewmen to the bottom of this godforsaken piece of the Pacific Ocean.

DIVING ODDS N' ENDS

Cousteau's Pneumothorax

According to Jacques Cousteau's biographers, the co-inventor of modern scuba gear suffered fractured ribs and a "punctured lung" (pneumothorax) in 1936, from an automobile accident. It took almost a year but he recovered fully. It was at that point that Cousteau began his hobby of spear fishing (with only a pair of Fernez goggles; scuba came much later, in the early 1940s).

Today, anyone with a history of traumatic pneumothorax would probably be advised not to take up scuba diving, because of the risk of another pneumothorax and possible air embolism. Fortunately Cousteau never got this advice (who knew?), and he went on to pioneer the sport.

Philipe and Jean-Michel Cousteau

Jacques and Simone Cousteau had two sons. Tragically Philipe, their younger son, died June 28, 1979, in a seaplane accident. Age 39, he was landing his seaplane on the Tagus River near Lisbon, Portugal, when it flipped over after touching the water. Everyone else on the plane survived. Philipe's wife Jan, two months pregnant at the time of the accident, gave birth to Philipe Pierre Jacques-Yves Arnault Cousteau on January 20, 1980.

The older son, Jean-Michel, born 1938, remains very active in diving and ocean conservation, speaking all over the world. He now heads the Cousteau Society and is on the board of the Historical Diving Society. The next item quotes his feeling about a subject of vital importance to all recreational divers, reef damage.

Effects of Gas Pressure at Depth: Nitrogen Narcosis, CO and CO$_2$ Toxicity, Oxygen Toxicity, and "Shallow-Water Blackout"

WHAT HAPPENS TO GAS PRESSURES AT DEPTH?

Any gas taken to depth in a scuba tank will be unaffected as long as it remains *in the tank*. Once it leaves the tank and enters the diver's lungs it will have the same pressure as the surrounding water, i.e., the ambient pressure. This statement is true for the two major components of compressed air (nitrogen and oxygen), as well as for any gaseous impurities (e.g., carbon monoxide).

WHAT IS NITROGEN NARCOSIS?

Nitrogen narcosis, also called "rapture of the deep" and "the martini effect," results from a direct toxic effect of high nitrogen pressure on nerve conduction. It is an alcohol-like effect, a feeling often compared to drinking a martini on an empty stomach: slightly giddy, woozy, a little off balance.

Nitrogen narcosis is a highly variable sensation but always depth-related. Some divers experience no narcotic effect at depths up to 130 fsw, whereas others feel some effect at around 80 fsw. One thing is certain: once begun, the narcotic effect increases with increasing depth. Each additional 50 feet depth is said to feel like having another martini. The diver may feel - and act - totally drunk. Underwater, of course, this sensation can be deadly. Divers suffering nitrogen narcosis have been observed taking the regulator out of their mouth and handing it to a fish!

In *The Silent World*, Cousteau wrote about his early experiences with the aqua lung:

> I am personally quite receptive to nitrogen rapture. I like it and fear it like doom. It destroys the instinct of life. Tough individuals are not overcome as soon as neurasthenic persons like me, but they have difficulty extricating themselves. Intellectuals get drunk early and suffer acute attacks on all the senses,

which demand hard fighting to overcome. When they have beaten the foe, they recover quickly. The agreeable glow of depth rapture resembles the giggle-party jags of the nineteen-twenties when flappers and sheiks convened to sniff nitrogen protoxide.

L'ivresse des grandes profoundeurs has one salient advantage over alcohol - no hangover. If one is able to escape from its zone, the brain clears instantly and there are no horrors in the morning. I cannot read accounts of a record dive without wanting to ask the champion how drunk he was.

The effect, thought due to a slowing of nerve impulses from inert gas under high pressure, is not unique to nitrogen; it can occur from many gases (though not helium). The effect is similar to what patients experience inhaling an anesthetic such as nitrous oxide (N_2O). With increasing pressure of inhaled N_2O there is a progression of symptoms, from an initial feeling of euphoria to drunkenness and finally to unconsciousness.

Every year there are diving deaths attributed to nitrogen narcosis, mainly among divers who exceed recreational depth limits. To prevent the problem commercial divers switch to a mixture of helium and oxygen (heliox) at depths exceeding around 170 fsw. Helium is much less soluble in tissues than nitrogen, and therefore is less likely to impair behavior (divers using helium still have to decompress to prevent DCS). Even setting aside the added cost and complexity, helium offers no advantage for recreational divers over ordinary air.

Because of similar (and additive) effects to excess nitrogen, alcohol should be avoided before any dive. A reasonable recommendation is total abstinence at least 24 hours before diving; by that time effects of alcohol should be gone.

Unlike the effects of alcohol, nitrogen narcosis dissipates quickly, as soon as the diver ascends to a safe level (usually less than 60 feet depth). There is also some evidence that some divers can become partially acclimated to the effects of excess nitrogen; the more frequently they dive the less each subsequent dive appears to affect them.

WHAT IS OXYGEN TOXICITY, AND CAN IT DEVELOP WHILE DIVING?

Oxygen toxicity is any injury or discomfort to the body from inhaling too much oxygen (see box). High concentrations of oxygen delivered at atmospheric pressure can harm the lungs. When diving, any given concentration of oxygen comes under higher pressure than atmospheric, thus increasing the amount inhaled and the potential for toxicity. Above atmospheric pressures, oxygen can also affect the central nervous system, and cause seizures and convulsions. Thus oxygen toxicity is a major potential hazard in some diving but not, as it turns out, recreational diving.

Oxygen is a vital gas, the absence of which leads to death in a few minutes. People with healthy lungs only need the amount of oxygen in the atmosphere, no more or less. Anything more than 21% oxygen is considered "supplemental oxygen."

Supplemental oxygen, like any drug, can be toxic at high doses; since oxygen is a gas the "dose" is based on both the percentage of oxygen inhaled and the ambient pressure. Patients who are ill from low blood oxygen receive a higher than normal percentage of oxygen as treatment (i.e., greater than 21%). Scuba divers, because of the increase in gas pressures with depth, inhale a higher than normal *oxygen pressure*; the percentage is the same, since compressed air is still 21% oxygen at any depth.

However, since *pressure* increases with depth, the deeper one dives the higher the total pressure of oxygen that is inhaled. Too high an inhaled oxygen pressure can be toxic to the lungs and central nervous

---

Oxygen toxicity

(see text for discussion)

Pulmonary effects (can occur at atmospheric pressure; threshold about .6 atm O_2)

    burning sensation on taking a deep breath
    cough
    pneumonia
    permanent lung damage

Central nervous system effects (requires pressures above atmospheric; threshold about 1.3 atm O_2)

    muscular twitching
    vomiting
    dizziness
    vision or hearing abnormalities
    anxiety, confusion, irritability
    seizures

---

system. Oxygen toxicity is the reason why very deep diving (e.g., greater than about 170 fsw) is safely accomplished not with compressed air, which contains 21% oxygen, but with a gas mixture that has a much lower percentage, e.g., 10% O_2. Such a low oxygen percentage would be dangerous at sea level, but at great depth, due to the high ambient pressure, it is more than adequate to sustain life.

Recreational scuba divers adhering to the dive tables have no significant risk of oxygen toxicity. At 35 feet depth, where RSD tables allow the diver to spend well over two hours on a non-repetitive dive, the PAO_2 (oxygen pressure in the lungs) is the same as from breathing 43% oxygen at sea level, i.e., non-toxic. At the maximum RSD depth of 130 feet, the PAO_2 from breathing compressed air is about the same as from breathing 100% oxygen at sea level. This level of oxygen would only begin to cause trouble if inhaled for at least an hour. The few minutes of bottom time that the tables allow at 130 fsw is simply not long enough to pose a significant risk from oxygen toxicity.

WHAT EXACTLY DETERMINES RISK OF OXYGEN TOXICITY?

The occurrence and type of oxygen toxicity correlate with the O_2 *concentration, the ambient pressure, the length of time supplemental O_2 is inhaled, and the diver's level of activity.*

Range of oxygen concentrations. The concentration of inspired oxygen can vary from zero to 100% (the maximum). The concentration in ordinary air is 21% (whether compressed or not, and regardless of the depth at which it is inhaled). *The higher the concentration of O_2 the greater the risk of oxygen toxicity.*

Range of ambient pressures. Ambient pressure can range from zero (outer space), to one atmosphere (sea level), to several atmospheres (in a hyperbaric chamber or underwater). On land, outside of a chamber, oxygen can be administered only at the surrounding atmospheric pressure, which can vary from 1 atmosphere (sea level) to about .33 atmosphere (summit of Mt. Everest). *The higher the ambient pressure, the greater the risk of oxygen toxicity.*

Length of time oxygen is inhaled. Supplemental oxygen can be given anywhere from a few seconds to lifelong. How long O_2 is given depends on the condition being treated, the concentration used, and the ambient pressure. *The longer supplemental oxygen is inhaled, the greater the risk of oxygen toxicity.*

Level of activity. This is the least quantifiable aspect of oxygen toxicity. Once the threshold of oxygen toxicity is reached (based on atmospheres of O_2), *the more active the diver the greater the risk of developing actual toxicity.*

Since air contains 21% oxygen, the amount of oxygen inhaled at sea level is .21 atm O_2; this amount is safe to breathe forever. From clinical experience it appears that patients can breathe .40 atm O_2 indefinitely, and possibly up to .60 atm O_2 for weeks at a time (equivalent to 40% O_2 and 60% O_2 at sea level, respectively), without apparent oxygen toxicity.

In healthy subjects, 100% oxygen at atmospheric pressure (1 atm O_2) causes chest discomfort, pain and cough after only a few hours. If inhaled continuously over 24 hours, 1 atm O_2 can lead to lung congestion (pulmonary edema) and, if continued, death. Obviously, doctors try not to use high concentrations of oxygen unless absolutely necessary. Patients who require 100% oxygen because of heart or lung disease are critically ill and will almost always be cared for in a hospital intensive care unit.

The most serious potential harm from inhaling supplemental oxygen at sea level pressure is lung injury, which develops slowly, over many hours. At depth the most serious harm from too much oxygen is a seizure, which can occur in just a few minutes of oxygen breathing.

HOW DO ATMOSPHERES OF O_2 RELATE TO OXYGEN TOXICITY?

Although potentially toxic, 1 atm O_2 does not cause seizures. However, when 100% oxygen is delivered at pressures two or more times sea level pressure, the *first* toxic manifestation can be a seizure. A seizure is a sudden electrical discharge from the brain that causes uncontrolled muscle movement. If seizures occur underwater the diver will likely be unable to breathe through the regulator and will drown (if rescue is not immediate).

Atmospheres of O_2 is the major determinant of oxygen toxicity; the risk increases directly with the atmospheres of oxygen inhaled. A diver breathing compressed air (21% oxygen) at 4.76 atmospheres (124 fsw) has the same risk of developing oxygen toxicity as when breathing 100%

1.3 atm O_2 =	100% O_2 at 9.1 fsw (pure oxygen)	
	32% O_2 at 101 fsw (Nitrox)	
	21% O_2 at 172 fsw (compressed air)	
1.5 atm O_2 =	100% O_2 at 16.5 fsw (pure oxygen)	
	32% O_2 at 122 fsw (Nitrox)	
	21% O_2 at 203 fsw (compressed air)	

O_2 at sea level (assuming the same level of activity). In either situation the diver is breathing *one atmosphere of oxygen (1 atm O_2)*.

Exposure to high oxygen pressures at RSD depths is not long enough to cause oxygen toxicity. Oxygen toxicity is mainly a concern for the deep diver, for divers breathing mixtures that contain more than 21% O_2 (e.g., Nitrox), and for patients undergoing hyperbaric oxygen therapy. The thresh-old beyond which oxygen toxicity is a major concern is about 1.3-1.5 atm O_2. The box shows some permutations for reaching this threshold.

HOW CAN OXYGEN TOXICITY BE MINIMIZED?

The risk of seizures from oxygen toxicity begins at 1.3 to 1.5 atm O_2. To reach this level on compressed air the diver has to exceed the RSD depth limits (see box on previous page). Divers who go deep (technical or other) can reduce the risk of oxygen toxicity by *decreasing* the concentration of inhaled oxygen. For example, a diver at 7 atm (198 fsw)

TEST YOUR UNDERSTANDING

1. When diving with compressed air, what is the *percentage of inhaled oxygen* at each of the following depths?

   a. 33 fsw
   b. 66 fsw
   c. 99 fsw

2. When diving with compressed air, what is the *atm of inhaled oxygen* at each of the following depths?

   a. 33 fsw
   b. 66 fsw
   c. 99 fsw

3. A diver is treated at sea level, in an emergency room, with increasing concentrations of oxygen (provided via loose-fitting face masks). For each concentration of oxygen inhaled, state the amount in *atm O_2*.

   a. 40%
   b. 60%
   c. 90%

---

might switch to a mixture containing just 4% oxygen (mixed with helium or helium and nitrogen). At sea level, 4% oxygen would not support human life; at 7 atm, 4% oxygen is about the same as breathing 28% oxygen at sea level. On the other hand, a diver breathing 21% oxygen at 7 atmospheres (198 fsw) would be at risk for oxygen toxicity as he would be inhaling 1.47 atm O_2.

Pure oxygen was used in re-breathing scuba equipment during World War II. Because of the risk of oxygen toxicity, military divers were limited to about 25 fsw, or 1.76 atm O_2. (The military now uses mixed gases with its re-breathing scuba apparatus for deeper diving). It is also because of oxygen toxicity that hyperbaric treatment schedules limit the breathing of 100% oxygen to only about 20 minutes at a time.

In summary, the risk of oxygen toxicity is directly related to the total atm of O_2, the length of time the O_2 is inhaled, and the level of physical activity. Examples of safe and unsafe oxygen concentrations are shown in Table 1.

TABLE 1.
Risk of Oxygen Toxicity with Supplemental Oxygen[*]

atm O_2 Inhaled	Time before O_2 toxicity may develop[**]	Depth equivalent in fsw breathing 100% O_2	Depth equivalent in fsw breathing 21% O_2 (compressed air)	
.21	never		0	
.42	indefinite		33	
.63	few hours		66	
.84	few hours		99	
1.00	few hours	sea level	124	
1.30	mins to hours	9.1	172	<— threshold[***]
1.50	mins to hours	16.5	203	
2.00	minutes	33	281	
3.00	minutes	66	438	
4.00	seconds	99	596	

fsw = feet of sea water

[*]   For the resting or sedentary individual; oxygen toxicity can develop more quickly with exercise

[**]   Pulmonary or central nervous system effects

[***] For risk of seizures

HOW DOES CARBON MONOXIDE TOXICITY OCCUR IN SCUBA DIVING?

Carbon monoxide (CO) is a tasteless, odorless, highly poisonous gas given off by incomplete combustion of petroleum fuel. Virtually every gasoline powered motor, including all cars that use hydrocarbon fuel, emit some carbon monoxide. All lighted cigarettes also give off carbon monoxide. The extreme toxicity of CO arises from the fact that, compared with oxygen, it combines about 200 times more readily with hemoglobin. As a result, any excess CO readily displaces some oxygen from the blood; the more CO there is, the more oxygen will be displaced.

CO-related problems while diving can occur two ways, one more infamous than the other. Probably the less appreciated problem is simply from smoking. All smokers (cigarette, cigar, pipe) have an elevated blood CO level and, sadly, many divers smoke (even on the dive boat!). There is no evidence that diving increases the blood CO level in smokers, but since CO competes with oxygen, the smoking diver is more hypoxic on entering and exiting the water than otherwise. Any stressful situation thus puts the diver at increased risk for an hypoxic-related event, such as heart attack.

While at depth, the hypoxic effect of excess CO will be somewhat (but not completely) mitigated by the higher blood oxygen level that also occurs at depth. In final analysis, we really don't know to what extent smoking causes problems in divers, but common sense (and basic physiology) makes it a dumb practice to smoke and dive.

The toxicity mechanism we hear more about is when enough CO is in the tank air to act as a life-threatening impurity. Fortunately this is a rare occurrence, but it happens, and the result can be truly disastrous. According to news reports in April 1994, soon after a German scuba diver's body was recovered off Key West, Florida,

> "investigators suspected something unusual...analysis [of air in the diver's tank] revealed carbon monoxide nearly three times the level considered acceptable."

The analysis reportedly showed 2500 parts per million (ppm) of CO in the tank's air, an extraordinary level. Non-smoking city dwellers inhale about 10 ppm. (Ten ppm is considered the maximal CO level permissible level in scuba tank air.) Cigarette smokers inhale between 30 and 60 ppm of CO; this amount binds from 5 to 10 percent of the blood with CO, which means 5-10% of the smoker's blood is unable to carry oxygen. An inhaled CO level of 2500 ppm would tie up over 60% of the blood and make anyone fatally hypoxic.

It was speculated that this diver's tank air was contaminated from a faulty air compressor. Air can certainly become impure when tank filling takes place near machine exhaust; the exhaust fumes can be taken up and compressed along with the surrounding air. At depth the pressure of any CO inhaled from a scuba tank is increased just like every other inhaled gas. However, unlike any other gas likely to be in the tank, even small amounts of CO can be harmful, because CO has a great affinity for hemoglobin and easily displaces oxygen from the blood.

Depending on the concentration of CO in the tank and the depth at which it is inhaled, the effects of CO toxicity may range from mild headache to confusion to a state of unconsciousness and death. Any CO impurity must be considered potentially dangerous at depth.

The incidence of faulty tank air is very rare, at least at reputable fill stations, so it is impractical to do on-site chemical analysis of every tank. Until air analysis becomes routine (if ever), testing must be up to the diver's senses, which means taking several breaths from the tank *before* entering the water. This practice helps provide a regulator check as well as a cursory check of the tank air. Certainly any headache (from CO) or bad taste (from other impurities) is warning that something may be wrong with the air. (Such a cursory check will likely not detect low levels of impurities, so sticking with a reputable fill station is probably your best protection.)

WHAT IS CARBON DIOXIDE TOXICITY?

Carbon dioxide is a gas byproduct of metabolism. Our body makes about 200 cc's of CO_2 every minute (more when we exercise) and expels it in the air we exhale. Plants take up the CO_2 and give off oxygen (photosynthesis). The concentration of carbon dioxide in the atmosphere is almost zero, and poses no risk when fresh air is compressed inside a scuba tank.

The partial pressure of carbon dioxide in a scuba diver's blood is a function only of metabolism and the rate and depth of breathing - the same factors that determine blood CO_2 concentration on land. Unlike other gases normally inhaled (nitrogen and oxygen), or gases that could be inhaled under abnormal conditions (CO and other gas impurities), *the CO_2 level in the blood is unchanged by the ambient pressure (i.e., the depth) per se.*

Scuba apparatus used in recreational diving is "open circuit," so exhalation of carbon dioxide is through the mouthpiece and into the water (it's all in the bubbles). Abnormal carbon dioxide accumulation in the blood can occur from too high a level of metabolism (from exercise) and/or inadequate breathing (usually not breathing deep enough). The medical term for high carbon dioxide in the blood is *hypercapnia*; when the level is high enough it can cause "CO_2 toxicity," which can lead to shortness of breath, headache, confusion and drowning (depending on severity).

Air density increases with depth, so the deeper you go the greater the work of breathing. Increased resistance to breathing can cause the diver to take shallow breaths, and shallow breaths make carbon dioxide elimination less efficient. If the diver also exerts herself heavily, her body will produce more CO_2, resulting in a "vicious cycle" of carbon dioxide buildup: heavy work (more CO_2 production) —-> shallow breathing (less efficient elimination of CO_2) —-> higher blood CO_2 (CO_2 toxicity).

Hypercapnia (and resulting CO_2 toxicity) is a major concern among deep divers, and also any diver who has to perform heavy work. It is much less of a concern for the typical recreational diver. Regular, deep breathing, and a properly functioning regulator, should eliminate risk of carbon dioxide buildup in recreational diving.

Some experienced divers practice "skip" breathing, which is holding the breath (on inhalation or exhalation) in order to conserve air. This might save air but it could also lead to CO_2 buildup, since by breath holding the diver is, in effect, under ventilating; if the diver under ventilates he will soon want to breathe even more, from the stimulus of an increasing CO_2 level. As a result, the diver who skip breathes enough to increase his CO_2 could end up depleting air supply faster than with normal breathing! Even without the obvious risk of pulmonary barotrauma (particularly if near the surface), skip breathing is definitely not recommended.

CO_2 BUILDUP WHEN DIVING: RISKS

Diving deep
Heavy work
Rapid, shallow breathing
"Skip" breathing

Apart from the practice of skip breathing, for recreational divers the depths achieved, the short times spent on deeper dives, and the open circuit design of scuba equipment make CO_2 toxicity an uncommon problem. Just be aware that, under some conditions, it can occur.

TEST YOUR UNDERSTANDING

4. A diver breathing compressed air has a seizure after 10 minutes at 66 fsw. Until the onset of seizure he is observed to have no breathing difficulty or any problem with equipment. Rank the following potential causes of his problem from 1 (most likely cause) to 5 (least likely).

   a. nitrogen narcosis
   b. CO toxicity
   c. CO_2 toxicity
   d. O_2 toxicity
   e. epilepsy (spontaneous seizures)

5. A diver breathing Nitrox I (32% oxygen, balance nitrogen) air has a seizure after 20 minutes at 140 fsw. Until the onset of seizure he is observed by his buddy to have no breathing difficulty or any equipment problem. Of the choices provided below what is the most likely cause? Can the other four conditions be ranked as in the previous question?

   a. nitrogen narcosis
   b. CO toxicity
   c. CO_2 toxicity
   d. O_2 toxicity
   e. epilepsy (spontaneous seizures)

WHAT CAUSES HEADACHE UNDERWATER?

Many divers mistakenly believe that any headache underwater is due to carbon dioxide buildup. For reasons discussed in the preceding section, CO_2 buildup is uncommon in recreational divers. Even with CO_2 buildup, headache may not be a symptom. In several studies the first symptom of CO_2 buildup was sudden blackout, with no headache or other warning signs.

More importantly, there are many other (and more plausible) causes for a headache while diving. The potential causes include: tank gas impurities (e.g., low levels of carbon monoxide); temporo-mandibular (jaw) joint ache from holding the mouthpiece too tightly; pressure of the mask against the forehead; a tight mask strap; salt water in the nasal passages; tension or anxiety; cold water; over breathing (hyperventilation); and squeeze on inadequately ventilated frontal sinuses.

In summary, headache is a sign that something is not right, but (in recreational divers) it is *not* a sure sign of CO_2 buildup.

TEST YOUR UNDERSTANDING

6. A diver breathing compressed air develops a headache after 20 minutes at 90 fsw. She is breathing fast and shallow and finds it difficult to inhale from her regulator. Tank psi is 1500 psi. The most likely cause of her headache is:

   a. nitrogen narcosis   c. CO_2 toxicity
   b. CO toxicity   d. O_2 toxicity

7. Of the choices a. through d. in Question 6, which one is the *least* likely cause of the diver's headache?

8. A diver is at 130 fsw hovering next to a wall, when he is seen to suddenly drift downward, seemingly oblivious to the increasing depth. His buddy catches up with him at 145 fsw and pulls him up to 100 fsw. The most likely explanation for the sinking diver's behavior is:

   a. nitrogen narcosis   c. CO_2 toxicity
   b. CO toxicity   d. O_2 toxicity

WHAT IS SHALLOW-WATER BLACKOUT?

As has been pointed out, diving without compressed air (breath-hold diving, skin diving) is very different from scuba diving, since the lungs compress on descent and decompress on ascent. Water pressure squeezing the lungs during a breath-hold dive is usually not great enough to cause problems from compression of the lungs (most breath-hold divers don't go deep enough to experience significant lung squeeze). Middle ear discomfort is a more common problem, and the breath-hold diver must swallow or blow against a pinched nose to equalize ear pressures.

Since, in a breath-hold dive, air compressed on descent merely expands back to its original volume on ascent, there is no danger of pulmonary barotrauma. But breath hold diving is not without hazard. Perhaps the most serious potential hazard for the breath-hold diver is "shallow-water blackout."

Shallow-water blackout is a sudden unconsciousness from lack of oxygen during a breath-hold dive. (The term was originally applied, in the 1940s, to blackout from CO_2 buildup seen with re-breathers; over the years the term's definition has been changed.) Shallow-water blackout doesn't always occur in shallow water; it can occur at any depth. However, for reasons which will be explained, the breath-hold diver is at greater risk for blacking out during ascent, near the surface.

To appreciate shallow-water blackout, consider the air hunger you feel during a breath-hold dive. When you hold your breath two things happen in the blood; CO_2 increases and O_2 decreases. The principle reason you feel air hunger is the increase in CO_2, *not* the decrease in O_2. Without the slight increase in CO_2 from breath holding, your sensation of air hunger would be delayed and you would stay down longer, even while your oxygen level is falling. This is an example where CO_2 buildup is a good thing!

The risk of shallow-water blackout is increased from *excessive* over breathing (hyperventilation) just prior to the dive. Hyperventilation lowers blood CO_2. At most one should take three to four deep breaths before a breath-hold dive; more than that can lower CO_2 sufficient to delay its buildup and therefore delay the urge to breathe and surface for air. In other words, blood CO_2 may be lowered so much by pre-dive hyperventilation, that it takes a relatively long time for CO_2 to build up underwater and cause "air hunger." The dive is prolonged but at the diver's peril. Blood oxygen will fall relatively quickly underwater compared to the buildup of CO_2. A critical hypoxic state can be reached before there is any drive to breathe, i.e., before there is any sensation of air hunger. This

Figure 1. Example of changes in oxygen and carbon dioxide that can lead to shallow-water blackout in a breath-hold diver. Direction of arrows indicates PO_2 and PCO_2 values above (up) or below (down) normal land values. Initial changes show a diver who has hyperventilated just prior to the dive. Actual point at which PO_2 and PCO_2 reverse, and the degree of change, will depend on depth of dive, time underwater, and work exerted on the dive.

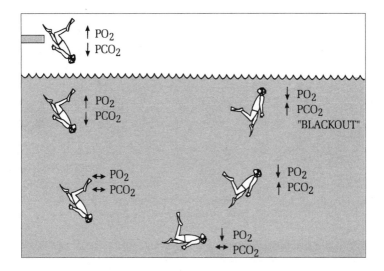

critical hypoxia is often reached on ascent, near the surface, hence the term "shallow-water blackout." However, it can occur at any depth and lead to sudden unconsciousness and drowning (Figure 1).

There is another factor that contributes to hypoxia, one that helps explain why blackout tends to occur near the surface. Even though the body utilizes oxygen throughout the breath-hold dive, at depth the water pressure effectively increases oxygen pressure in the lungs and the blood. All the while, of course, the diver is metabolizing oxygen, so the *total amount* available is steadily declining. Paradoxically, however, being deep is somewhat protective, because the pressure of oxygen in the lungs and blood is *higher* than it would be at the surface with the same breath holding time. However, as the breath-hold diver rises toward the surface, the pressure of oxygen in his lungs falls precipitously, not only because his body continues to utilize oxygen, but also because the surrounding pressure falls. Near the surface the breath-hold diver's blood oxygen pressure falls to a critical level and he blacks out. (Ambient pressure falls on ascent from a scuba dive as well, but the oxygen supply is continuously replenished with fresh air from the tank).

A CASE OF "SHALLOW-WATER BLACKOUT"

A young scuba instructor working on a liveaboard dive boat, and one of the boat's male guests, decide to go breath-hold diving one afternoon. They, and two other boat guests along just for the ride, take a dingy out to the site of a famous wreck.

Each of the breath-hold divers carries four pounds of lead weight to assist in descent, and while one dives the other stays in the water as a spotter. While the non-diving guests remain in the dingy, the divers each make a breath-hold plunge. The first dive for each lasts about 1.5 minutes, at a depth of 60 to 70 feet.

On the scuba instructor's second breath-hold dive, he goes a little deeper and stays on the wreck a little longer. Over 2 minutes into his dive, he is seen to ascend quickly from the wreck, then stop at 10 feet from the surface; at that point he shows no movement. The spotter dives down and drags the unconscious diver to the surface. The rescuing diver provides in-water mouth-to-mouth resuscitation and, with the aid of the two other people, lifts the by now semi-conscious diver into the dingy. The rescued diver fully regains consciousness but remembers nothing about what happened.

A few minutes later they are back on the liveaboard. The dingy observers reveal what an awful sensation they felt as the limp instructor was pulled to the surface; they thought he might be dead. The rescued scuba instructor only complains of having some chest discomfort and feeling fatigued. He is also observed to have blue nail beds (cyanosis). He is given 100% O_2 and, when he claims to feel better, goes to lay down in his cabin. A few hours later he feels worse and has a fever; the captain decides to motor to the nearest town, where the diver is hospitalized. Diagnosis: pneumonia (presumably from aspiration of some sea water.) He is given antibiotics and the next day is released; he eventually recovers fully.

Youth, diving experience and excellent physical condition allowed the scuba instructor to stay down much longer than the average person; this was also his (almost fatal) undoing. What happened is that his delayed urge to breathe made him attempt an ascent too late; just 10 feet from the surface he blacked out from *lack of oxygen*. Had there not been an experienced spotter on the surface the instructor would surely have drowned.

Answers to TEST YOUR UNDERSTANDING

1. a, b, c. All are 21% oxygen.

2. a. .42 atm O_2 b. .63 atm O_2 c. .84 atm O_2

3. a. .40 atm O_2 b. .60 atm O_2 c. .90 atm O_2

4. 1st., epilepsy; 2nd., CO toxicity (due to contaminant in the tank air). These are the only two plausible causes among the five listed. CO_2 toxicity would be unlikely due to the short time of the dive, the shallow depth, and the lack of a breathing or equipment problem. Nitrogen narcosis would also be unlikely at this depth. Oxygen toxicity would not occur at this depth after breathing compressed air for 10 minutes.

5. 1st. O_2 toxicity. The other four causes are all possible but unlikely. Epilepsy can cause seizures at any time; a "first-ever" seizure under water is unlikely to be epilepsy, so the pre-dive medical history would be very important. CO_2 toxicity usually does not present with seizures, but it can lower the threshold for developing oxygen toxicity. Nitrogen narcosis also does not cause seizures. Finally, CO toxicity is always a concern in sudden and unexplained underwater catastrophes, but it occurs only with major contamination of tank air.

6. c. Headache, fast and shallow breathing, and trouble inhaling from the regulator all suggest CO_2 toxicity.

7.   d. O$_2$ toxicity would be the least likely cause, since she has only spent 20 minutes at 90 fsw.

8.   a. The diver went deep and lost concentration, a sure indication of nitrogen narcosis.

REFERENCES AND BIBLIOGRAPHY

See references Sections B-E, plus the following (*Especially recommended).

*Edmunds C, McKenzie B, Thomas R. *Diving Medicine for Scuba Divers*. J.L. Publications, Melbourne, 1992.

*Gilliam B, Von Maier R. *Deep Diving. An Advanced Guide to Physiology, Procedures and Systems*. Watersport Publishing, Inc. San Diego; 1992.

Lanphier EH. Carbon dioxide poisoning, in Waite CL, ed., *Case Histories of Diving and Hyperbaric Accidents*, pages 199-213.

Lanphier EH, Rahn H. Alveolar gas exchange during breath hold diving. J Appl Physiol 1963;18:471-477.

Lanphier EH, Rahn H. Alveolar gas exchange during breath holding with air. J Appl Physiol 1963;18:478-482.

Lanphier EH. Breath-hold and ascent blackout. In *The Physiology of Breath-hold Diving*, UHMS Pub. No. 72(WS/BH) 4/15/87, pages 32-43.

Leitch DR. A study of unusual incidents in a well-documented series of dives. Aviation, Space, and Environ Med 1981;52:618-624.

*Lippmann J. *Deeper into Diving* Aqua Quest Publications, Inc., New York, 1992.

*Lippmann J. *The Essentials of Deeper Sport Diving*. Aqua Quest Publications, Inc., New York, 1992.

Martin L. Hypercapnia Revisited. Sources, Journal of the National Association of Underwater Instructors. November/December 1994, pages 52-54.

DIVING ODDS N' ENDS

Most Frequently Asked Question of Scuba Divers by People Who Have Never Dived (and Never Intend To):

"Aren't you afraid of sharks?"

Standard Answer: "Of all the things most scuba divers worry about, meeting a shark is not high on the list." The facts:

1) More people are killed by lightning or bee stings each year than by sharks. Since 1965 the annual recorded number of shark attacks is about 40-100 worldwide; the number of shark-related deaths per year is 5-10. Very, very few diving-related deaths appear to have anything to do with shark attack. Overall, considering the millions of people who enter the ocean for pleasure worldwide, shark attack is very rare.

2) Only a few of the 360+ known species of shark pose any threat to humans. These include the great white, mako, tiger, white-tipped, hammer-head and lemon sharks.

3) Through active hunting, and use of large fishing nets which trap sharks, people have posed a far greater threat to sharks than vice versa.

4) On most recreational dives just seeing a shark is considered a thrill. Guided shark dives (no petting allowed) are growing in popularity and are offered in many sites around the world. In Australia you can even sign up for an underwater encounter with the great white shark; they put you in a 'shark proof' cage and drop the cage in the water.

DIVING ODDS N' ENDS

ama DIVERS of Japan and Korea

Professional breath-hold divers of Korea and Japan, known scientifically as "ama" divers, have been practicing their art for over 2000 years. They dive daily, usually to shallow depths, but have been known to go very deep. One study of working ama divers found that their total in-water time averaged about 180 minutes/day for 115 dives/day (Hong 1991). The average time per dive was about 30 seconds. Total bottom time per day was 27 minutes.

DIVING ODDS N' ENDS

There Has To Be A Better Ending (*Sphere*)

In his 1985 novel *The Sphere* Michael Crichton conjures up an exciting story about discovery of a giant vessel found at the bottom of the sea. It has been there 300 years (based on coral encrustation), but is made of materials unknown on earth. Is it from the past? Or from the future? After some exciting hypothesizing and equally exciting underwater action scenes, the reader aches to see how all the unanswered questions will be resolved. Crichton probably ached also.

In the end he has the protagonists simply *forget* what they experienced. Literally. His characters give their reasons, and one can't fault a master writer for choosing a "mind game" ending. Nonetheless, the ending is unsatisfying because it seems so *implausible*. The reader can accept an alien intelligence at the bottom of the sea, but not that mere mortal humans can will themselves to forget all about it.

DIVING ODDS N' ENDS

Sheck Exley and Jim Bowden

Sheck Exley, a pioneer of deep cave diving, died at age 45 on April 6, 1994. He failed to surface during a record-breaking attempt to 1000 feet/307 meters in the Zacatón sinkhole in northeast Mexico (located about 60 miles north of Tampico). He and partner Jim Bowden dove at the same time, using two separate descent lines, so they were relatively unaware of each other's position during the dive. (Each was trying to break Exley's previous open circuit scuba world depth records: 867 feet, 1989, Mante Mexico; and 863 feet, 1993, Bushmansgat, South Africa.) (Exley 1994, Hamilton 1994).

Bowden surfaced after reaching a new world record of 915 feet, as measured by one of two computers he carried; the other measured 924 feet (Taylor 1994). When Exley's body was finally pulled up, his depth meter read 904 feet (Zumrick 1994).

Exley wrote several books on cave diving safety, and pioneered safety rules that were widely adopted by all cave divers. "He was not a daredevil; he was the forerunner who spent his life preparing himself mentally and physically for underwater challenges. He was simply the best and most experienced diver that we had." (DeLoach 1994)

Dive Tables and Dive Computers: Their History and Utility

WHY DO DIVERS NOT ROUTINELY USE DIVE TABLES?

There is probably no more intimidating subject to many divers than dive tables and their high tech cousins, dive computers. Everyone learns to use "no decompression" tables during the basic open water course, but most newly-certified divers seem to quickly forget what they learned. From simple observation it is apparent that few recreational divers bother consulting any printed table when diving. Nonetheless, most divers do dive "by the tables." There are two explanations for this paradox.

- It is common to make some mistakes with dive tables in a classroom, where there is good lighting, a stable desk and all the time in the world to calculate and check answers. Understandably, new divers often feel awkward and unsure when figuring out dive tables under open water conditions, which may include a rocking, crowded boat with no convenient place to sit and calculate. Dive tables are difficult unless one uses them routinely, so most recreational divers (particularly those who dive infrequently) never learn to feel comfortable with them. The typical recreational diver seems happy to let others worry about dive tables, recognizing that he or she can dive safely at a resort, where the day's dives *are* planned by the tables but *by someone else*. For example, diver Jill may be told she can do a first morning dive to 80 feet for 30 minutes and, after an appropriate surface interval, dive to 50 feet for 40 minutes. After these two dives she may be back on shore by noon. The resort then offers either an afternoon shallow dive commencing around 2 p.m., or a night dive. In any given scenario, the dives are planned and executed by standard dive tables; all Jill has to do is show up and not exceed the resort's planned dive profiles. In effect, someone else employs the tables for her safe diving.

- Other divers may use a dive computer which, unlike printed tables, take into account multi-level diving. Dive computers give more latitude than the tables, since tables assume you spend all bottom time at maximum depth. The dive computer incorporates a complex algorithm for nitrogen uptake and elimination, so it is actually a highly sophisticated set of tables, more detailed and reliable than anything printed that requires human calculations. Of course computers can be abused, but divers who use them properly are, in effect, "diving by the tables." (Manufacturers recommend that printed tables be taken on a dive as backup in case of computer loss or failure, but this is not a common practice.)

HOW IS A DIVE TABLE USED?

Before discussing the origin of dive tables it will be useful to walk through a modern dive table. Figure 1 shows the U.S. Navy Dive Table for no-decompression diving. You may be familiar with other dive tables. When using PADI, NAUI or other recreational tables, you will find different letter group designations and times. In particular, the times allowed at depth are less than allowed by the U.S. Navy. However, in principle all dive tables are the same. They all include three parts: 1) no-decompression time limits; 2) surface interval times; 3) residual nitrogen times.

The first part of the U.S. Navy Table includes the depth in the two left hand columns, the no-decompression time limits in the third column and then a string of letters called "Group Designation," with a column of numbers under each letter. Each letter is important if you do a repetitive dive. If you dive only once for the day (i.e., make no repetitive dive), the letters and the columns of numbers under them would be unnecessary.

Let's say you plan a dive to 60 feet/18.2 meters. The no-decompression table shows you can stay at that depth for up to 60 minutes and then surface without having to make a decompression stop. (Other tables allow a shorter time at this depth. In any case, standard practice is to do a 3-5 minute safety stop at 15 feet/3 meters.) Depending on how long you actually stay at 60 fsw, you choose the appropriate letter group. If you stay only 10 minutes you are in letter group B; 25 minutes, E; the full 60 minutes, J; etc. For any depth between the depths shown, you must use the next highest depth. For any time between the times shown, use the next higher time.

Before continuing it is important to emphasize just what these letters represent. Each letter represents an amount of extra nitrogen accumulated on the dive. *The higher the letter the more extra nitrogen is accumulated.* Each letter also represents a length of time it will take that extra nitrogen to leave the body (off-gas) once the diver is on the surface. *The higher the letter the longer it will take the extra nitrogen to off-gas.* This time is the 'residual nitrogen time,' an important concept in dive tables. If your next dive takes place beyond the residual nitrogen time range for all the group designation letters in the table, then the letter group is superfluous; the rest of the table also becomes unnecessary. For the U.S. Navy table shown, this length of time is 12 hours; if you have a surface interval more than 12 hours between consecutive dives the letter group designation is not relevant. (In other words, the letter groups are not needed if you don't plan a repetitive dive.)

Letter groups are used on repetitive diving because you will accumulate more nitrogen on the next dive, which *must be added* to the residual nitrogen of the preceding dive. Instead of worrying about the actual quantity of nitrogen, the letter groups indicate the length of time it will take the residual nitrogen to leave the body (i.e., the residual nitrogen time); this time can then be used to calculate an appropriate length of time for your next dive.

Now enter the second part of the U.S. Navy Table. Here you start with your letter group designation. Let's assume you dove to 60 feet for

Figure 1. First part of U.S. Navy Dive Tables. See text for discussion. Reprinted from U.S. Navy Diving Manual, Vol., 1.

TABLE 7-3

No Decompression Limits and Repetitive Group Designation Table for No-Decompression Air Dives

Depth (feet/ meters)	No-Decompression Limits (min)	Group Designation														
		A	B	C	D	E	F	G	H	I	J	K	L	M	N	O
10	3.0	60	120	210	300											
15	4.6	35	70	110	160	225	350									
20	6.1	25	50	75	100	135	180	240	325							
25	7.6	20	35	55	75	100	125	160	195	245	315					
30	9.1	15	30	45	60	75	95	120	145	170	205	250	310			
35	10.7	310	5	15	25	40	50	60	80	100	120	140	160	190	220	270	310
40	12.2	200	5	15	25	30	40	50	70	80	100	110	130	150	170	200
50	15.2	100		10	15	25	30	40	50	60	70	80	90	100		
60	18.2	60		10	15	20	25	30	40	50	55	60				
70	21.3	50		5	10	15	20	30	35	40	45	50				
80	24.4	40		5	10	15	20	25	30	35	40					
90	27.4	30		5	10	12	15	20	25	30						
100	30.5	25		5	7	10	15	20	22	25						
110	33.5	20			5	10	13	15	20							
120	36.6	15			5	10	12	15								
130	39.6	10			5	8	10									
140	42.7	10			5	7	10									
150	45.7	5			5											
160	48.8	5				5										
170	51.8	5				5										
180	54.8	5				5										
190	59.9	5				5										

Figure 1 (continued). Parts 2 and 3 of U.S. Navy Dive Tables. See text for discussion. Reprinted from U.S. Navy Diving Manual, Vol. 1.

Table 7-4 Residual Nitrogen Timetable for Repetitive Air Dives

Locate the diver's repetitive group designation from his previous dive along the diagonal line above the table. Read horizontally to the interval in which the diver's surface interval lies.

Next read vertically downward to the new repetitive group designation. Continue downward in this same column to the row which represents the depth of the repetitive dive. The time given at the intersection is residual nitrogen time, in minutes, to be applied to the repetitive dive.

* Dives following surface intervals of more than 12 hours are not repetitive dives. Use actual bottom times in the Standard Air Decompression Tables to compute decompression for such dives.

** If no Residual Nitrogen Time is given, then the repetitive group does not change.

Changes based on NEDU Report 13-83

Repetitive group at the beginning of the surface interval — surface interval ranges (hours:minutes) leading to each new group designation:

Starting group	Surface interval ranges →
A	0:10–12:00*
B	0:10–3:20 · 3:21–12:00*
C	0:10–1:39 · 1:40–4:49 · 4:50–12:00*
D	0:10–1:09 · 1:10–2:38 · 2:39–5:48 · 5:49–12:00*
E	0:10–0:54 · 0:55–1:57 · 1:58–3:24 · 3:25–6:34 · 6:35–12:00*
F	0:10–0:45 · 0:46–1:29 · 1:30–2:28 · 2:29–3:57 · 3:58–7:05 · 7:06–12:00*
G	0:10–0:40 · 0:41–1:15 · 1:16–1:59 · 2:00–2:58 · 2:59–4:25 · 4:26–7:35 · 7:36–12:00*
H	0:10–0:36 · 0:37–1:06 · 1:07–1:41 · 1:42–2:23 · 2:24–3:20 · 3:21–4:49 · 4:50–7:59 · 8:00–12:00*
I	0:10–0:33 · 0:34–0:59 · 1:00–1:29 · 1:30–2:02 · 2:03–2:44 · 2:45–3:43 · 3:44–5:12 · 5:13–8:21 · 8:22–12:00*
J	0:10–0:31 · 0:32–0:54 · 0:55–1:19 · 1:20–1:47 · 1:48–2:20 · 2:21–3:04 · 3:05–4:02 · 4:03–5:40 · 5:41–8:50 · 8:51–12:00*
K	0:10–0:28 · 0:29–0:49 · 0:50–1:11 · 1:12–1:35 · 1:36–2:03 · 2:04–2:38 · 2:39–3:21 · 3:22–4:19 · 4:20–5:48 · 5:49–8:58 · 8:59–12:00*
L	0:10–0:26 · 0:27–0:45 · 0:46–1:04 · 1:05–1:25 · 1:26–1:49 · 1:50–2:19 · 2:20–2:53 · 2:54–3:36 · 3:37–4:35 · 4:36–6:02 · 6:03–9:12 · 9:13–12:00*
M	0:10–0:25 · 0:26–0:42 · 0:43–0:59 · 1:00–1:18 · 1:19–1:39 · 1:40–2:05 · 2:06–2:34 · 2:35–3:08 · 3:09–3:52 · 3:53–4:49 · 4:50–6:18 · 6:19–9:28 · 9:29–12:00*
N	0:10–0:24 · 0:25–0:39 · 0:40–0:54 · 0:55–1:11 · 1:12–1:30 · 1:31–1:53 · 1:54–2:18 · 2:19–2:47 · 2:48–3:22 · 3:23–4:04 · 4:05–5:03 · 5:04–6:32 · 6:33–9:43 · 9:44–12:00*
O	0:10–0:23 · 0:24–0:36 · 0:37–0:51 · 0:52–1:07 · 1:08–1:24 · 1:25–1:43 · 1:44–2:04 · 2:05–2:29 · 2:30–2:59 · 3:00–3:33 · 3:34–4:17 · 4:18–5:16 · 5:17–6:44 · 6:45–9:54 · 9:55–12:00*
Z	0:10–0:22 · 0:23–0:34 · 0:35–0:48 · 0:49–1:02 · 1:03–1:18 · 1:19–1:36 · 1:37–1:55 · 1:56–2:17 · 2:18–2:42 · 2:43–3:10 · 3:11–3:45 · 3:46–4:29 · 4:30–5:27 · 5:28–6:56 · 6:57–10:05 · 10:06–12:00*

NEW GROUP DESIGNATION / Residual Nitrogen Times (Minutes)

Repetitive Dive Depth feet / meters	Z	O	N	M	L	K	J	I	H	G	F	E	D	C	B	A
10 / 3.0	**	**	**	**	**	**	**	**	**	**	**	**	279	159	88	39
20 / 6.1	**	**	**	**	**	**	**	399	279	208	159	120	88	62	39	18
30 / 9.1	**	**	469	349	279	229	190	159	132	109	88	70	54	39	25	12
40 / 12.2	257	241	213	187	161	138	116	101	87	73	61	49	37	25	17	7
50 / 15.2	169	160	142	124	111	99	87	76	66	56	47	38	29	21	13	6
60 / 18.2	122	117	107	97	88	79	70	61	52	44	36	30	24	17	11	5
70 / 21.3	100	96	87	80	72	64	57	50	43	37	31	26	20	15	9	4
80 / 24.4	84	80	73	68	61	54	48	43	38	32	28	23	18	13	8	4
90 / 27.4	73	70	64	58	53	47	43	38	34	30	26	22	18	14	10	7
100 / 30.5	64	62	57	52	48	43	38	34	30	26	22	18	14	10	7	3
110 / 33.5	57	55	51	47	42	38	34	31	27	24	20	16	13	10	6	3
120 / 36.6	52	50	46	43	39	35	32	28	25	21	18	15	12	9	6	3
130 / 39.6	46	44	40	38	35	31	28	25	22	19	16	13	11	8	6	3
140 / 42.7	42	40	38	35	32	29	26	23	20	18	15	12	10	7	5	2
150 / 45.7	40	38	35	32	30	27	24	22	19	17	14	12	9	7	5	2
160 / 48.8	37	36	33	31	28	26	23	20	18	16	13	11	9	6	4	2
170 / 51.8	35	34	31	29	26	24	22	19	17	15	12	10	8	6	4	2
180 / 54.8	32	31	29	27	25	22	20	18	16	14	11	10	8	6	4	2
190 / 59.9	31	30	28	26	24	21	19	17	15	13	10	10	8	6	4	2

Residual Nitrogen Times (Minutes)

30 minutes; you are therefore in letter group F. The second part of the table asks "Mr. (or Ms.) F, how long are you to remain on the surface?" The answer is the surface interval time (SIT). The longer your SIT, the more the residual nitrogen from the first dive will be dissipated, and the less nitrogen you will have on entering the water again.

Note that the second part of the table is a range of surface intervals. Immediately to the right of letter F is the surface interval 10 minutes to 45 minutes (0:10-0:45). The next surface interval ranges from 46 minutes to one hour 29 minutes (0:46-1:29). Choose the surface interval that includes your SIT. Suppose your SIT is one hour 35 minutes; this SIT falls into the surface interval 1:30-2:28.

Note that all surface intervals are associated with another letter group designation. Beneath the column that contains the surface interval 1:30-2:28. is the letter D; again, the lower the letter, the less extra nitrogen remains in your body. The highest surface interval shown is 12 hours because the Navy tables assume you are rid of all excess nitrogen after 12 hours.

The third part of the table is for the next or repetitive dive. Using the letter group from the second part of the table, follow the column down until you reach the *row* which represents the depth of the repetitive dive. The time shown in the column is the residual nitrogen time, in minutes, to be applied to the repetitive dive.

For example, suppose your first dive of the day and surface interval are the same as in Question 4; in that case your letter group designation is E. Moving down the column under the E, the residual nitrogen times for all the depths shown range from 120 minutes at 20 feet to only 10 minutes at 190 feet. What is the residual nitrogen time you must use in planning your next dive to 50 feet? Looking at the row that contains 50 feet, we see it is 38 minutes. This is the length of time that must be subtracted from the next dive to determine the length of time you can spend at 50 feet. On a first dive to 50 feet you could spend (according to the U.S. Navy Table) up to 100 minutes. Now, on this repetitive dive, your maximum time is 100 minus 38 minutes, or 62 minutes. A repetitive dive must take into consideration the amount of residual nitrogen in your body after preceding dive(s). In terms of nitrogen, diving to 50 feet is very different for a repetitive dive than for a first dive.

TEST YOUR UNDERSTANDING

5. Your first dive is 70 feet for 40 minutes, followed by a surface interval of one hour. You plan your next dive to 50 feet. Using the U.S. Navy Tables, how long, in minutes, can you stay at that depth on your second dive without a decompression stop?

    a. 100
    b. 56
    c. 44

6. Your first dive is 60 feet for 33 minutes, followed by a surface interval of 45 minutes. You plan your next dive to 45 feet. Using the U.S. Navy Tables, how long in minutes can you stay at that depth on your second dive without a decompression stop?

    a. 100
    b. 53
    c. 47

WHAT IS THE ORIGIN OF DIVE TABLES?

The first dive tables were devised by the Englishman John Scott Haldane and colleagues in the period 1906-1908, following their landmark experiments on goat decompression. Why goats? As stated in the original paper (Boycott 1908):

> ...goats were very suitable animals in that slight symptoms were presented to our notice in a definite objective form. The lesser symptoms of caisson disease cannot be neglected, and there are reasons for supposing that their occurrence is not exactly conditioned by those experimental circumstances which in a more severe form produced serious and fatal results. They cannot be properly detected in mice or guinea-pigs or even in rabbits. Goats, while they are not perhaps such delicate indicators as monkeys or dogs, and though they are somewhat stupid and definitely insensitive to pain, are capable of entering into emotional relationships with their surroundings, animate and inanimate, of a kind sufficiently nice to enable those who are familiar with them to detect slight abnormalities with a fair degree of certainty.

> The animals, 85 in number, used in the present experiments were a mixed collection of ordinary English goats of no particular breed...The commonest symptom which we have observed [of decompression sickness] consists of the exhibition of signs indicating that the animal feels uneasy in one or more of its legs. The limb, most commonly a fore-leg, is held up prominently in the air and the animal is evidently loth to bear weight upon it.

These decompression pioneers found that goats could avoid the bends if ambient pressure did not drop by more than half at any one time. Thus, in a hyperbaric chamber, a goat could go from a depth of 165 ft. (6 atm) to 66 ft. (3 atm), or from 99 ft. (4 atm) to 33 ft. (2 atm), without encountering the bends. A change in pressure greater than this 2:1 drop did lead some goats to manifest limb pain. A result of these experiments was the first set of "dive tables" listing depths and times at depth that could prevent decompression sickness. Decades before their work, the Frenchman Paul Bert had pointed out the importance of very slow decompression to prevent symptoms of caisson disease, but Bert's "experiments were not sufficient to furnish data as to what rate of decompression would be safe. Nor has subsequent human experience in engineering undertakings solved this problem" (Boycott 1908). In contrast to any prior work, the research on goats provided the theory, the data *and* feasible guidelines for safe decompression (the 1908 paper by Boycott, et. al. runs to 120 pages).

WHAT IS THE THEORY BEHIND DIVE TABLES?

The theory behind dive tables is based on our limited understanding of how nitrogen is taken up on compression (descent) and given off on decompression (ascent). This is a complex subject, all the more so because there is really no unified theory to account for all observations. Haldane's original theory, and one that has more or less stood the test of time, is that nitrogen is taken up and given off in "exponential" fashion. The rate of tissue nitrogen uptake is highest following an increase in ambient pressure; the rate of uptake then decreases as time passes. Similarly, after a lowering of ambient pressure the rate of nitrogen output is greatest, then gradually falls off as time passes (Figure 2).

Haldane assumed that the rate of uptake and output were the same. For example, if it takes two hours to fully saturate a tissue after a pressure increase, it will take two hours for the loaded nitrogen to leave when the pressure decreases, and the rate of leaving will be a mirror image of the rate of entry (Figure 2).

Haldane also knew that the rate of nitrogen uptake and elimination are not uniform within the body; there is a spectrum of uptake and elimination times among all the different tissues and even among the same type of tissue located in different organs. This spectrum exists because of different solubilities of nitrogen in various tissues (fat, bone, cartilage, muscle, tendon, etc.), and because of different rates of blood flow (perfusion) to those tissues.

Figure 2. Exponential rise and fall of nitrogen in tissues with change in ambient pressure.

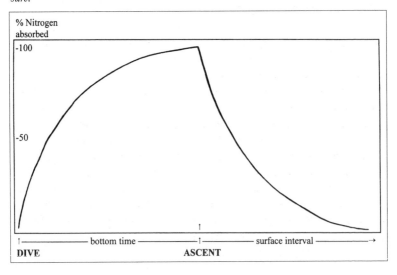

Perfusion can vary by type of tissue (none for the cornea of the eye; high for all nerve and brain tissue), or by activity (less perfusion for muscles at rest than for muscles exercising). To account for the various tissue types, and the enormous range in perfusion, designers of tables theorized a fixed set of "compartments," each with its own "half-time." It is important to keep in mind that they are not actual anatomic compartments, and not even types of tissues, but only theoretical constructs to cover the range of possible nitrogen uptake and output times within the body.

The idea of using theoretical compartments is simply to approximate what is happening in the body. Rather than worry about the actual half-times of many specific tissues with their varying rates of blood flow, scientists (starting with Haldane) simply said something like: 'Let's just divide all the tissues with their varying blood flow into several compartments. If we include what is likely the fastest tissue half-time (usually 5 minutes) and the slowest tissue half-time (several hours), we should be able to simulate what actually happens throughout the body.' In their pioneering work Haldane and his colleagues assumed five such compartments, with half-times of 5, 10, 20, 40, and 75 minutes.

Understand then, this is just a model for the real world. What really happens is far more complex than any model, which is one reason why any model should be tested as widely as possible. By assuming uptake and excretion times for the various compartments, Haldane and others were able to arrive at tables for avoiding the bends *which work in practice*. And keep in mind that "work in practice" means most of the time, not all the time.

WHAT IS "SATURATION"?

"Saturation" and "half-time" are two very important concepts in the design of decompression tables. Models for both printed tables and computer algorithms are based on assumptions of half-times to "full saturation" for various tissue compartments.

In the context of decompression theory, saturation means how "filled up" a tissue is with a gas such as nitrogen. Tissues can be unsaturated, partly saturated, or fully saturated with nitrogen (or any other inert gas). Full saturation means that blood or tissue has all the nitrogen it can hold *for the ambient pressure to which it is exposed*. It also means that the pressure of gas in the tissue equals the pressure of gas in the ambient air.

Thus "saturation," at least in terms of an inert gas such as nitrogen, refers both to an amount of gas and to the pressure of that gas. Any tissue that is fully saturated with nitrogen at a given pressure could still hold more nitrogen at a higher pressure.

TEST YOUR UNDERSTANDING

7. The pressure of nitrogen in any tissue of the body at sea level is .78 atm N_2. If the pressure of nitrogen in a tissue is higher than .78 atm, more gas will dissolve in that tissue; this statement follows from:

   a. Boyle's law   b. Henry's law   c. Charles' law

8. Assume that compartment X in a diver's body is fully saturated with nitrogen at two atmospheres (33 fsw). This means that compartment X (choose all correct statements):

   a. holds all the nitrogen it can hold at two atmospheres.
   b. has a nitrogen pressure twice that at one atmosphere.
   c. is in equilibrium with the ambient nitrogen pressure.
   d. is a fast tissue.

9. Assume that compartment X in a diver's body is fully saturated with nitrogen at two atmospheres (33 fsw). The diver then quickly descends to 66 fsw. At that point compartment X (choose all correct statements):

   a. is no longer fully saturated with nitrogen.
   b. is half saturated with nitrogen.
   c. begins loading additional nitrogen.
   d. is a slow tissue.

HOW DO HALF-TIMES AFFECT NITROGEN LOADING AND UNLOADING?

Given enough time, a diver at 33 fsw will eventually saturate all body tissues to two atmospheres of total gas pressure. Of this total gas pressure, the partial pressure of nitrogen, PN_2, will be 2 x .78 = 1.56 atm How long will it take *all the tissues* to reach two atm total pressure (and a PN_2 of 1.56 atm)? In other words, how long for all the tissues to become fully saturated at the new ambient pressure?

The answer is complex, because the body does not load up on nitrogen evenly. A spectrum of nitrogen loading rates exists because of different tissue types and rates of perfusion; as a result, half-times range from minutes to hours. (Remember, a half-time is the time it takes any given tissue or compartment to fill with one half the nitrogen it will accumulate on reaching full saturation at a given pressure.)

Fat tissue has a long half time because it takes fat a long time to saturate with nitrogen when exposed to a higher pressure (it has a high solubility for nitrogen) and because perfusion of fat is relatively poor compared to other tissues; it is therefore a *slow tissue*. Nerve tissue is considered to have a fast half time because it takes a shorter time than most tissues to load up on all the nitrogen it can contain when the pressure increases (moderate solubility), and because it is so very well perfused. (The *fastest tissue* is blood in contact with the lungs, since it picks up nitrogen quickly from the inhaled air. Half-times of tissues used for dive table modeling do not include blood.)

Let's look more closely at a *single* compartment, one with a half-time of 20 minutes taken to 33 fsw (Table 1). A 20-minute half-time means that half the nitrogen that will enter that compartment will do so in the first 20 minutes, at which point the nitrogen pressure will be

$$0.78 + 1/2 \,(.78) = 1.17 \text{ atm } PN_2.$$

That leaves $1/2$ (.78) PN_2 to go before the compartment is fully saturated with the final nitrogen pressure of 1.56 atm Note that when the compartment is fully saturated its PN_2 will equal the ambient pressure, which is also the gas pressure in the lungs.

Although the first 0.39 atm of nitrogen (1/2 of .78) entered in 20 minutes, the next 0.39 atm of nitrogen *does not* enter in the next 20 minutes. This is because the rate of entry slows as the compartment fills; it loads nitrogen according to the exponential curve shown in Figure 2. In the next 20-minute period, half of the amount of nitrogen that can enter

---

TABLE 1.

Half-times to full saturation with nitrogen for a compartment with 20-minute half-time, at depth of 33 fsw (two atm).

half-time period	length of half-time (minutes)	total elapsed time (minutes)	Percent of full saturation	PN_2* of: lungs	comp.**
First	20	20	50	1.56	1.17
Second	20	40	75	1.56	1.365
Third	20	60	87.5	1.56	1.46
Fourth	20	80	93.75	1.56	1.51
Fifth	20	100	96.875	1.56	1.535
Sixth	20	120	98.5	1.56	1.55

* measured in atmospheres of nitrogen
** compartment

will do so; the same thing holds for each subsequent 20 minute period, until the compartment is fully saturated.

Mathematically, an exponential curve (Figure 2) will never reach 100%; each additional half-time will only get the pressure (or concentration) half way to the final 100%. For practical purposes in designing decompression tables, six half-times is considered full saturation. After six half-times the compartment is 98.5% saturated (and another half-time would add only an extra 0.75%).

The concept of six half-times to full (98.5%) saturation holds true regardless of the pressure change or the length of the half-time. At 66 fsw the body (or any tissue or theoretical compartment) could hold 3 x 0.78 atm of nitrogen; at 99 fsw, 4 x 0.78 atm of nitrogen, etc. The rate at which nitrogen approaches these pressures will depend only on the half-time of the individual compartment; in each case the percentage of loading will be the same after six half-times (98.5%).

Table 2 shows the first six half-times for the *same* 20-minute half-time compartment as in Table 1, this time taken to a depth of 99 fsw (4 atm). Notice that at either depth, each succeeding half-time adds a lesser *quantity* of nitrogen to the compartment (as reflected in the pressure of nitrogen). In the first half-time, half the total nitrogen that will be taken up due to the higher ambient pressure enters the compartment. Subsequent half-times load less and less nitrogen. (The same process reverses when the ambient pressure is lowered; see Figure 2.)

TABLE 2.

Half-times to full saturation with nitrogen for a compartment with 20-minute half-time, at depth of 99 fsw (four atm).

half-time period	length of half-time (minutes)	total elapsed time (minutes)	Percent of full saturation	PN_2* of: lungs	comp.*
First	20	20	50	3.12	1.95
Second	20	40	75	3.12	2.535
Third	20	60	87.5	3.12	2.83
Fourth	20	80	93.75	3.12	2.97
Fifth	20	100	96.875	3.12	3.05
Sixth	20	120	98.5	3.12	3.085

* measured in atmospheres of nitrogen
** compartment

SO WHAT DO HALF-TIMES AND SATURATION HAVE TO DO WITH DIVE TABLES?

Haldane reasoned that if he knew what pressure change *will not* cause DCS, and also the rate various tissues saturate and desaturate with nitrogen, a table could be designed to prevent DCS. Experimentally his group showed that goats did not develop DCS if any stage of decompression was no greater than 2:1. Right away, therefore, he determined it is safe to dive indefinitely to 33 fsw. (We now know this is not correct. The goats were compressed for only a few hours, not long enough for the very slow tissues to fully saturate; the longest half-time is much longer than the 75 minutes Haldane assumed, probably more like 12 hours. If a diver stays at 33 fsw until full saturation, decompression is mandatory to prevent the bends. In recreational diving, shallow-depth dives are not long enough to reach full saturation.)

Haldane's main concern was for deeper dives. What about a dive to 99 feet (4 atm)? At this depth one must be concerned about decompression, and therefore tissue half-times. Lets look at five different compartments, each with its own half-time, at 99 fsw (Table 3). We see that the five minute compartment controls the dive, i.e., it determines that a decompression stop is mandatory at 30 feet, so the diver can let off nitrogen accumulated in the fast tissues. If the diver did not stop on ascent at 30 feet he would exceed the safe 2:1 decompression ratio and greatly increase his chance of developing the bends.

From considerations such as these Haldane and colleagues were able to design the first set of dive tables.

TABLE 3.

Nitrogen loading at depth of 99 fsw (four atm) after 20 minutes, for five different theoretical tissue compartments with half-times of 5, 10, 20, 40 and 80 minutes. (fsw = feet sea water)

half time (min)	No. periods	% saturation	atm N_2	atm N_2 for 2:1 drop	fsw for 2:1 drop
5	4	93.75	2.97	1.49	30
10	2	75	2.54	1.27	16
20	1.0	50	1.95	0.98	6.6
40	0.50	25	1.37	< 0.78	surface*
80	—-tissue not at risk for bubbles—			< 0.78	surface*

* can surface without experiencing a 2:1 drop in ambient pressure

WHAT IS SUPERSATURATION?

Supersaturation occurs when the nitrogen pressure in the tissue is higher than the ambient pressure. To some extent a state of supersaturation always occurs on ascent from a dive; for a brief period the nitrogen pressure in some of the tissues will be higher than in the lungs and blood, since they (lungs and blood) will be the same as the ambient pressure (Figure 3).

Supersaturation is not a problem if it is held to a small degree. When the degree of supersaturation is large, bubbles can form and cause decompression sickness. Bubbles form because the exit of nitrogen from supersaturated tissue is too great for the gas to merely dissolve in the blood.

In a sense supersaturation and decompression go hand in hand. Whenever the nitrogen pressure is higher in the body (or any part thereof) than in the ambient environment, decompression will start (nitrogen will start to leave the supersaturated tissue). In fact every time you fly in an airplane, drive up a mountain or ascend in an elevator, your tissues become transiently supersaturated with nitrogen and start to decompress, i.e., nitrogen starts to leave. Clearly, from an evolutionary viewpoint, decompression is something the human body is designed to handle - up to a point.

Haldane surmised, from his experiments with goats, that the human body could actually tolerate a two-fold degree of supersaturation before

Figure 3. Supersaturation. When the ambient pressure decreases the amount of nitrogen in the tissues suddenly becomes higher than can be sustained by the lowered ambient pressure; nitrogen begins to exit the tissues. In this figure nitrogen pressures are assumed to be 1000 mm Hg in the tissues and 800 mm Hg in the blood and lungs.

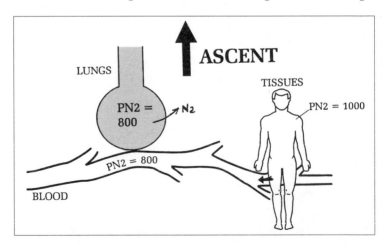

bubbles would form, i.e., a halving of ambient pressure. As pointed out earlier, we now know this is not always a safe degree of supersaturation, particularly after long shallow dives. A supersaturation of 1.5:1 is safer. When the amount of tissue nitrogen is no more than 1.5 times the level called for by the ambient nitrogen pressure, decompression sickness is unlikely to occur.

HAVE THE TABLES BEEN MODIFIED FOR RECREATIONAL DIVING?

Haldane's tables were first adopted by the British Navy, and later (1915) by the U.S. Navy. In the 1930s these tables were modified by the U.S. Navy, based on empiric observation of DCS incidence in sailors diving various profiles in a hyperbaric chamber. In its modifications the U.S. Navy always allowed for a certain percentage of bends in its divers, realizing that zero percentage is not realistic for deep diving, and that a decompression chamber is available for immediate treatment (at least on training dives).

When scuba diving began to emerge as a popular activity, American training agencies adopted the U.S. Navy tables, with slight modifications. In recent years PADI developed a set of dive tables specifically for recreational use, following studies using a technique called doppler ultrasound.

WHAT IS DOPPLER ULTRASOUND?

Doppler ultrasound is a laboratory method of detecting bubbles in the blood. Sound waves beyond the range of human hearing (ultrasound) are transmitted through a probe (about the size of a short pencil) pressed against the chest, over the diver's heart. The probing starts immediately after the completion of an actual or simulated (chamber) dive. As bubbles move through the heart - and toward the point of the probe - they reflect sound waves coming from the probe. The reflection of sound waves as the blood passes through the heart is "read" by the doppler probe as bubbles. The device can also determine the size and relative quantity of the bubbles.

Bubbles are never normal in the blood, so any detected are presumed to arise from nitrogen leaving tissues too quickly. Although bubbles are the root cause of decompression sickness, finding them in the blood does not always mean the diver has DCS; they could be "silent," meaning too small or too few to cause any problems. In fact many divers manifest silent bubbles.

To cause symptoms the bubbles must reach a "critical size." Finding only tiny bubbles is usually considered not significant; finding larger bubbles is a great concern because of their potential to cause symptoms at any time. With doppler ultrasound many different divers and dive profiles can be tested, especially with a hyperbaric chamber where the conditions are easily controlled. Gradually, over time, a safe dive table can be devised for the population that was tested. (With or without bubbles, any symptoms of DCS during a controlled test means the *table has failed that diver*.)

PADI uses its proprietary tables, but other training organizations use modifications of U.S. Navy or yet other tables, such as the Canadian DCIEM tables (Defense and Civil Institute of Environmental Medicine). The most important test for any table is probably the test of time. As any table designer will admit, a table isn't worth much unless it has been tested in the field.

DOES DIVING "BY THE TABLES" GUARANTEE A DIVER WON'T DEVELOP DCS?

Obviously not. The original tables were based on many assumptions and experimental work on goats. Haldane's observation, that bends could be avoided if ambient pressure did not decrease by more than half at any one time, was later shown to be invalid for shallow dives of long duration.

Haldane also assumed five tissue compartments for nitrogen uptake and elimination, but later analysis have found that nine or more compartments, with much longer half-times for the slowest compartment, is a more reliable assumption. The prevention of decompression sickness remains an imperfect science, but research and much testing since 1908 have helped refine dive tables considerably.

Since Haldane's era, the U.S. Navy has refined and tested tables extensively. Through the 1980s the Navy tables were the standard for all recreational diving, even though they were based on the square wave concept (i.e., the total time is assumed spent at the deepest depth). In the 1980s Diving Science and Technology, a scientific arm of PADI, created tables specifically for the recreational diver. DSAT used doppler ultrasound testing after both in-water and hyperbaric chamber dives.

There are theoretical problems with Doppler ultrasound testing, not the least of which is that much of the testing is carried out in a hyperbaric chamber. (In the DSAT tests some of the dives were conducted in open water.) A hyperbaric chamber can create the pressure changes of diving but little else. Water temperature, the feeling of water against the skin, visibility conditions (which may affect breathing and level of stress), ocean currents, the fear of drowning - these and numerous other factors simply can't be simulated in any dry chamber.

Another, and perhaps greater, drawback of the doppler technique is that bubble *detection* may not correlate with development of DCS. It has not been shown that bubbles detected in blood coursing through the heart signifies bubbles in the tissues, around the nerves, in the brain, etc. In addition, *not* detecting bubbles in the blood right after a dive doesn't mean they won't show up later. There may be an excess amount of nitrogen in some very slow tissues that won't release bubbles for several hours (or longer).

The mechanisms that cause DCS are not well understood, and bubble detection is simply a technique to monitor one aspect of the problem in a group of volunteer divers. That the tables work when tested on a small group does not, of course, guarantee that they will work for everyone, all the time. The population of recreational scuba divers is simply too diverse for any table to be tested for all the varying characteristics of people (age, weight, percentage of body fat, level of fitness) and dives (depth, time, rate of ascent, water temperature, visibility levels, etc.) that will encompass all situations.

Since different people can react differently to decompression, no table can be considered 100% safe. The standard dive table is thus only a *conservative guide* to safe diving for the whole population, and not a personal safety guide for each diver. It is a fact that some people diving within standard dive table limits *have* developed DCS.

There is no perfect table, nor will there ever be. Nonetheless, years of experience with available dive tables shows they are far better than nothing and, miraculously, seem to keep most divers from ever getting bent. Only a few hundred DCS cases are reported to DAN every year, which is a small number for such a potentially hazardous activity that is practiced millions of times a year. (See Section P.)

WHAT IS THE DIFFERENCE BETWEEN SQUARE WAVE AND MULTI-LEVEL DIVING?

Dive tables are conservative in large part because they assume all bottom time is spent at the deepest point reached. This type of diving is called *square wave*: down to a depth, level off for a set time, then up to the surface, at an ascent rate no faster than 60 feet a minute. Figure 4 shows two sequential square wave dives as envisioned by the dive tables; the second dive is always at a shallower depth than the first.

Simple observation on dive trips suggests that most recreational dives are not square wave at all; they are instead "multi-level." The diver descends some distance at one rate; down further to maximum depth at a different rate; up a little from the bottom at one rate; up a little further at a different rate; perhaps down again to see something missed; up some more; down a little; up; up some more; safety stop; surface. The variations are infinite. Figure 4 also shows two multi-level dive profiles. The first multi-level profile is typical of that observed on many scuba dives, with slight "ups and downs" as the diver gradually makes his way to the surface. The second multi-level dive (Figure 4) shows a smoother ascent from the deepest point reached early in the dive. Note that these dive profiles illustrate the twin rules for all dives: 1) in any given dive reach the deepest point early; 2) in repetitive dives make the deepest dive first.

Because dive tables calculate all bottom time at the deepest point reached (i.e., as a square wave), each multi-level dive is always at an average depth *less* than what the tables would assume for the same dive. As a result, in a multi-level dive (what most recreational divers do), *less*

Figure 4. Two square wave dives (solid line) and two multi-level dives (dashed line). See text for discussion.

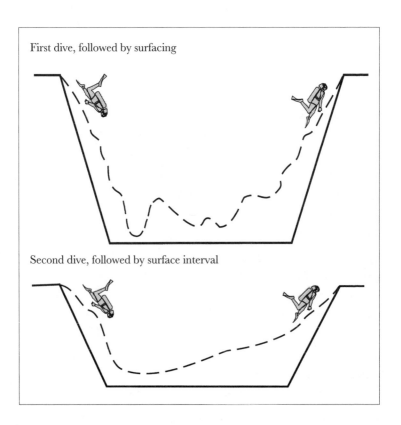

First dive, followed by surfacing

Second dive, followed by surface interval

nitrogen is actually absorbed into the diver's tissues than is assumed by the standard dive tables.

Until the advent of dive computers in the early 1980s, printed tables were all one could go by to dive safely and avoid DCS. Even the PADI Wheel, which was specifically designed in the late 1980s for multi-level diving, cannot account for the fact that what you plan and what you dive are often very different. With the PADI Wheel you may plan the following dive: 50 feet for 20 minutes followed by 40 feet for 10 minutes followed by 30 feet for 8 minutes. Chances are you won't dive that plan. Too many factors affect buoyancy, the length of time spent at a given depth, ascent and descent rates, etc., to execute a multi-level dive exactly as planned. Instead the diver needs some device that tracks the dive *as it occurs*; that device is the dive computer.

WHAT IS THE ORIGIN OF DIVE COMPUTERS?

Until the early 1980s almost all recreational diving was taught by the standards of U.S. Navy tables. Because the Navy tables are not based on multi-level diving profiles, scientists developed algorithms that take into account changes in nitrogen uptake with *continuous changes* in depth. These algorithms were mainly theoretical models until the microchip revolution made them accessible and workable in a hand-held computer. When the algorithm is programmed into a computer that also senses depth (a simple depth gauge) and measures time, you have a "dive computer."

The first commercially available dive computer was the Orca Edge, in 1983. Since then dive computers have become smaller and more versatile. They are now manufactured by many companies, and incorporate one of several algorithms for calculating nitrogen uptake and elimination.

WHAT DO DIVE COMPUTERS DO?

Based on the algorithm used, the dive computer (Figure 5) tracks depth and time every second or so; with this information it continuously computes nitrogen uptake and elimination in the various theoretical compartments assumed by the algorithm. (Among the various computer models the number of compartments ranges from about 6 to 16.) Using measurements of depth and time at depth, the computer calculates the nitrogen saturation and de-saturation of each compartment, and rapidly converts this information into a digital readout for the diver. Keeping track of multi-level diving is no problem for the computer. At the same time the computer performs other functions, such as tracking rate of ascent. Not all dive computers function alike, but most are able to provide the following information:

during the dive
- depth
- number of the dive (first, second, etc.)
- time elapsed since dive began
- how many minutes may be spent at current depth before a decompression stop becomes mandatory
- speed of ascent, and some type of message flashed if it is too fast
- water temperature

after the dive
- maximum depth reached
- length of time that can be spent at various depths on the next dive
- when it will be safe to fly (time to desaturation)

Dive computers are constantly evolving, and many on the market offer additional features, such as air integration for registering tank pressure (replacing the stand alone air gauge), information about how long air will last at the diver's current rate of breathing, various log or bookkeeping functions, and algorithms for nitrox and perhaps other types of mixed gas diving. Regardless of what features a dive computer has, none can account for individual diver characteristics such as age, weight,

Figure 5. A dive console with computer (middle) and compass (right).

percent of body fat and degree of physical conditioning. Although a computer could be designed to accept this type of information, the existing algorithms (like all commercially-available tables) are population-based; they are not designed specifically for the person who buys and uses the computer. (Professional and technical divers sometimes use customized tables, a practice not yet feasible for recreational divers.)

ARE DIVE COMPUTERS PREFERRED OVER DIVE TABLES?

Unlike printed tables, dive computers keep track of where you've been and for how long, and thus give an accurate display of your dive profile. At the same time, based on the algorithm employed, the computer shows if your dive is within the no-mandatory-decompression ("no decompression") limits. Tables cannot track your dive, of course, but they can, if followed, keep you within the no-decompression limits.

So which is better? Some argue that the printed tables are safer because they assume an average depth greater than actually achieved on most dives, and therefore provide a greater margin of safety. This is true in theory. However, even if you went to the exact depth intended (say 55 feet, and stayed the shorter time shown on the tables for a 60-foot depth), the chance for making human error in calculating a repetitive dive is high. Finding the right designated letter group, determining surface interval, keeping an accurate record, etc., all leave much room for making mistakes. Even assuming you accomplished a square-wave dive, you are unlikely to match a computer for computation and record keeping.

Also, all divers know how hard it is to keep track of depth. Many (?all) divers have had the experience of planning a dive to a certain depth, say 60 feet at a wall or over a wreck, and finding they are "suddenly" at 70 or 80 feet; they don't remember descending deeper, but the depth gauge doesn't lie. Or, the diver may not even check his depth gauge and therefore be unaware he went deeper than planned. The computer, of course, not only stores the depth continuously but uses the information to compute when the diver needs to surface, decompress, etc. Obviously tables cannot account for unexpected or unplanned changes in depth. Thus repetitive, multi-level or deep (>60 ft.) diving should be safer with a properly-used computer than with printed tables. This statement does not mean computers are "better" than tables. Computers make it easier for the typical recreational diver to keep track of the dive, and to stay within safe limits while, in many instances, also increasing bottom time.

HOW ACCURATE ARE DIVE COMPUTERS?

This is a subject of much debate in the dive community. The real question is, "If I use the computer properly, will it keep me from getting the bends?" Obviously, the computer *computes* accurately; but is the algorithm on which it is based sufficient to prevent the bends? The answer is both "yes" and "no."

No, because some divers using computers properly *have* developed DCS; documented cases are reported to Divers Alert Network every year. The reason(s) are unknown, but most likely have to do with individual susceptibility and diving at or close to the computer's limits. There is significant variation among computers in the times allowed at various depths (because the algorithms differ), but too little is known about this variation to blame any particular algorithm for a DCS problem. There is surprisingly little published information about the various computer algorithms in terms of actual testing; however, there is also no evidence that any particular algorithm is "dangerous" or "unsafe." (If there is, I am unaware of it).

The answer is also "yes", because the vast majority of divers who follow their computer do not develop the bends, even though their profiles may exceed what would be allowed with square-wave-based dive tables. In one respect, at least, computer algorithms are more conservative than tables – in their allowed rate of ascent. Dive computers have long allowed for an ascent rate much slower than the training agencies' old recommendation of 60 ft./minute. (Training agencies now recommend an ascent rate no faster than 30 feet/minute.) Some computers allow for different rates of ascent, faster at deeper depths, then slower at shallower depths. A typical allowed rate of ascent above 60 fsw is 30 to 35 feet/minute; if the diver is raising faster than this rate the computer will flash SLOW or provide an audible signal to the diver.

In summary, a modern dive computer, used wisely, is accurate - but not infallible.

WHAT ARE ODD DIVE PATTERNS?

Odd dive patterns include those dives that violate the twin rules of reaching the deepest point early in any dive, and of making each subsequent dive shallower than the one before it. Odd dive patterns, which are thought to increase the risk of decompression sickness, include (Figure 6):

on a single dive
- bounce diving

- reverse time profile
- sawtooth profile

on consecutive dives
- second dive deeper than first, third deeper than first or second, etc.

Figure 6. Odd dive patterns (not recommended). S=start of dive; F=finish.

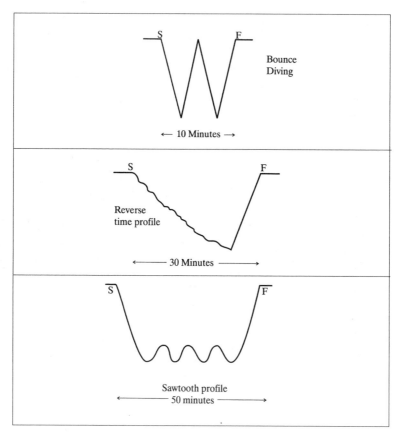

Odd dive patterns obviously differ from either of the multi-level patterns shown in Figure 4 The reverse time profile (reaching the deepest point late in the dive) effectively shortens the time available for off-gassing (decompression), since nitrogen is being continually accumulated until the very end of the dive. When the deepest point is reached first, as is recommended, some of the nitrogen loaded at the deepest depth is being unloaded throughout the dive, during the gradual ascent to the surface.

Bounce and sawtooth diving probably increase DCS risk because of silent bubble formation at depth. On ascent any silent bubbles that form begin to release nitrogen harmlessly. However, if the diver quickly returns to the deepest depth, more nitrogen will enter the tissues; *that* nitrogen, on re-ascent, will then flow into the existing bubbles, which expand further. Thus, the risk of DCS increases by diving immediately after formation of any silent bubbles; bounce or sawtooth diving is one way to do this.

HOW ARE COMPUTERS ABUSED?

There are many ways dive computers can be improperly used or abused. Like any tool, the dive computer cannot keep a person from hurting himself or herself. Perhaps a dive computer's greatest drawback is that it may impart a false sense of security to the diver.

"The best dive computer is the human brain" is a frequently quoted slogan. Rely mindlessly on a dive computer and you are asking for trouble. In no particular order, here are some ways a dive computer can be improperly used or abused, and increase the risk of a diving accident.

1) By exceeding the computer's limits, such as: ascending too fast; repetitive diving to depths greater than allowed; staying too long at depth when you should be ascending; flying before the computer says it is safe.

2) Pushing the limits of the computer. There is frequent debate about whether a given computer is "conservative" or "liberal" in the diving it allows. Regardless, it is foolish to push the limits of any dive computer (or dive table, for that matter). If you have made four dives in a day, and the computer says you can do a fifth dive to 40 feet for 18 minutes, and you decide to do that dive for 18 minutes "because the computer says I can," you are pushing the envelope of safety and increasing your risk of DCS. Common sense says it would be safer to either not dive or, if you do, go to less than 40 feet or for less than 18 minutes (or both).

3) Diving odd patterns (Figure 6). The computer will track them and may not sound any alarms. However, in theory these patterns increase risk of DCS.

4) Ignoring non-computer factors. The computer algorithm assumes a "typical" or average population of divers. The computer does not know if its owner was up all night with an upset stomach, had three martinis for breakfast, is dehydrated, or is using a thin lycra skin in

water that calls for a heavy wet suit. All of these factors might increase risk for DCS but they are unknown to the computer.

5) Not using the computer on all repetitive dives. If some part of a diver's console is malfunctioning, he may borrow someone else's, and end up using a different computer, or perhaps none. He may reason: "It's only one dive." If it is his only dive in the past 24 hours, no problem (assuming the dive is planned by the tables). But if it is one of several repetitive dives, he is making a big mistake; the computer will know nothing about his nitrogen uptake on previous dives, and its calculations will be invalid for protecting him from DCS. This will also be the case for all subsequent repetitive dives, no matter which computer he uses.

6) Relying on the computer worn by a dive buddy. Dive buddies *never* have identical dive profiles. A buddy team, where only one buddy has a computer, should dive by the tables and not by the computer. Relying on a buddy's computer, especially for repetitive diving, is very risky.

7) Letting the computer separate a dive team. If each member of a buddy team has his/her own computer, and the algorithms differ, the *pair* must dive by the more conservative computer. If the diver with the more liberal computer stays down (because the computer says he can) while the one with the more conservative computer ascends, the situation becomes a "same ocean, same day dive," not a buddy dive. Staying together as a buddy team should take precedence over any computer's algorithm.

8) Not maintaining the computer properly. The computer is no good if its battery runs out at 75 feet. Low battery signals should not be ignored.

9) Using a computer at altitude when it is programmed for sea level. Altitude diving (above 2000 feet) requires a different set of dive tables than what is used at sea level. (Many computers now automatically adjust for altitude.)

TEST YOUR UNDERSTANDING

10. Two divers go as a buddy team to 60 fsw. Only diver B has a computer. Using tables, Diver A determines she can dive to 60 fsw for 40 minutes. Twenty minutes into the dive they are both at 40 fsw. Diver B's computer shows he can stay at this depth another 30 minutes. Which one of the following statements is correct?

    a. Both divers should surface after 40 minutes bottom time.
    b. Both may surface after 50 minutes bottom time.
    c. Diver A should surface after 40 minutes, while diver B can stay an extra 10 minutes.
    d. A compromise of 45 minutes total bottom time should be reached, and then both should surface.

11. A diver goes to 60 fsw with her computer; at 10 a.m. it shows a 'no decompression time' of 35 minutes. At 10:15 a.m. she is at 42 fsw; her computer shows a no decompression time of 40 minutes. Assuming she stays at 42 fsw until ascent begins, she should be at her safety stop by:

    a. 10:35 a.m.   d. 10:20 a.m.; her computer is malfunctioning
    b. 10:40 a.m.   e. the time her tank pressure reaches 500 psi
    c. 10:55 a.m.

12. A tissue compartment has a half-time of 10 minutes. After a doubling of ambient pressure how many minutes will it take for the compartment to become fully (98.5%) saturated?

    a. 20   c. 40   e. 60
    b. 30   d. 50

13. A compartment is considered fully saturated at 6 hours. It's half time in minutes is:

    a. 20   c. 40   e. 120
    b. 30   d. 60

14. A diver goes to 99 fsw breathing a nitrox mixture (68% nitrogen, 32% oxygen) and stays 15 minutes. How many half-times would it take for his 30-minute compartment to become fully saturated (98.5%) with nitrogen at that depth?

    a. 4   c. cannot determine without more information
    b. 6

TEST YOUR UNDERSTANDING

15. State whether each of the following statements about nitrogen loading is true or false.
    a. A compartment with a 30-minute half-time will gain the same percentage of nitrogen when going from 30 fsw to 60 fsw as when going from 60 fsw to 120 fsw.
    b. On a dive to 33 fsw some compartments, if at depth long enough, will end up with a PN_2 greater than 2.0 atm
    c. Assume two divers, A and B, of identical weight and body composition, go to 33 fsw. Diver A stays 60 minutes and diver B stays 120 minutes. At the beginning of ascent the two divers will have the same amount of nitrogen in their tissues.
    d. Assume that it takes 12 hours for a body to fully saturate at a depth of 33 fsw. If diver A has been at this depth for 24 hours and diver B has been there for 13 hours, the two divers should have the same PN_2 in their tissues.
    e. "Fully saturated" with nitrogen means the tissue holds all the nitrogen it can ever hold, no matter what the circumstances.
    f. A diver whose tissues are 'fully saturated' with nitrogen at 33 fsw will change to 'partly saturated' if she descends to 66 fsw.

16. State whether each of the following statements about computers is true or false.
    a. Diving within the computer's limits will prevent any diver from getting the bends.
    b. All dive computers used by recreational divers give essentially the same 'no decompression times' for the same dive profiles.
    c. It is acceptable for two divers to use one computer if they plan to hold hands the entire dive.
    d. Computers can extend the length of a dive over the time allowed by dive tables.
    e. The computer can remember numbers and perform calculations more reliably than people.
    f. The computer algorithm is more reliable than the information provided in a standard set of printed dive tables.
    g. "The best dive computer is the human brain" means that if the depth reading or the 'no decompression time' on the computer don't seem correct during a dive, you should ignore them and use your intuition.

Answers to TEST YOUR UNDERSTANDING

1. c. 60 minutes (use the next highest depth, which is 60 feet)

2. b. Letter group G

3. Letter group H. Since you dove to 36 feet, you use 40 fsw as your depth in the table; the letter group after the first dive is therefore I. Entering the second part of the table, your surface interval time of 35 minutes is in the surface interval 0:34-0:59 minutes. Moving down that column you reach the new letter group H.

4. Letter group E

5. c. 44 minutes. After your first dive you are in letter group H. After an hour surface interval you are in letter group G. For a planned second dive to 50 feet your residual nitrogen time is 56 minutes, which must be subtracted from the bottom time shown in part one for a dive to 50 feet. One hundred minutes minus 56 minutes = 44 minutes bottom time on the second dive.

6. b. 53 minutes. After your first dive you are in letter group G. After a 45 minute surface interval you are in letter group F. For a planned second dive to 45 feet you must use the next higher row, 50 feet; your residual nitrogen time is 47 minutes, which must be subtracted from the bottom time shown in part one for a dive to 50 feet. One hundred minutes minus 47 minutes = 53 minutes bottom time on the second dive.

7. c. Henry's law.

8. a, b, and c are true.

9. a and c are true.

10. a. A buddy team with only one computer should dive by the tables.

11. c. 10:55 a.m. The no decompression time lengthens as the depth becomes shallower. Her computer is working fine.

12. e. 60 minutes

13. d. 60 minutes

14. b. 6 half-times.

15. a. true
    b. false. The maximum PN_2 at 33 fsw is 2.0 atm
    c. false. Diver B will have much more nitrogen in his tissues since he is exposed to the ambient pressure for a longer period; at this depth and time neither diver is fully saturated with nitrogen.
    d. true. Since full saturation occurs in 12 hours, both divers have the same nitrogen pressure in their tissues (two atm PN_2 at 33 fsw).
    e. false. Fully saturated means a tissue holds all the nitrogen it can for the ambient pressure to which it is exposed.
    f. true

16. a. false
    b. false
    c. false
    d. true
    e. true.
    f. false. Statements 'e' and 'f' serve to clarify the term 'reliable' in regards to dive computers. Computers are certainly more reliable than people at remembering information and making calculations. However, the computer algorithm itself is not more reliable than the information available in a set of printed tables.
    g. false. The slogan means that one should always employ common sense and not become a slave to a computer. Computers invariably compute accurately, but they cannot imbue any diver with the ability to make correct decisions.

REFERENCES AND BIBLIOGRAPHY

See references for Sections B-E, plus the following.

Cole B. *Decompression and Computer-Assisted Diving.* Best Publishing, Flagstaff, AZ, 1993.

Hamilton RW, Rogers RE, Powell MR, Vann RD. *The DSAT Recreational Dive Planner: Development and validation of no-stop decompression procedures for recreational diving;* 1994. Hamilton Research, Ltd., 80 Grove Street, Tarrytown, NY 10591-4138.

Huggins KE. *Microprocessor Applications to Multi-Level Air Decompression Problems.* Michigan Sea Grant Publications, 2200 Bonisteel Blvd., Ann Arbor , MI 48109; 1987.

Lang MA, Hamilton RW. *Proceedings of the American Academy of Underwater Sciences Dive Computer Workshop,* Univ. of California Sea Grant Publication # USCSG-TR-01-89, 1989.

Lewis, JE., Ph.D., Shreeves KW. *The Recreational Diver's Guide to Decompression Theory, Dive Tables and Dive Computers,* 2nd Ed. International Padi, Inc., Santa Ana, CA, 1993.

Lippman J. A Statistical Review of Dive Computer Safety. Alert Diver, May/June, 1994; p. 16.

Loyst K. *Dive Computers: A Consumer's Guide to History, Theory and Performance.* Watersport Publishing, Inc., San Diego, 1991.

Spencer MP. Decompression limits for compressed air determined by ultrasonically detected blood bubbles. Jour Appl Phys 1976;40:229-235.

Stangroom JE. *Decompression Demystified. Modern Decompression Theory in Plain English.* The Hope Valley Press, Derbysire (England), 1991.

Wienke BK. *Basic Decompression Theory and Application.* Best Publishing, Flagstaff, AZ, 1991.

DIVING ODDS N' ENDS

Scuba Diving in Hawaii

For scuba divers perhaps the principal difference between Hawaii and most other popular warm water sites is...the absence of soft coral. Hawaii's lack of soft coral is attributed to both the islands' north Pacific location (strong winter winds between September and May, with heavy surf conditions) and the fact that the sea bed near the islands is covered with volcanic lava. The result is much hard coral but no soft coral. Other differences in the scuba experience have to do with the Hawaiian islands' remote location - the most geographically remote islands on earth. Many fish species common elsewhere are not found in Hawaii (e.g., groupers, clown fishes), while an estimated 20% of the species in Hawaii are found *nowhere else* (e.g., the lemon butter-fly fish, *Chaetodon milaris*; the Hawaiian sharpnosed puffer, *Canthigaster jactator*).

NOTES

Stress, Hyperventilation, and Hypothermia

WHAT IS STRESS?

Stress is a term frequently used by divers to describe uncomfortable or dangerous experiences. The dictionary defines stress as "physical, mental or emotional strain or tension." The diver who says "I was stressed" usually means something like: "I found myself in a difficult situation and was uncomfortable, anxious, fearful." Or, "I was not in full control of the situation, my heart was pounding, and for a while I felt pretty tense." The sudden onset of stress is usually accompanied by specific physiologic changes such as sweating, headache, fast heart beat and over breathing (hyperventilation).

WHY IS AN UNDERSTANDING OF STRESS IMPORTANT FOR DIVERS?

Stress is such an important concept in diving - avoiding it when possible, confronting stress without panic when it does occur - that the subject is an integral part of "Stress and Rescue" courses offered by the scuba training agencies. Recognition and proper handling of stress are keys to safer, more enjoyable diving.

Stressful situations leading to panic probably account for many preventable fatal scuba accidents. In Stress and Rescue courses divers are taught that in any stressful situation you must STOP - BREATHE - THINK - ACT, in order to avoid a panic reaction.

IN ANY STRESSFUL SITUATION:

STOP
BREATHE
THINK
ACT

WHAT IS A PANIC REACTION?

Panic - defined as a chaotic and inappropriate response to a stressful situation - puts the diver's life in jeopardy. Rather than belabor this point I will provide examples of several stressful situations, comparing reactions by the panicked or near-panicked diver and the stress-trained diver. (The diver's thoughts are in single quotation marks.)

1) **Howard, diving alone, finds himself snagged in some kelp 45 feet below the surface. As he tries to swim away he is pulled back deeper into the kelp bed.**

Panic reaction. 'I'm caught! What is this? I can't get away! Oh my god! I've got to twist around and get out of this stuff!' With each attempt at moving away Howard finds himself more restricted. He begins to over ventilate and run low on air. He's not sure if the kelp is around his body or just his BC. He decides to ditch the BC and make an emergency ascent. He risks drowning.

Stress-trained reaction. STOP. 'I'm caught in some kelp. Can't seem to move. Have to stop and figure this out.' BREATHE. 'Must control my breathing. Take slow, deep breaths while I work on this. I should have at least 1000 psi left.' THINK. 'Since I can't move away, I have two options. Try to cut it with my knife or try to ditch my BC and tank.' ACT. Howard slides his right hand down his leg and grasps his knife, which he always takes with him into the kelp bed. Slowly, carefully, he brings it up to waist level and begins to cut all kelp he can see or feel. Making slight rotational movements he continues to cut a wider and wider area. In a short few minutes he is able to turn completely and cut the last remaining kelp, around his ankle. Then he sheathes the knife and makes a slow ascent to the surface.

2) **John, 50 feet down, finds that he has run out of air. His buddy is nowhere to be seen.**

Panic reaction. 'Oh my god I'm going to die! How did this happen? I can't breathe! Where the hell's my buddy? He left me!' John sees the surface far away and starts kicking up as fast as possible. Panicked and unthinking, he holds his breath and experiences an air embolism on reaching the surface.

Stress-trained reaction. STOP. 'I'm out of air, for sure. And I can't see my buddy. No time to start looking for him.' BREATHE. 'That's the problem. Can't inhale water.' THINK. 'I must have a good half minute of air in my lungs. I remember the first rule of diving: never hold your breath. OK, I've got to make an emergency ascent. Must be sure to exhale all the way up. Better ditch my weight belt.' ACT. John unbuckles his weight belt and it falls quickly away. He uses the power inflator to inflate his BC a little, finding there is enough air remaining for that purpose. He slowly kicks upward while continuously exhaling, all the while concentrating on the bubbles coming out of his lungs. In only a few seconds he surfaces, and then manually inflates his BC. He has saved himself by coping properly with an extremely stressful situation.

3) **Bill, a newly certified diver, signs on for a morning wreck trip with Macho Divers. He is diving alone but is told he can buddy up on the boat. Sure enough, he is teamed with Rambo, who has made "hundreds of dives" in the area. Near the wreck site the dive master informs the group that the first dive will be to 90 feet on the wreck, over twice the depth Bill has ever reached before.**

Near-panic. Bill is anxious: 'I can't back out now.' He rationalizes: 'This dive should really be no different from the two I made to 40 feet in my certification course.' He is fearful: 'What if I can't keep up with my buddy? Do I follow him inside the wreck? Or wait for him outside? Will I have enough air to last? Oh damn, what choice do I have? If I say something they'll think I'm chicken. I'll just go down and see what happens. But what if there's a problem?' Doubt-ridden, anxious and hyperventilating, Bill makes the dive. A few minutes later, while hovering over the wreck and trying to keep up with Rambo, Bill is shocked to discover his air gauge reads only 1100 psi. He aborts the dive and ascends quickly, forgetting to make a safety stop.

Stress-trained reaction. STOP. 'First dive to 90 feet? This is not a safe situation at my level of training.' BREATHE. 'No need to panic. Glad I'm not in the water. My breathing is even; no one around me even senses my concern. THINK. 'I've never been that deep and now is not the time to go, especially with this Rambo buddy.

No chance he's going to stay close by me. I'm getting goose bumps just thinking about all the bad things that can happen down there.' ACT. Bill tells the dive master he's a new diver and isn't comfortable with this first dive to 90 feet; he would rather sit it out and make the second dive to 50 feet, with the whole group. "No problem" says the dive master. Rambo is teamed up with someone else. Bill has a safe and successful shallow dive later that morning.

4) **Mary loses sight of her buddy during a drift dive. She becomes disoriented and decides to surface. Back on the surface, she sees that the dive boat is far away. There is about a two-foot chop on the surface.**

Panic. Mary starts screaming: "Help! Help!" She flails her arms wildly but no one sees her. Her regulator falls behind the tank and she cannot grasp it. She forgets to use her snorkel. A wavelet rushes over her and she swallows a mouthful of water. She begins choking and coughing, and feels certain she is going to die. When finally spotted by the boat captain, she is water logged and choking. Mary is picked up and rushed to shore for medical examination.

Stress-trained reaction. STOP. 'Well, I'm far from the boat. Not a good situation.' BREATHE. 'Must take slow, deep breaths. Don't want to hyperventilate. Could get dizzy that way.' THINK. 'They won't hear me if I yell, and I don't have any signaling device. Surely they'll find me soon. I just have to be patient. As long as I have air in my tank there's no danger of drowning. Let's see...um, that's good, 1500 psi. OK, I'll be fine. Just be patient.' ACT. Mary inflates her BC and tucks the regulator mouthpiece into her vest so she can get it without fumbling. She begins breathing through her snorkel, and lays back to relax and conserve energy. Periodically, she waves her arms back and forth, the universal diver's signal for "I need help," in case someone from the boat looks her way. She spends a relaxing 10 minutes in the water until picked up by the boat.

There are many potentially stressful situations that can occur when diving. Every month the pages of *Skin Diver* and other scuba magazines report how experienced and novice divers handle them, sometimes well, sometimes not so well. The key steps to handling any stressful situation: first, recognize when it occurs; second, STOP - BREATHE - THINK - ACT.

HOW DO I KNOW WHEN I'M IN A STRESSFUL SITUATION?

A stressful situation can develop within seconds, or build up over minutes to hours. True emergencies, such as an entrapped or injured diver, or an out-of-air situation, are obvious stressful situations. However, any time there is an element of fear, tension or uncertainty there is a stressful situation which, if not handled properly, can lead to a bad outcome.

If you experience these feelings, you are in, or are approaching, a stressful situation. This is not necessarily bad. Stressful situations are part and parcel of diving. The important thing is to recognize stress so it can be contained. For example, the mere *occurrence* of any of the following questions in the mind of the diver signals a potentially stressful situation. Remember to STOP - BREATHE - THINK - ACT.

before a dive
- Should I make that third dive this afternoon?
- Should I rent this equipment even if it has no octopus?
- Should I dive with this cold/sinus infection?
- The water looks rough from shore. Should I do this boat dive today?
- Should I do this night dive? They all say it's going to be great, but I'm really tired.

during a dive
- Should I take a chance and enter that cave/wreck?
- Should I turn around with only 1000 psi in my tank, or go further?
- My computer just died. Should I abort this dive or just stay with my buddy until he's ready to surface?
- Should I try to pet that moray eel?
- Should I try to pick up that spiny urchin hiding under the rock?

Handling stress does not mean taking no risk, or always sitting out a dive when a doubt arises, or insisting only on perfect conditions. After all, diving by definition is riskier than not diving. Handling stress means doing what is best for you in any difficult or tense situation, consistent with your level of training; above all, it means never, never panicking.

What constitutes stress, and a stressful situation, is largely diver-dependent. An open water student may experience stress on her very first pool dive. Someone who has only dove in Caribbean waters may feel stress in a cold water lake. A highly experienced diving instructor may feel stress while diving in a cave. The point is, every scuba diver is at risk for encountering stressful situations. Every diver needs to learn to handle stress. STOP - BREATHE - THINK - ACT.

WHAT IS HYPERVENTILATION?

Hyperventilation is one of the commonest physiologic responses to stress and anxiety. Hyperventilation simply means breathing more than is necessary for the amount of carbon dioxide your body produces. "Breathing more" means breathing faster and/or deeper than necessary to keep the blood carbon dioxide at an optimum level. To a large extent the **BREATHE** step in handling stress is a reminder to take slow, deep breaths and *not* hyperventilate.

Hyperventilation lowers the partial pressure of CO_2 in the blood ($PaCO_2$) and makes the blood more alkaline than normal. Normal blood $PaCO_2$ ranges between 35 and 45 mm Hg; hyperventilation brings it to less than 35 mm Hg. The lower the $PaCO_2$, the worse the symptoms.

Hyperventilation can occur very quickly, within seconds. You can hyperventilate right now. First, make sure you are sitting down. Take several deep, rapid breaths. Your CO_2 level will fall and you will probably begin to feel tingling in your fingers and a little lightheaded (if you keep hyperventilating you will definitely feel lightheaded).

The next few paragraphs describe the consequences of hyperventilation in general, and then the consequences peculiar to diving.

General consequences. So-called involuntary hyperventilation is a common phenomenon. We see it in kids and grownups, in friends, relatives, patients. The person becomes anxious and starts to over breathe. This leads to a low blood CO_2 level. If the problem occurs quickly the body doesn't have time to adjust, and several symptoms can manifest: palpitations (feeling your heart beat); numbness and tingling in the fingers and around the mouth; headache and dizziness. In the most severe cases there can be muscle spasms of the arms, low blood pressure and fainting.

The symptoms of acute hyperventilation are often "cured" by having the hyperventilator breathe into a paper bag held over the mouth and nose; this leads to re-breathing exhaled carbon dioxide, which raises the blood $PaCO_2$ toward normal. The bag should be removed as soon as the symptoms abate and the patient can be reassured that he is OK. At that point the problem causing the stress or anxiety can be investigated. Because the hyperventilator on land has an unlimited air supply, hyperventilation alone is never fatal.

When diving. All the general consequences of hyperventilation apply underwater, and more. Underwater, of course, the supply of air is *very limited.* The hyperventilating diver uses air much faster than normal, so the dive is cut short. Instead of a planned bottom time of 30 minutes on a dive to 60 feet, for example, the hyperventilating diver may have only five minutes because of a rapidly diminishing air supply. On one memorable dive to 50 feet an overweighted, hyperventilating diver thought her tank was leaking because 10 minutes into the dive she was down to only 1200 psi! Back on the boat she asked the dive master to check her equipment. Her equipment was fine.

The numbness and tingling from hyperventilation can mimic the bends and cause a stressful situation. If the diver doesn't recognize the problem, anxiety and further hyperventilation can ensue. In the most extreme cases the diver can become lightheaded and lose control of the situation. The regulator could fall out of her mouth, she could experience muscle spasms, end up in a panic state and risk drowning. All from simply over breathing.

TEST YOUR UNDERSTANDING

1. Someone who has symptoms from "hyperventilating" will always have: (choose one answer only)

   a. a fast breathing rate
   b. deeper breathing than normal
   c. numbness or tingling in the fingers
   d. an arterial PCO_2 lower than 35 mm Hg
   e. a history of anxiety

2. An open water scuba student goes to 30 fsw with his instructor. After about five minutes the student finds it difficult to inhale through his regulator and starts to breathe fast. The student gives an out-of-air sign and the instructor signals him to surface. On the surface the student appears anxious and is noted to be breathing fast. The instructor helps him get back onto the dive boat. The student complains of numbness and tingling in his hands and around the mouth. What is the most likely cause of his problem?

3. What is the principal difference between hyperventilating on land and while scuba diving?

Probably most people hyperventilate to some extent when first learning to dive. By appreciating the problem it can be avoided. Be conscious of your breathing. When not stressed, slow, moderate-sized breaths are preferred. Try to avoid deep, sighing breaths, as well as short, shallow breaths.

WHAT IS HYPOTHERMIA?

Hypothermia is a lower than normal body temperature. Normal body temperature is about 37°C (98.6°F). Water temperature less than this will drain heat away from the body and, over time, cause hypothermia. The most susceptible areas for heat loss are the head, underarms and groin. This is why a hood is so important in cold water diving.

Water conducts heat about 25 times faster than air. Because of rapid heat conduction by water, and lack of much natural insulation, the human body cannot defend against low water temperatures as well as against low air temperatures. That is why 75°F in the air feels quite comfortable with light clothing, but the same water temperature requires a full wetsuit for comfort.

For medical purposes, hypothermia is defined as a central body temperature equal to or less than 35°C (95°F). Hypothermia can be divided into three stages based on the body temperature: mild, moderate and severe (Table 1).

Up to a point we can maintain normal central body temperature when exposed to cooler temperatures, even though we may feel cold.

TABLE 1.
Classification of Hypothermia

Mild: 34°-36.5°C (93° - 95°F)
Blood pressure usually normal but may be high or low; victim may have trouble speaking, walking, remembering; shivering often present when temperature reaches 95°F.

Moderate: 28°-33.5°C (82.4° - 92°F)
Victim begins to lose consciousness; heart rate slowed; victim may have heart rhythm disturbance with low blood pressure.

Severe: Below 28°C (82.4°F)
Victim in shock; no response to pain; very slow heart rate; victim at high risk for sudden death from heart rhythm disturbance.

Feeling cold or chilly is not the same thing as hypothermia, but may be a precursor to true hypothermia. True hypothermia is a medical emergency that, uncorrected, can be fatal. However, water temperature has a variable effect on a given individual; its physiologic effects depend not just on individual tolerance, which varies from person to person, but also on the length of the exposure and the type of protection worn.

For most divers, water temperatures above 90°F feel hot, and temperatures between 84°F and 89°F feel quite comfortable, at least initially. We often see divers enter water in the mid 80s without a wetsuit, or with only a non-insulating protective "skin" worn to avoid abrasions. Even so, heat loss is occurring at these "warm" temperatures, because they are still lower than normal body temperature. For each degree of water temperature lower than 84°F, an increasing percentage of people feel the need for thermal protection with a wet suit.

There are data regarding how long an unprotected person can stay immersed in water at various temperatures before hypothermia occurs; obviously the colder the water, the faster body temperature will fall and the more likely the victim will succumb. According to the National Oceanic and Atmospheric Association (NOAA), a body temperature of 91.4° F (33°C) is lethal for about 50 percent of all people who reach this level from water exposure.

Recreational divers in warm waters (>75°F) will likely not develop hypothermia during one dive. They may, however, feel chilled and uncomfortable, lose some body heat, and enter into a stressful situation: not a pleasurable dive. The major warning sign of impending severe hypothermia is shivering, which usually occurs when body temperature reaches 95°F. The shivering diver should exit the water.

It is always better to have a little too much protection than too little. Protection for the diver means some type of worn garment covering most of the skin surface, either a wet or a dry suit. One can always open a wet suit zipper if the water feels too warm. Once chilled, however, there is little one can do except get out of the water.

A wet suit is a form-fitting suit, usually made of closed-cell neoprene, which means it contains air cells that are an inherent part of the fabric. The wet suit allows water to enter between the suit and the diver's skin. This layer of water is then warmed by the diver's skin and serves to retard heat loss during the dive. Wet suits, depending on their thickness and use of hood and gloves, can be protective down to the 50°F to 55°F range. Note that the closed air cells of neoprene are compressed with depth, so the wet suit loses much of its insulating ability the deeper one goes.

Below 50°F, a dry suit is usually necessary for proper thermal protection. (Some divers feel any water temperature less than 60°F mandates a dry suit.) No water can enter a dry suit, so the diver stays dry throughout the dive. A dry suit is typically composed of 1/4 inch closed-cell neoprene with nylon backing. Instead of water, a layer of air (delivered from the tank) is kept in place between the inside of the dry suit and the undergarments worn by the diver (thermal underwear is recommended). Boots are also an integral part of the dry suit. The amount of air inside a dry suit is controlled by the diver; since it can markedly affect buoyancy throughout the dive, special training is necessary for proper use.

The range of wet suit thicknesses and temperature effectiveness are shown in Table 2, compared with the dry suit. Note that the protection afforded by both types of suits will be enhanced if the diver also wears a hood and gloves. The neoprene wet suit sizes are based on the English system of measuring thickness. In most countries wet suits are marketed by metric thickness, e.g., 1, 3, 5 mm, so the corresponding thickness in inches will vary accordingly.

TABLE 2.

Wet Suit Thickness and Water Temperature

| wet suit thickness: | | water temperature |
inches	mm	range*
1/16	1.6	75-85°F/ 24-30.5°C
1/8	3.2	70-85°F/ 21-30.5°C
3/16	4.8	65-75°F / 18-24°C
1/4	6.4	50-65°F / 10-18°C
3/8	9.5	45-60°F / 7-15.5°C
	Dry suit	<60°F/<15.5°C

* Tolerance to cold will vary according to the diver's body makeup, plus use of hood and gloves. There are no hard rules about what wet suit to wear at what water temperature; it is largely a matter of preference and diver tolerance. The temperatures shown are the approximate ranges for comfort for the specified protective gear.

WHAT IS THE TREATMENT OF HYPOTHERMIA?

You may be called on to assist or aid a hypothermic or chilled diver. There are formal hypothermia protocols and whenever possible victims

TEST YOUR UNDERSTANDING

4. Listed below are four "mechanisms." Choose the two mechanisms by which wet suits protect against hypothermia.

    a. insulation (prevention of radiation heat loss)
    b. thermal equilibrium between water under the wet suit and the diver's skin temperature
    c. continuous circulation of water between the suit and the diver's skin
    d. compression of neoprene air cells with depth, which keeps heat from escaping

5. What is the recommended procedure for a diver who feels chilled and begins to shiver 10 minutes into a planned 40 minute/50 fsw dive? The diver is wearing a wet suit appropriate for the water temperature.

    a. Stay as deep as possible to increase wet suit compression and thus thermal insulation.
    b. Exercise by using arms in a swimming motion; plan for a somewhat shorter dive since this technique will increase air consumption.
    c. Tighten the BC to prevent flow of water between it and the wetsuit.
    d. Ignore the sensation until your teeth chatter and you can no longer comfortably hold the regulator in your mouth.
    e. Make a sign to your dive buddy that you are chilled and then exit the water. Expect your buddy to follow you up unless there is someone else he/she can buddy up with.

should be handled by a knowledgeable professional. Issues such as CPR or hypoxia may also need management in any hypothermic diving injury.

Treatment of hypothermia can be divided into passive rewarming, active surface rewarming, and active core rewarming. In the field, away from a medical facility, you will probably only be able to accomplish the first two.

PASSIVE REWARMING - remove all wet clothing; use dry, unheated blankets, dry clothes, and a warm room environment.

ACTIVE SURFACE REWARMING - use heated blankets or hot water bottles applied to skin. If the victim is fully alert, give warm liquids; this will help correct any associated dehydration. Alcohol and caffeine beverages such as coffee and tea should be avoided. Immersion techniques, such as placing the victim in a tub of hot water, are not generally recommended.

ACTIVE CORE REWARMING (by medical personnel only) - instillation of warm fluids into the veins; placement of warm fluids through a tube into the victim's stomach; inhalation of warm respiratory gases; dialysis (removal of blood for warming outside body, then returning the blood to the victim).

WHAT IS HYPERTHERMIA?

Hyperthermia, or over heating, is much less common than hypothermia. The main reason is that open water (oceans, lakes, rivers) is naturally cooler than body temperature. However, while wearing a thick wet suit on hot days, any diver can become overheated and develop true hyperthermia out of the water. The body temperature rises, which is the same as developing a fever. The threshold body temperature that puts the diver at risk is about 102.2°F (39°C). Signs of hyperthermia include rapid breathing, feeling warm or hot, mental confusion, fatigue, muscle cramps, nausea, and exhaustion.

The higher the temperature above 102°F the worse the problem. Hyperthermia is considered life threatening whenever body temperature reaches 105-106°F; such a fever places the diver at risk of cardiovascular collapse, shock and death. Treatment requires that any wet suit be removed as quickly as possible. If recently in the water the diver will be wet, but the skin will be warm and pulse rapid. (If hyperthermia occurs before entering the water the victim will appear hot and *dry*, with flushed skin and a rapid pulse.)

The major complications from hyperthermia are dehydration and shock. Emergency first aid requires cooling the body temperature by any means available: wrapping in a wet blanket, immersion in water, spraying with cool water. Generally the body temperature should not fall below 101°F with first aid treatment, as too rapid cooling can precipitate hypothermia. Since a thermometer may not be available in the field, it is best to cool the person slowly rather than quickly.

Answers to TEST YOUR UNDERSTANDING

1. d. Of the answers provided, only a low $PaCO_2$ is invariably present, since it is part of the definition of hyperventilation. All of the other symptoms are often found, but are not part of the definition (they could be due to other causes, including DCS).

2. Hyperventilation. Although hyperventilation and the bends may be difficult to distinguish after a dive, in this situation the shallow depth and short length of time virtually rule out the bends.

3. On land you cannot run out of air so hyperventilation, per se, is not life threatening. Under water a hyperventilating diver can run out of air, panic, or have some other catastrophe, and thereby risk drowning.

4. a. and b. Note that answer d, compression of neoprene air cells at depth, actually diminishes the wet suit's thermal protection.

5. e. Exit the water. Exercise is likely to worsen the hypothermia since it brings cold blood from the extremities to the central part of the body.

DIVING ODDS N' ENDS

Cold Water Diving

Some of the best diving is in cold water, which I define as water colder than 75°F. I've seen no poll on this, but from numerous articles the following U.S. areas seem to be favorites for cold water diving:

1. Central Florida springs (72°F year round)
2. Southern California, including Catalina island
3. Monterey Peninsula (central California)
4. Wreck diving off the Atlantic Coast, from North Carolina to New York
5. Northwest U.S. (San Juan Islands)
6. Wreck diving in Great Lakes region
7. Bonne Terre Mine (near St. Louis)

Diving with Non-air Gas Mixtures: Nitrox, Heliox, Trimix, et. al

WHAT IS NITROX?

Nitrox is a gas mixture of oxygen and nitrogen, but with a higher oxygen percentage than found in ordinary air. As a result of its higher oxygen concentration, the percentage of nitrogen in nitrox is always *lower* than in air. There are two standard mixtures of Nitrox recognized by NOAA for diving: Nitrox I and Nitrox II (see Table 1).

TABLE 1.

COMPOSITION OF AIR, NITROX I AND NITROX II

	%OXYGEN	%NITROGEN*
Air	21	79
Nitrox I	32	68
Nitrox II	36	64

* Included are trace inert gases such as argon, krypton and neon which together make up less than one percent.

Nitrox is usually prepared by mixing pure oxygen from one source (e.g., a tank of 100% oxygen) with air, until the desired oxygen concentration is reached (either 32% or 36%). Adding oxygen to air always lowers the percentage of nitrogen in the final nitrox mixture, because the sum of gas percentages cannot add up to more than 100%. The process requires quality control to assure the desired oxygen concentration is reached, and that the two gases are thoroughly mixed in whatever container holds the nitrox.

Synonyms of nitrox include "enriched air nitrogen" (EAN) and "oxygen-enriched air" (OEA). No matter what it is called, nitrox is not air and should not be called air. Also, when nitrox is discussed in relation to a specific dive profile it must always be qualified with the exact percentage of oxygen used; nitrox I and nitrox II have different risks.

WHY NITROX?

Nitrox provides a lower percentage of nitrogen than ordinary air. In this way less nitrogen will enter the body at a given depth and decrease the risk of two nitrogen-related problems: decompression sickness (DCS) and nitrogen narcosis. Both DCS and nitrogen narcosis result from increased nitrogen pressure, the former from bubble formation on ascent and the latter from nerve inhibition at depth.

It cannot be over emphasized that nitrox does NOT allow one to go deeper than with air. Instead, the decreased nitrogen percentage provides two advantages, which define the two principal reasons nitrox is used:

1) as a *time extender* for dives to recreational depths, i.e., ability to dive longer at a given depth than allowed for by standard air tables, without increasing the risk of developing DCS;
2) to *lessen the risk of developing DCS* for dive profiles that adhere to the standard air tables.

WHAT ARE THE HAZARDS OF NITROX?

Nitrox evolved from military and commercial diving, both considered professional activities. In professional settings, the blending process is tightly controlled, divers are highly trained, and a hyperbaric chamber is likely to be available at the diving site. In non-professional use of nitrox, it has become clear that a principal potential hazard is *oxygen toxicity*.

Going to any depth increases the partial pressure of oxygen that is inhaled. The recreational diver who goes to 130 fsw on compressed air has a blood oxygen (and nitrogen) pressure almost five times that at sea level. While at depth, the principal hazard of excess nitrogen pressure is nitrogen narcosis. But there is also an increased risk of oxygen toxicity. The oxygen pressure at 130 feet when diving with ordinary air would lead to oxygen toxicity if the diver stayed long enough. Because the recreational dive tables allow for only a short time at 130 feet, oxygen toxicity is not a problem.

When the percentage of inhaled oxygen is increased the risk of oxygen toxicity increases, particularly with deeper dives (100 to 130 feet). With nitrox you can stay at a given depth longer because there is less nitrogen in your body (and hence less risk of narcosis and DCS), but stay too long and you risk oxygen toxicity. Since the *first* manifestation of oxygen toxicity can be seizures, diving with nitrox can lead to drowning.

Simply put, nitrox is a two-edged sword: less nitrogen good, more oxygen bad. Oxygen toxicity is the limiting factor when diving with nitrox. Thus, to the usual major concerns associated with scuba diving (DCS and AGE), nitrox adds the possibility of oxygen toxicity. Anyone diving with nitrox needs to be aware of this potential hazard. Table 2 compares the atmospheres of oxygen (atm O_2) inhaled with air and with Nitrox I, when diving to 100 fsw and 130 fsw.

TABLE 2.
atm O_2 WITH AIR AND NITROX I

depth	atm	air (21% O_2)	Nitrox I (32% O_2)
100 fsw	4.03	.85	1.29
130 fsw	4.94	1.04	1.58

WHY ISN'T NITROX ROUTINELY USED BY RECREATIONAL DIVERS?

For several reasons the use of nitrox by recreational divers is controversial. Nitrox has to be specially prepared; proper use requires special training; and there are differences in philosophy about what should be included in the purview of recreational diving.

As nitrox entered into non-professional diving a significant problem became apparent: poor quality control. The same quality control achievable in military, scientific and commercial applications was not always found in facilities promoting nitrox to the recreational diver.

Compressed air for scuba diving is universally available because, basically, air is air. The air compressor used to fill a tank to 3000 psi either works or it doesn't. There is little to go wrong. Impurities can enter compressed air but that problem is preventable by good maintenance and proper positioning of the compressor with respect to environmental exhausts.

Nitrox is different. Nitrox has to be specially prepared, and without good quality control the resulting mixture may not contain the specified amount of oxygen. You can be sure that compressed air has 21% oxygen because that's the composition of air, but you can't be sure a tank of Nitrox I has 32% oxygen, and not 30% or 34%. A couple of percentage points one way or the other could make a difference in the safety of the dive. Nitrox experts recommend that the composition of tank gas be measured *before each dive*. Because of the need for special equipment (in preparing the mixture and then measuring its makeup), most dive shops are not equipped to offer nitrox.

A second reason nitrox is not routinely used is that it requires additional training. Air-trained divers are *not* trained to dive with nitrox. Nitrox diving requires more education about the risks of oxygen toxicity and the importance of measuring the gas composition before diving. No air-certified diver should use nitrox unless accompanied by a qualified nitrox instructor (or has otherwise completed an accredited training course).

The third reason has to do with differences in philosophy. Some people in the dive industry believe nitrox complicates the recreational experience, and that it should be used only by the "technical" diver, never by the casual diver who puts on scuba gear once or twice a year. People of this philosophy readily concede the potential benefits of nitrox, but believe the potential hazards far outweigh those benefits for recreational divers and the recreational diving industry. They are openly afraid the casual diver will abuse the mixture, that the typical dive shop will not be able to maintain adequate quality control, and that the overall result will be an increase in diving accidents and bad publicity for the industry. These people don't want to see nitrox promoted to the recreational diver.

On the opposite side are many scuba enthusiasts who see this attitude as regressive, as inhibiting growth of the industry and enrichment of the scuba experience. They are passionate about the benefits of nitrox, and feel anyone who is certified for open water can be properly trained in use of nitrox, and that it should be widely available. They point out that exceeding the limits can (and does) happen with compressed air, and feel nitrox is no more dangerous than air if used properly. They also point out how scuba has changed dramatically in the last three decades, and see nitrox as just one more evolutionary advancement whose "time has come."

In truth, both groups have good arguments. Nitrox would complicate the scuba experience, and not just for the occasional diver, but for the dive operator who must make it available. On the other hand, nitrox does offer advantages if properly used. It is probably just a matter of time before nitrox becomes an option to compressed air at many dive resorts. Like other aspects of recreational diving (for example, the dive computer), nitrox can be a great benefit if divers learn to use it wisely *and* do so.

For all the reasons indicated, nitrox diving comes under the general heading of technical diving. It is a semantic argument whether or not nitrox should instead be part of "recreational diving." Anyone who chooses to dive with nitrox should just be aware of its benefits and potential hazards, and obtain proper training. As long as those goals are accomplished, it is not particularly relevant what label the activity goes by.

BUT IS NITROX DANGEROUS?

Nitrox has actually received "bad press" from much of the recreational dive community, for reasons explained above. The bad press is largely undeserved because nitrox, per se, is not dangerous. In fact, its purpose is to make diving safer than with compressed air, by lowering the risk of decompression sickness. Problems occur when nitrox is abused, such as staying longer on deep dives or going deeper than allowed. The hazards include:

- using an improperly mixed gas composition
- going deeper than allowed
- staying longer than allowed at a given depth

If all nitrox divers limited themselves to 130 feet *and* used the standard air tables, nitrox would be safer than diving with air, as the risk of decompression sickness and nitrogen narcosis should be lower. This is a big "if." After all, one of the two reasons divers use nitrox is because it allows them to stay down *longer* than with compressed air (since less nitrogen is taken up for a given time at depth).

TEST YOUR UNDERSTANDING

1. You are diving with nitrox I to a depth of 60 feet. Your computer, designed for air use only, states you can stay at this depth for 40 minutes. Since you are using nitrox, you can:

   a. stay an extra 5 minutes
   b. stay an extra 10 minutes
   c. stay no longer than your computer indicates
   d. do what you want

2. For nitrox I at recreational depths and times, compared with compressed air, all of the following are true *except one*:

   a. less risk of nitrogen narcosis
   b. more risk of oxygen toxicity
   c. less risk of decompression sickness
   d. less risk of arterial gas embolism
   e. more risk of improper air mix

3. Valid reasons for objecting to use of nitrox in recreational diving include all of the following *except one*:

   a. greater cost than air
   b. more difficult to prepare
   c. special knowledge and training required
   d. greater risk of Type II decompression sickness
   e. greater risk of oxygen toxicity

WHO CERTIFIES FOR NITROX DIVING?

In the past decade many reliable Nitrox training facilities have opened up around the country. Many of these are regular dive shops that have decided to enter the field of nitrox diving; they train divers under the auspices of a national certification agency.

In the early days of nitrox diving there were only two agencies which sanctioned nitrox and arranged for standards of use: ANDI (American Nitrox Divers International) and IANTD (International Association of Nitrox and Technical Divers). Now there are several nitrox training programs, including those developed by traditional open water agencies such as PADI (see Section S for listings).

WHAT IS HELIOX?

Heliox is a mixture of helium and oxygen used for very deep diving, usually to greater than 220 feet. Helium's great advantage is that it does not lead to nitrogen narcosis. Helium diving requires as much or more decompression time as nitrogen, so there is no saving there. Beyond 300 feet heliox may cause the 'high pressure nervous syndrome,' a shaking sensation that can be incapacitating. Another disadvantage of helium is that it conducts heat about six times faster than nitrogen, so divers get colder than with air diving. A third problem is caused by the fact that helium is much less dense than nitrogen or air; as a result, the vocal cords vibrate much faster and divers sound like Donald Duck. Professional divers can use voice unscramblers to make their speech intelligible.

Overall, helium offers no advantage for recreational divers. Diving with heliox is strictly for technical and commercial divers.

WHAT IS TRIMIX?

Trimix is a mixture of oxygen, helium and nitrogen. Nitrogen, usually in a small percentage (e.g., 15%), is added back to heliox to create trimix, in order to lessen the risk of the high pressure nervous syndrome seen with helium breathing. Nitrogen slows down nerve conduction.

Trimix is used for the deepest dives, usually greater than 400 feet. Like Heliox, Trimix is strictly for non-recreational use: military, scientific, commercial, and advanced technical diving.

ARE THERE OTHER GAS MIXTURES USED FOR SCUBA DIVING?

Several other gas mixtures have been used, such as hydrogen-oxygen, argon-oxygen, and neon-oxygen. These mixtures are all in the realm of technical and experimental diving. The goal with any non-air mixture, of course, is to dive deeper or longer than can safely be accomplished with compressed air. It is apparent that, for a long time to come, recreational diving as we know it will be done only with mixtures of oxygen and nitrogen.

Answers to TEST YOUR UNDERSTANDING

1. c. Unless your computer is designed to incorporate nitrox diving, you must follow the standards for air diving.

2. d. Less risk of arterial gas embolism is *not* afforded by nitrox.

3. d. There is no greater risk of Type II DCS with nitrox.

REFERENCES AND BIBLIOGRAPHY

See references for Sections B-E, plus the following.

Mount, T, Gilliam B: *Mixed Gas Diving*. Watersport Publishing Co., San Diego, 1993.
Betts EA. *Introduction to Enriched Air Diving*. American Nitrox Divers Association, 74
    Woodcleft Avenue, Freeport, N.Y. 11520; 1994.

DIVING ODDS N' ENDS

Highest-altitude Dives

In the 1993 *Guinness Book of Records*, the record altitude dive was listed as 16,200 ft. in the Himalayan lake Donag-Tsho (Nepal). The dive was accomplished by Frank B. Mee, Dr. John Leach and Dr. Andy McLean on March 4, 1989, to a depth of 92 feet.

In the 1994 Guinness book, the record was changed to a dive made years earlier, by Richard Weihrauch of Germany. He is credited with diving in a shallow crater lake inside the dormant Mexican volcano Popocatépetl, which is at an altitude of 16,509 ft. This dive was made on November 20, 1983.

Ah, but records are made to be broken. The 1997 Guinness states that in 1994 and 1995, several divers, including Johann Reinhard and Henri Garcia, explored a shallow crater lake situated between Chile and Bolivia. The altitude? An incredible 19,357 ft.

DIVING ODDS N' ENDS

The Compleat Goggler - Guy Gilpatric

Guy Gilpatric pioneered the modern sport of spear fishing when he discovered how easy it was to hunt for fish with watertight goggles (see Section A). His book, *The Compleat Goggler*, published in 1938, was widely read at the time. Less well known is an article by the same name, published in the Saturday Evening Post October 6, 1934. Excerpts:

...The first thing you need, to be a successful goggle fisher, is a body of good clear water. Personally, I use the Mediterranean Sea, and there is still plenty of room in it; but parts of the Atlantic, most of the Pacific and all of the Mexican Gulf and the Caribbean will do just as well, and I know of many American lakes and streams which provide grand goggling. Next you need a pair of watertight goggles. I made my first pair myself from an old pair of flying goggles, plugging up the ventilating holes with putty and painting over it. The ones I now use were built for pearl diving...

...Here are some of the things we have learned: When you have let out your breath to go down, go down feet first until you are completely underwater; then, but not until then, lean forward and swim toward the fish. If you go down head first, you break the surface as you dive and drag with you air which rises in silver bubbles like sparks behind a rocket. All this frightens the fish. A feet-first descent doesn't cause a ripple or a bubble. Remember that though your lungs are empty and that you are therefore heavier than water, a couple of strokes with your free hand will shoot you up to the surface. Although you cannot remain under as long with empty lungs as with full, because you have no air to exhale as sort of last-gasp reserve, you save strength and avoid water disturbances because you have no buoyancy to struggle against. My useful limit underwater is about fifty seconds; a goggle-fishing disciple of mine can stay two minutes, which I thought extraordinary until I heard of a Red Sea pearl diver's record of six minutes. This time seems incredible, but I have it on good authority...

DIVING ODDS N' ENDS

Ocean Facts

- The world's oceans are one vast interconnected body of water, commonly referred to as the *world ocean*. The world ocean covers approximately 142,000,000 sq. miles, or 70.1% of the earth's surface, and has three main divisions: the Pacific Ocean (63,800,000 sq. miles); the Atlantic Ocean (33,420,000 sq. miles); and the Indian Ocean (28,350,500 sq. miles). Many geographers consider the Arctic and Antarctic oceans extensions of the other three divisions.

- The volume of the world ocean is approximately 326,000,000 cubic miles.

- The salt content varies by location, and averages about 35 parts per thousand (ppt) by weight; the range is 33 to 36 ppt.

- The deepest part of the ocean so far measured is a section of the Pacific's Mariana Trench, southwest of Guam: 36,198 ft. The bathyscaphe *Trieste* visited this trench in 1960, reaching a depth of 35,820 ft. (see Section A). The deepest parts of the Atlantic and Indian Oceans are, respectively, the Puerto Rico Trench (28,374 ft.) and the Java Trench (23,376 ft.). Average depths of the three oceans are similar: Pacific, 12,925 ft.; Atlantic, 11,730 ft.; Indian 12,598 ft.

- The continental shelf is the gently sloping floor of the ocean surrounding the continents, from sea level to a depth of about 600 feet. Its width varies from almost nothing to 800 miles, with an average about 30 miles. Where the shelf leaves off the continental slope begins, reaching depths of 5,000 to 11,000 feet.

- Scientists divide all living things in the ocean into three groups: the plankton, the nekton and the benthos. Plankton includes all plants and animals that drift about with the tides and currents; they are subdivided into phytoplankton (microscopic plants such as diatoms) and the larger zoo-plankton, which includes animals like the jellyfish and copepods.

- The nekton comprises all animals that can swim about, including fishes, squids and whales. An estimated 13,300 species of fish live in the sea, ranging in size from 40 feet (whale shark) to less than one inch long (gobies).

- The benthos includes all bottom-dwelling life, both plants (kelp, sea grasses) and animals (starfish, corals, anemones)

Women and Diving

DOES ONE'S SEX AFFECT SCUBA DIVING?

There are two answers to this important question. The short answer is "no." Much has been written about the difference between men and women divers, and no self respecting dive columnist would stop with such a simple answer. But the fact is, the differences between men and women regarding scuba diving are, with one exception, *minor and not significant.* The one exception, of course, is pregnancy, which I will discuss in a later question.

The long answer is that women, on average, have smaller lungs, a lower aerobic capacity, a greater percentage of body fat, and less upper body strength than men, and these differences have some effects on diving. Women tend to use less air/minute than men (because of their smaller lung volume), but in recreational diving that is rarely an important factor. Women may not have the same capacity for extreme physical exertion as men, but that too is of little consequence in recreational diving. Since women have a higher percentage of body fat than men, in theory they should have better tolerance to cold water. Although some think the higher percentage of body fat increases the risk of DCS, there is really no solid evidence to support this belief (discussed below).

The long answer also recognizes that the menstrual period poses some concern for women, but this is not ordinarily a limitation. The long answer must also include the observation that men as a group seem to take more risks than women, and as a result show up more frequently in mortality statistics associated with cave, deep, and mixed gas diving.

However, except for pregnancy, the anatomic differences between men and women are simply not a big deal when it comes to scuba diving. Either sex can learn to become quite proficient both as a recreational diver or as a scuba diving professional.

ARE WOMEN AT GREATER RISK THAN MEN FOR DEVELOPING DECOMPRESSION ILLNESS?

Women have on average 10% more subcutaneous fat than men. Since fat tissue can hold five times more nitrogen than blood, it has been suggested that women might be more susceptible to decompression sickness (DCS) than men. However, the few studies in this area are inconclusive. Some studies have suggested an increase in DCS among women, while others have not found any difference. If you read the literature on the subject, there appears to be "some controversy"; however, I believe this merely reflects that the data are insufficient to show a difference one way or the other. Not controversial, of course, is the risk of DCS *simply from diving*. Women need to be every bit as cautious as men in this activity. Until some respected agency comes out with a different set of dive tables for men and women, it is safe to assume the risk for DCS is the same or about the same, and not worry about it.

As for the other component of decompression illness - arterial gas embolism - there are no reports of an excess incidence in women. Also, the incidence of patent foramen ovale (a theoretical predisposition to arterial embolism) is the same in women and men.

Overall, women do not seem over-represented in DAN's yearly compilation of diving accident statistics. Of course, the great unknown (as with many other diving accident statistics) is the number of people at risk. Personal experience, as well as the vast panoply of scuba literature, suggest as many women as men enjoy recreational diving.

When scuba first became popular there were very few women divers (Jacques Cousteau's wife Simone was probably the very first, in the 1940s). Now, about half of newly-certified divers are women. There is nothing in scuba instructors' collective experience to indicate that women have a greater risk than men for developing decompression illness.

In summary, inconclusive studies, as well as lack of any perceived gender-related problems by professionals in the field, suggest there is no increased risk of DCS and AGE among women divers.

WHAT ABOUT PSYCHOLOGICAL DIFFERENCES BETWEEN MEN AND WOMEN REGARDING SCUBA DIVING?

As already mentioned, men on average seem to take more risks than women. Apart from this observation, which may account for the disproportionate number of men who engage in technical (as opposed to recreational) diving, there seem to be no important psychological differences between men and women that would affect scuba diving.

DO CHANGES DURING MENSTRUATION POSE ANY RISK?

Again, there are no conclusive studies to answer this question. Repeated exposure to hyperbaric pressure has not been shown to affect hormone regulation, ovulation, or menstruation.

Many women are concerned that menstrual bleeding itself could attract sharks or other predators. However, with tampons this is simply not a problem. It is not even clear that it would be a problem without a tampon; the amount of blood that would be released into the water from menstruation during a 30 or 45-minute dive is minuscule. Some women have experienced a greater menstrual flow when diving, but this has not posed any significant problem either. Thus, it appears safe to dive during the menstrual period providing, of course, the woman feels healthy. Obviously any woman who suffers severe menstrual cramps, headaches, or other symptoms related to her period should refrain from diving until fully recovered.

DO ORAL CONTRACEPTIVES POSE A RISK TO WOMEN DIVERS?

There are no data to indicate that use of oral contraceptives increases risk of diving accidents. We know that oral contraceptives and smoking increase the risk of stroke, but smoking is bad for divers in any case. Oral contraceptives have also been associated with increased rates of blood clotting ("thrombo-embolic" disease) and mild hypertension, particularly in women over age 35. However, if oral contraceptives cause the woman no problem on land, there should be no problem underwater.

WHAT ABOUT DIVING DURING PREGNANCY?

A short exposure to increased ambient pressure, per se, appears of no consequence to the fetus. However some studies on pregnant animals have shown an increased rate of fetal abnormality from decompression sickness, particularly among sheep; different studies in other animals have not shown an ill effect on the fetus. Like many other medical conditions, the available studies on this issue are inconclusive.

Based on what is known about pregnancy, and about diving, my recommendation (and that of most physicians) is that pregnant women should not dive. There are three reasons for this blanket recommendation. First, pregnancy is only nine months, a relatively short period in one's life; it is simply not worth taking any unnecessary risks by subjecting the unborn child to an abnormal environment. The body experiences marked pressure changes underwater, changes that are believed to be safe for adults who follow recreational guidelines. However, considering that accidents do occur, diving is riskier than not diving. We have so little information about decompression on the developing fetus, and much of the information is conflicting, that common sense suggests any risk is simply not worth taking.

The second reason against diving while pregnant has to do with treatment of diving injuries. If a pregnant diver does develop DCS or gas embolism, she will be referred for hyperbaric therapy. Hyperbaric therapy poses a theoretical risk to the unborn child, because of the high oxygen pressures. The developing eye of a fetus is particularly prone to oxygen toxicity. Although non-diving pregnant woman have been successfully treated with hyperbaric therapy (for carbon monoxide poisoning), there is always concern a fetus could be harmed, especially if multiple treatments are needed.

It has been recommended by some authors that pregnant women who do dive stay shallower than 33 feet (less than 2 atmospheres total); the rationale is that shallow diving should at least prevent any risk of the bends. However, there are no data to support this recommendation, and a sensitive fetus might not like *any* increase in nitrogen or oxygen pressure. Certainly the risk of air embolism is not diminished by staying shallow.

The third reason against diving is that pregnancy is often accompanied by changes which could make a dive uncomfortable, if not downright hazardous. These changes include frequent bouts of nausea ("morning sickness"), gastric reflux (from the enlarged uterus), and discomfort from increased abdominal girth. In theory a woman could become nauseous on the dive boat (abetted by any sea sickness), experience regurgitation underwater, and then lose her weight belt as she tries to adjust it for her larger size - all on one dive!

In summary, it is a strong recommendation that any woman who is pregnant (or thinks she may be, or is trying to become) refrain from diving.

HOW SOON CAN ONE DIVE AFTER PREGNANCY?

I would leave this decision up to the woman and her obstetrician. The answer should depend on how quickly the woman has regained her strength, whether the delivery was vaginal or by C-section, whether there are any post-partum complications, etc. A general recommendation is that the woman should be able to return to diving when she feels back to her baseline health *and* has medical clearance to resume strenuous activity.

WHAT SHOULD BE DONE IF A WOMAN INADVERTENTLY DIVES WHILE PREGNANT?

Although diving during pregnancy is definitely not recommended, on occasion a woman may dive without knowing she is pregnant (i.e., very early in gestation). This event should not be cause for alarm.

There is certainly no evidence to warrant pregnancy termination because the fetus was briefly exposed to higher pressures. However, if the dive was complicated by injury to the woman, then the specifics of the case need to be discussed with the diver's obstetrician and, if necessary, a dive medicine specialist.

SHOULD WOMEN EXPECT SPECIAL TREATMENT WHEN SCUBA DIVING?

Ideally, no. The stereotype of a weak, mechanically disinterested, and/or uncoordinated female is out of date and harmful to both sexes. Any woman who expects that manual chores will be done for her (carrying her tank, attaching the regulator, etc.) *because* she is a woman, loses the opportunity to learn important skills and remain self-sufficient. Any man who abridges a woman's chance for self-sufficiency by insisting on doing things for her not only demeans her but also perpetuates an outdated stereotype. Also, if the woman is his dive buddy, he may weaken skills she may one day need to help *him*.

Scuba diving is a level playing field; it is no place for machismo behavior or sexism of any sort. Equality certainly reigns at the professional level. Hundreds of women instructors teach open water and advanced courses to men and women. Women run dive shops, operate dive boats and lead diving expeditions. Resorts that carry tanks, attach BC's or perform other dive-related chores for its customers do so for men and women alike. Obviously, scuba diving is no longer "a man's world" as it was perhaps a generation ago. Today, it should be as acceptable for a man to ask a woman for help with equipment or some other problem, as vice versa. When diving, women and men should want - and expect - to be treated as equals.

REFERENCES AND BIBLIOGRAPHY

An * indicates references that are especially recommended. Medical textbooks and journal articles can be obtained from most public libraries via inter-library loan.

Bernhardt TL, Goldman RW, Thombs PA, et al. Hyperbaric oxygen treatment of cerebral air embolism from orogenital sex during pregnancy. Critical Care Medicine 1988;16:729-30.

Bolton ME Scuba diving and fetal well-being: A survey of 208 women. Undersea Biomed Res 1980;7:183-9.

Bolton-Klug ME, Lehner CE, Lanphier EH, Rankin JHG. Lack of harmful effects from simulated dives in pregnant sheep. Amer Jour Obstetrics and Gynecology 1983;146:48-51.

Cole M. Women and diving. SPUMS J 1989;19:56-60.

Cresswell JE, St. Leger-Dowse M. Women and scuba diving. British Medical Journal 1991; 302:1590-1.

Newhall JF. Scuba diving during pregnancy: a brief review. Am J Obstet Gynecol 1981; 140: 893-4.

*O'Neill E, Morgan EJ. *When Women Dive. A Female's Guide to Both Diving and Snorkeling.* Watersport Publishing, Inc., San Diego, 1992..

Robertson AG. [Letter]. Decompression sickness in women. Undersea Biomed Res 1992; 19:217-8.

Robinson TJ. [Letter]. Decompression sickness in women divers. Undersea Biomed Res 1988;15:65.

Taylor MB. Women in diving. Alert Diver. May/June 1990; p. 1-6.

*Taylor MB. Women and diving. Chapter 13 in: Bove AA, Davis JC; *Diving Medicine,* 2nd Edition, W.B. Saunders Co., Philadelphia, 1990.

Van Hoessen KB, Camporesi EM, Moon RE, et al. Should hyperbaric oxygen be used to treat the pregnant patient for acute carbon monoxide poisoning? JAMA 1989;261:12039-43.

Zwingelberg KM, Knight MA, Biles JB. Decompression sickness in women divers. Undersea Biomed Res 1987;14:311-7.

DIVING ODDS N' ENDS

Coral Reef Facts

- There are two main types of coral, *hard* and *soft*. Living coral reefs are made up of hard corals, which take calcium out of the seawater and excrete skeletons of calcium carbonate (limestone). They are found only in warmer waters (>65°F or 18°C) because the polyps don't survive in colder temperatures. Coral reefs are also found only at shallow depths because of their need for sunlight to survive.

- Soft corals, often found on or around hard coral reefs, don't excrete a limestone skeleton. Soft coral includes gorgonions (sea fans and sea whips), which have internal skeletons of a flexible, horny substance.

- The individual coral polyp is a coelenterate, a large group of animals that includes jellyfishes and sea anemones. The coral polyp is typically less than one inch in diameter. It is the ability of coral polyps to form colonies that gives the fantastic shapes and colors visible on a coral reef.

- Coral reefs occupy only 0.17% of the world ocean, or some 238,000 square miles. The three types of coral reefs are: 1) fringing reefs, submerged platforms that extend from the shore into the sea; 2) barrier reefs, which follow the shoreline but are seperated from it by water; and 3) atolls, ring-shaped coral islands in the open sea; an atoll is often the rim of an open volcano, and is most common in the South Pacific.

- The world's largest reef system is the Great Barrier Reef which runs for about 1250 miles down the eastern coast of Australia; second in size is the Belize Barrier Reef.

- One of the biggest natural predators of coral is the crown-of-thorns starfish, which has destroyed many coral formations. Other natural hazards include boring marine worms and storms.

DIVING ODDS N' ENDS

Ciguatera and Scombroid Poisoning

Two major types of fish poisoning are called ciguatera and scombroid. They are very different.

Ciguatera poisoning is the most frequently reported seafood-related disease in the U.S. It occurs from toxins (ciguatoxin and others) supplied by dino-flagellates that are ingested by plant-eating fish. As these smaller fish are ingested by larger carnivorous fish, the toxin increases in quantity, until the larger fish is caught and eaten by humans. Thus larger and older fish tend to be more toxic. Most commonly implicated fish: barracuda, snapper, jack and grouper.

The dino-flagellate is named *Gambierdiscus toxicus*. Common in the Caribbean and Indo-Pacific islands, *G. toxicus* has been found in over 400 species of tropical reef fish. No known processing procedures, including cooking, are protective, so ciguatera poisoning is hard to prevent; presence of the toxins in fish does not affect their appearance, smell or taste.

Symptoms of ciguatera poisoning may begin minutes to hours after eating the fish, and include abdominal cramps, diarrhea, skin itching, skin tingling, headache, muscle aches, confusion, and facial pain. After initial recovery the victim may have sensory changes for months. Death can result from respiratory muscle paralysis. The average duration of illness is about 8 days.

Treatment is supportive, although some patients have markedly improved with intravenous mannitol, a drug used to treat brain edema (excess water on the brain). Improvement of confusion in the treated patients suggests they were suffering from brain edema.

* * *

Scombroid poisoning resembles an acute allergic reaction. It comes from eating the breakdown products of certain types of fish which are improperly prepared for consumption.

Scombroid poisoning can occur from eating fish of the Scombridae family (origin of its name), including mackerel, tuna and bonito; it can also occur from eating non-Scombridae fish such as mahi-mahi, bluefish and amberjack. Bacterial decomposition after the fish is caught produces high levels of histamine and other toxic substances in the fish's flesh. Although at one time histamine was thought to be the sole culprit, other substances probably account for many of the symptoms.

The responsible toxin or toxins cause an immediate reaction (within 30 minutes of eating), characterized by facial flushing, sweating and a burning sensation of the mouth and throat. Other symptoms include nausea, vomiting, pain, large skin welts, blurred vision and asthma. Symptoms usually last anywhere from 4 to 24 hours, rarely longer.

Treatment is usually symptomatic. Antihistamines may be effective. At least one report has found intravenous cimetidine effective; this is a type of histamine blocker used to treat stomach ulcers.

Medical Fitness for Diving: Guidelines Real and Imagined

ARE THERE REGULATIONS REGARDING WHO MAY SCUBA DIVE?

No. There are no local, state or federal laws regulating recreational scuba diving. Some regulations apply to certain aspects of equipment, such as tank inspection and air compressor maintenance, but there are no regulations regarding *divers*.

New applicants for certification may be required to obtain medical clearance if they acknowledge a problem on their health questionnaire, but there is nothing to compel an applicant to admit an active medical problem. On the other hand, relatively few physicians are familiar with scuba diving, so an encounter between diver-with-medical-question and a physician may not result in correct advice or information. Even when physicians are knowledgeable in this area, there is apt to be disagreement about what disqualifies people from diving.

WHO IS *FIT* FOR DIVING?

Before discussing medical conditions that might prohibit diving, it will be useful to discuss fitness in a general sense. In Section B, I explained that diving requires at least a sound mind, heart and lungs. Beyond these basics, much has been written about physical fitness for diving, including the subjects of exercise, nutrition, and physical stamina.

Clearly one does not have to be an athlete or body builder to dive. On the other hand, diving is not recommended for true "couch potatoes" either. It is probably risky to be sedentary in life style - overweight, no exercise, no routine physical exertion on the job or otherwise - and then go diving. Diving physicians believe that the more physically fit the individual, the less risk in diving. There are several cogent reasons for scuba divers to be physically fit.

1) Diving can be strenuous. It can require sudden bursts of physical exertion such as when swimming against a current, climbing onto an unsteady boat, or rescuing a buddy. Obviously the more fit you are, the better you can handle heightened physical requirements. Many a diver has "tired

out" and had to be rescued because he didn't have the stamina for unexpected physical stress.

2) Physically fit people tend to use less air than the unfit. Hyperventilation and panic stress reactions are more likely to occur in the physically unfit.

3) Physical fitness reduces the risk of heart attack, which is a major cause of diving fatality.

4) Physical fitness may reduce the risk of developing DCS.

Apart from the exercise jocks, how does someone know if they are physically fit? Sophisticated exercise testing can give numbers to go by, but such tests are cumbersome, expensive and hardly necessary (with the exception of testing for underlying heart disease). In truth, if the question is just about overall physical fitness, and not about underlying heart disease, *you* are probably the best judge. You are probably *physically fit* for scuba diving if you can swim several laps in the pool without difficulty (the basic swimming test for enrollment in a scuba certification course), ride a bicycle for half an hour, or jog a half mile without collapsing. Certainly if you perform aerobic exercise regularly you are probably physically fit.

You are probably *physically unfit* if you don't regularly exercise, or you are short of breath with simple efforts like stair climbing or brisk walking, or you exceed 20% of your ideal body weight and/or smoke heavily. In other words, the question of physical fitness for an activity like scuba diving is mostly one of common sense. Common sense suggests that, since a scuba diver's life may depend on heavy physical exertion at some point, you should not be grossly overweight, should not smoke, and you should engage in some aerobic exercise on a frequent basis. The exercise could be bicycling, running, swimming, racquet sports, or any other aerobic activity. (Exceptions to this recommendation are physically impaired people who may take special training to go scuba diving; see below.)

CAN ONE DIVE WHILE TAKING A DECONGESTANT?

Generally, yes. Decongestants are commonly employed to clear up nasal inflammation and to help shrink mucous membranes in the head. They are not treatment for infection of ears or sinuses, but only for symptomatic relief of mild head congestion. Over-the-counter decongestants commonly employed include Dimetapp, Sudafed, and various acetaminophen (Tylenol) preparations combined with an antihistamine.

Some caveats: you should feel well, not have any side effects from the medication (such as drowsiness or dizziness), and be able to clear your ears without difficulty.

WHAT CONDITIONS SHOULD PROHIBIT DIVING?

Table 1 lists conditions that physicians involved in dive medicine generally regard as permanently prohibitive of scuba diving. Table 2 lists conditions that are self-limiting or treatable, and that would prohibit diving only until resolved or adequately treated. Table 3 lists chronic conditions that might or might not prohibit diving, depending on a medical assessment. In reviewing these lists, keep in mind the following:

- As explained above, scuba diving can be a physically demanding activity when everything goes well; it can become more so when there are adverse conditions such as waves, current, poor visibility, faulty equipment, etc. People not in good health should not dive.

Table 1.
Conditions that should prohibit scuba diving
(* Surveys reveal that some people
with these conditions do engage in scuba diving; see text.)

Any significant, exercise-limiting problem. Examples: angina [heart pain], chronic asthma, heart failure, cardiomyopathy [heart muscle weakness], cardiac arrhythmia that limits exercise, pulmonary insufficiency, high blood PCO_2 or low PO_2 (an indication of serious respiratory insufficiency), vertigo or other nervous system instability.

Presence of non-ventable air spaces, e.g., bullous emphysema, blebs.

History of air embolism from ruptured lung

History of spontaneous pneumothorax

Serious ear problems, such as: permanent perforation of tympanic membrane; chronic middle or inner ear infection; Meniere's disease

Psychiatric or emotional instability

*Epilepsy requiring drug treatment for prevention of seizures

*Diabetes requiring insulin for control of blood sugar levels

*Asthma requiring drug treatment for control of symptoms

Alcoholism or other dependency on mind-altering drugs

Sickle cell disease

Hemophilia or other severe clotting disorders

Cystic fibrosis

Diffuse scarring in the lungs from any cause (e.g., idiopathic pulmonary fibrosis, sarcoidosis, pneumoconiosis)

The problem is in defining "good health." From the diver's point of view, he or she should feel well, not be fatigued, and have no medical problem that might affect diving.

• From the physician's point of view, good health means at least a good heart and lungs, a sound mind, and no significant problem with ears or sinuses. Any impairment of heart or lung function, any mental impairment, or any blockage of ears or sinuses could be disastrous underwater. There are other medical problems, of course, which can affect safe diving, but the main concerns are heart, lung or mental impairment, and blockage of air passages in the head.

• Someone physically disabled from a musculoskeletal problem, such as leg or arm paralysis, might safely scuba dive under certain conditions. There are programs to train physically-disabled divers, who then can dive with unimpaired buddies. The Handicapped Scuba Association trains scuba instructors who wish to certify disabled people for diving (see Section S).

TABLE 2.
Conditions or situations that should delay scuba diving until resolved or treated

Anemia (low blood count)
Sinusitis or sinus infection
Ear infection (any type)
Head or chest cold
Continuous cough
Pregnancy
Acute orthopedic or musculoskeletal problems that impair underwater movement (e.g., a broken arm or leg)
Use of anti-anxiety or sedative medications
Any acute impairment in vision (e.g., eye infection, need for an eye patch)

• A non-diver with any of the conditions in Table 1 will invariably be advised not to take up the sport. However, experienced divers who develop any of these conditions (among those that can be acquired) often keep on diving. There is documentation that some asthmatics who use medication, some insulin-dependent diabetics, and some epileptics taking anti-seizure medication, do dive. If these people feel fit and secure with their skills, they may never ask anyone "for clearance." Alternatively, some experienced divers with these and other medical problems are concerned enough to consult a diving specialist. Depending on the problem, the specialist may do an evaluation and then offer advice based on the specific findings.

This dual standard between new and experienced divers is not as illogical as it may first appear. For most divers it takes at least 50 dives to feel fully comfortable in the water. Some skills like buoyancy control only come with experience and much trial and error. A specialist in diving medicine will be more inclined to allow an experienced diver to return to scuba after, say, a heart operation, than for a similar patient who has never been underwater to take up the sport. Whether medically condoned or not, the fact is that many people with some of the medical conditions listed in Table 1 do scuba dive.

TABLE 3.

Chronic conditions that require careful medical evaluation before diving.

Any chronic orthopedic or musculoskeletal problem that impairs underwater movement

Any chronic heart condition, including cardiomyopathy, arrhythmias, heart failure, heart valve disease, and coronary artery disease.

History of decompression sickness, Type I ("the bends") or Type II (neurologic, pulmonary or cardiac involvement)

Asthma without current symptoms (see Section O)

Any recent respiratory infection, e.g., pneumonia, bronchitis, sinusitis

History of pulmonary embolism (blood clot in the lungs)

History of thoracic, chest or heart surgery

Use of anti-coagulants (blood thinners)

Hypertension under treatment

Massive obesity

Non-insulin-dependent diabetes

Any history of ear or sinus surgery

• Determining medical suitability for diving is often a matter of opinion. Given the existence of a medical problem about which there are differing opinions, many physicians will opt for the safe route and rule against diving. It is up to the patient to take any medical advice, of course. An alternative water activity that can carry great pleasure with little risk is snorkeling - using mask, fins, and snorkel to swim on the surface while viewing underwater marine life.

- Boyle's law explains why patients with wheezing, sinus congestion, colds and ear infections should not dive until fully recovered; and why patients with bullous lung disease (abnormal pockets of air within the lungs) should never dive. Any air space that cannot be vented or equalized presents serious potential hazard to the scuba diver. Divers with prohibitive medical problems may rationalize that they can avoid trouble by staying shallow, e.g., diving to less than 35 feet. While shallow diving will prevent nitrogen narcosis and decompression sickness, the risk of barotrauma is actually greater near the surface, because of the larger percentage change in air space volume (see Section D).

- Any doubtful case should be discussed with, or referred to, a diving medicine specialist (see Section R for information on DAN).

WHY ARE SOME CONDITIONS CONTROVERSIAL FOR DIVING?

Controversy results from disagreement among specialists about who should not dive. These disagreements usually appear in journal articles, in public forums such as scuba diving conferences, and when physicians and scuba instructors talk among themselves. There are five reasons for controversy about medical fitness for diving; these reasons are listed in the box and then explained in detail.

MEDICAL FITNESS FOR DIVING:
REASONS FOR CONTROVERSY

1. Objections for a given medical condition are largely theoretical
2. Lack of good evidence to support theoretical objection
3. Wide variability for each condition
4. Affected people with the condition do dive
5. Differences in philosophy about participation

---

1. For many conditions there are sound theoretical objections to diving, and these objections are often put forth by acknowledged medical experts. Thus, it "makes sense" to write in a medical journal that anyone who might have an asthma attack underwater, or who might develop a heart attack while diving, should not participate. It also makes sense that, if a diver's lungs trap air, there is a high risk of lung

rupture and air embolism; or that, if a diver ever had a seizure before diving, he might have another seizure at depth and drown. Since scuba diving is voluntary and recreational, it is hard to argue against such seemingly plausible, albeit theoretical, objections.

2. On the other hand, someone who really wants to dive has a right to say, "show me why not." And guess what? Typically, there is no good evidence to *prove* that more accidents occur among divers with theoretically risky conditions such as asthma, diabetes or epilepsy. This does not mean that diving with these and other medical conditions is safe, only that an increased risk can't be proved or disproved.

So the diver legitimately asks: if my condition is supposed to be so risky for diving, how come you can't prove it? There are several possible reasons why proof may be lacking.

- First, diving accidents are relatively rare, so it's hard to show any trend among specific causes. Less than 1000 diving accidents are reported to DAN each year out of hundreds of thousands or perhaps millions of divers (among North American residents); of the accidents, only about half are confirmed as meeting criteria for DCS or AGE. Thus, there may not be enough injured divers with a specific condition (e.g., asthma) to prove anything statistical.

- A second reason is that most scuba diving deaths are either due to an unforeseen event that could occur anywhere (such as sudden death from heart attack), to some catastrophe like "out of air," to entrapment in an overhead environment (e.g., a cave), or to panic; when these deaths are examined closely (including autopsies) there is no evidence to show that asthma, diabetes, epilepsy (or most other conditions considered 'at risk' for diving) played a significant role. The one major underlying condition often found on close examination of diving deaths is heart disease.

- Third, the theoretical objections may be correct, but only for the extremes of a given condition. People with Condition X who scuba dive may have the most stable state of that condition. Patients with the more severe form of Condition X may have selected themselves out of the diving population, either because they were advised against diving or because they experienced problems and dropped out on their own. This happened to one physician with asthma, who wrote about his experience in a medical journal (Martindale 1990).

Whatever the reasons, doctors and scientists like to prove things with studies, but studies *proving* an increased risk are lacking for all conditions listed in the Tables. Common sense prevails, of course, when there is obvious impairment. Only a fool would demand a "study" to prove that someone short of breath from emphysema or heart failure should not scuba dive.

3. Each diagnosis pertains to a diverse group of patients with a wide range of symptoms. Some asthmatics have symptoms only once every 10 years, whereas others have trouble every day. The statement that "asthma prohibits diving" will seem illogical if it is applied equally to both extremes.

   Similarly, some patients with diabetes require meticulous control of blood sugar with twice daily insulin injections, and other patients can be well controlled by diet alone. To state that "diabetics" should not dive is far too broad a prohibition, and sure to engender disagreement and controversy. In the real world, such broad and unqualified prohibitions serve no useful purpose.

4. It is a fact that many people with asthma, diabetes, epilepsy and other medical conditions *do dive*. Arguments against diving with a history of these and other "risky" conditions will not mean much to people who have been diving with the disease for years, without a mishap. This is certainly one reason for the controversy about asthma and diving (Section O).

5. Finally, controversy arises because of simple differences in philosophy about participation. Some physicians have a liberal attitude, exemplified by the statement that patients "should lead full lives without any personal restrictions" (Dreifuss 1985). Other physicians are more cautious, as exemplified by the statement that a patient "should take up another sport less risky for him and others" (Millington 1988). This variation in philosophy about risk-taking is prominent in opinions about asthma and diving (Section O).

The bottom line is that no one should be excluded from diving because of a diagnostic label, whether it be "asthma" or "diabetes" or whatever. Exclusion for a medical problem should take into account the person's current state of health, recent medical history, and a careful assessment of what is likely to occur under ordinary diving conditions. Sometimes evaluation is easy, sometimes difficult. Here are two examples.

Easy Decision: A 22 year-old man was referred by a disabled diving group for an evaluation. His diagnosis was Duchenne muscular dystrophy, a condition that weakens the muscles of the arms and legs. The diving instructor was prepared to begin training him in scuba, provided that he was otherwise fit. The request for evaluation was not unreasonable, since at the time the young man was driving a car and living independently. On exam he had some mild weakness of his upper arms, and a few other motor abnormalities related to muscular dystrophy. However, most disturbing was his recent history of shortness of breath. On further evaluation I found that he also had weakened heart muscle and heart failure, a complication of his basic disease. This finding made him physically unfit to scuba dive.

Difficult Decision: A 27 year-old man came for evaluation because "I foolishly checked asthma on my health form" (for a scuba certification course). He had a history of mild asthma and admitted to using an asthma inhaler "a couple of times" during the year. I explained that anyone needing an asthma inhaler probably should not scuba dive. This didn't concern him because, he said, he had already made several dives in resort courses and had experienced no problem. Furthermore, a buddy of his "uses an inhaler and has no trouble diving." Lung exam revealed no wheezing but a breathing test showed what doctors call a slight obstruction to air flow. However, he claimed to feel normal and thought that any prohibition to his diving was "ludicrous" because "I already dive." He just wanted to be certified, he said, and made it clear that he "could just start all over again with another dive shop." I agreed to reserve judgment until some more tests were done, but he did not return as scheduled. Presumably he went elsewhere.

WHY ARE SOME CONDITIONS CONSIDERED PROHIBITIVE FOR SCUBA DIVING?

Tables 1 through 3 include many common medical conditions, some of which warrant further discussion. (Asthma, which poses one of the most difficult decisions regarding fitness for scuba diving, is discussed at length in the next Section.) In all cases, of course, the individual with a medical situation should seek out personal medical advice.

Massive Obesity. There are two major concerns with massive obesity. One is the limitation of physical fitness. Massive obesity, which can be defined as either 50 pounds or 30% over ideal body weight, limits exercise, imposes a strain on the heart, and makes any physical activity riskier. Massively obese patients are simply not in "good shape" compared to normal weight people, and can be presumed to have increased risk for scuba diving.

The other concern with obesity is the increased risk of DCS. Fat takes up more nitrogen than other tissues and releases it more slowly, and many experts feel the massively obese person is at greater risk for

DCS. This may well be true but, like most issues relating to actual occurrence of DCS, there are no hard data to prove the point.

One rule of thumb is that an obese person should reduce bottom time in proportion to the extra weight. For example, a 20% overweight diver should shorten bottom time by 20%, so a 45 minute bottom time is reduced to 36 minutes. Obviously, this rule would mean that someone two to three times ideal body weight will have very little bottom time! For a diver triple his ideal body weight at, say, 450 lbs., a 45 minute bottom time drops to 15 minutes!

Diabetes. Diabetes is an imbalance of blood sugar due to insufficient insulin, the hormone that regulates blood sugar. Diabetics are prone not only to swings in blood sugar, but also to vascular disease that can affect the heart, kidneys, eyes, and other organs.

Concerns about diabetics and diving (Dembert 1986, Dembert 1987, Brouhard 1987, Wedman 1987) are similar to those for asthma. Whereas the decision point for asthma and diving often revolves around whether the diver takes medication to control symptoms, the decision point for diabetes often revolves around the need for insulin, a drug that can be used only by injection. Those requiring insulin to control blood sugar tend to have more severe diabetes, and "insulin-dependent" diabetics are more prone to large swings in blood sugar. The main concern is that an insulin-dependent diver might develop an "insulin reaction" underwater. An insulin reaction is the body's response to a very low blood sugar (hypoglycemia). Hypoglycemia, which occurs from too much insulin for the amount of carbohydrate in the blood, may arise from omitting a meal, from exercising, or from injecting too much insulin at any one time.

The effects of an insulin reaction, which can range from mild sweating to dizziness to coma, could be fatal underwater. Most physicians recommend that insulin-dependent diabetics not scuba dive. However, many insulin-dependent diabetics do dive, and without apparent difficulty.

A survey by DAN (Dear, et. al. 1994) among readers of Alert Diver was responded to by 116 diabetics, of whom 84 were insulin-dependent; 35% had been diving longer than 10 years and the median number of dives per diver was 100. Only one person had experienced decompression illness (AGE).

Seventy-two percent of the 116 diabetic divers checked their blood sugar before a dive and 52% checked it after a dive. Although the survey found "a significant incidence of hypoglycemia," the authors concluded that "Some diabetics can scuba dive safely," but "bias in the sample undoubtedly exists because the sample does not include diabetics who have discontinued diving because of complications."

Interestingly, 12% of divers reported low blood sugars while diving, but 44% reported experiencing hypoglycemia during exercise. Dr. Guy Dear, the senior author of the study, noted in Alert Diver: "...most divers told us that they carried out a variety of techniques to maintain a normal or elevated blood glucose while diving. These included eating extra candy, altering the dose of insulin or other drugs, and carefully regulating both the time of the dive and their meals of the day. The sample size of our survey was too small to make any meaningful comment about whether diabetes is a risk factor for decompression illness" (Dear 1994).

This information is similar to the asthma situation (Section O); many asthmatics use an inhaler and dive without apparent difficulty, but you will find neither condition (diabetes or asthma) sanctioned for diving. As Dr. Dear notes, "The decision of whether a new diver who has diabetes should be allowed to dive ultimately remains between the diver and his or her physician. This applies also to an established diver who is newly diagnosed as having diabetes."

Non-insulin-dependent diabetics may control their blood sugar with diet alone, or with a pill. For both insulin and non-insulin users, a decision about diving should be based not only on the theoretical risk of a hypoglycemic reaction, but on overall health. Diabetes is a major cause of heart, kidney and eye disease, so these areas should also be checked before the patient begins any underwater activity.

In summary, if the diabetic has well-controlled blood sugar levels, has no significant complications of the disease, and understands how to control for changing glucose needs with exercise, there should be no prohibition on diving. In this context, "well-controlled," "significant," and "understands" are terms best determined by the diabetic patient and a knowledgeable physician.

Epilepsy. Epilepsy poses some of the same concerns as diabetes and asthma. Instead of an asthma attack or insulin reaction underwater, the concern is for a seizure (Dreifuss 1985, Hill 1985, Meckelnburg 1985, Millington 1985, Green 1992). A seizure underwater will almost always lead to drowning, and for this reason most physicians would rule against diving for anyone who is at risk. Practically speaking, this means anyone who requires medication to suppress seizures.

A remote history of one seizure (perhaps related to some acute medical problem such as fever or infection), that has not required any medication, should not prohibit diving. Any potential diver with a seizure-related question should either not dive or else seek evaluation by a neurologist.

Anemia (low blood count). There are many causes and types of anemia and it is impossible to generalize about fitness for diving. The major problem from anemia is lack of oxygen carrying capacity and limitation of exercise tolerance. Mild anemia, often present in menstruating women, may pose no problem, but severe anemia can be life threatening in any exertional situation.

Sickle cell anemia is a genetic disease characterized by "sickling" or distortion of the oxygen-carrying red blood cells. Present almost exclusively in blacks, the disease is characterized by severe anemia (low blood count) and episodes of severe joint pains. In advanced cases organs like the lungs and the heart can become permanently damaged.

The painful "crises" seen in sickle cell anemia are thought to arise from increased sickling of the red blood cells, which can occur from stress, heavy exertion, hypoxia (low oxygen), etc. Each crisis usually requires treatment with strong pain medication and, occasionally, hospitalization. (A sickle crisis after diving would be indistinguishable from a severe case of the bends.) Physicians universally recommend that patients with sickle cell disease not scuba dive.

A disease genetically related to sickle cell disease, but vastly different clinically, is *sickle cell trait.* People with the trait have part of the abnormal gene found in sickle cell disease, but don't have the anemia, the painful crises or other problems associated with the disease. (Diagnosis requires a special blood test.) People with *sickle cell trait* are advised not to risk extremes of stress or any low-oxygen situation (e.g., mountain climbing), since under extreme conditions the "trait" cells can sickle (become distorted in shape). However, recreational scuba diving (where the oxygen levels are actually increased during a dive) does not pose any apparent increased risk to people with the trait. It is possible that an episode of decompression sickness may be made worse in someone with the trait (as there may be local tissue hypoxia), but this is theoretical only. As with most issues in this section, data are lacking to prove an increased risk.

If someone with sickle trait wishes to scuba dive, I recommend they first consult a physician to confirm the diagnosis and assure there is no accompanying blood disorder. If the only condition is sickle cell trait then there is no clear reason to prohibit recreational scuba diving. To be on the safe side, I recommend that such individuals dive very conservatively in order to minimize risk of developing DCS (e.g., 60 feet maximum depth, no more than two dives a day, and wait 24 hours to fly after any diving).

Thoracotomy (operation in which the chest has been opened such as with almost all heart surgery). Although some authors feel that thoracotomy is a contraindication to diving because of undetectable air trapping from scars or adhesions in the lungs, there are no studies on the subject. (It is interesting that Jacques Cousteau suffered an accident in 1936 that broke several ribs and punctured his lung; see Diving Odds N' Ends, Section H.) A post-thoracotomy patient who insists on diving should have a thorough physical exam, plus chest x-ray and CT scan; the presence of any air pocket should preclude diving (Mellem 1990). If the tests are equivocal, and the patient insists on diving, a hyperbaric chamber trial might be arranged to observe the effects of pressure changes under controlled conditions (Millington 1988).

Sarcoidosis and *pneumoconiosis*. These are medical terms for two different diseases that can affect the lungs in similar fashion. The cause of pneumoconiosis is inhaled dust, such as coal mine dust or silica dust. The cause of sarcoidosis is unknown. Both diseases can lead to permanent scarring of the lungs.

Although it has been stated that these diseases preclude recreational scuba diving (Hickey 1984), the extent of disease rather than the diagnosis should be the governing factor. Sometimes sarcoidosis doesn't involve the lungs, or involves the lungs and then disappears altogether; in other words, the natural history of sarcoidosis is variable. Anyone with a history of sarcoidosis who wishes to dive should consult with a lung disease specialist and, if questions remain, a diving medicine specialist. A chest CT scan and lung function tests would be most helpful in determining the overall extent of any lung involvement. Any breathing impairment should rule out scuba diving.

Pneumoconiosis may be evaluated similarly. Sometimes the diagnosis is a mistake, from over interpreting a chest x-ray. The disease may be so minimal that it affects lung function not at all. As with sarcoidosis, a chest CT scan and lung function tests should be done to determine overall lung involvement. Any impairment should rule out scuba diving.

Pulmonary fibrosis. This is the medical term for diffuse scarring of the lungs. It can occur as the result from either of the two diseases mentioned above, but can also occur spontaneously, from no known cause;

in the latter case it is called *idiopathic* pulmonary fibrosis, IPF. Diffuse lung scarring can be fatal. Anyone with this disease should not dive. Fortunately IPF is rare.

Chronic obstructive pulmonary disease (COPD). This is the umbrella term for both "chronic bronchitis" and "emphysema," two chronic lung conditions that are almost always due to long term cigarette smoking. Diagnosis is confirmed by the patient's history (usually shortness of breath on exertion and history of heavy smoking), an abnormal pulmonary function study, and chest x-ray. The chest x-ray may show some "air trapping" or even bullae ('holes') in the lungs. In some cases the chest x-ray can be normal, but the breathing tests will still show air flow obstruction. Unlike asthmatics, where the air flow obstruction is episodic and largely unpredictable, patients with COPD have permanent air flow obstruction. Anyone with COPD should not scuba dive.

Coronary artery disease (CAD). This type of heart disease is the most common in the U.S. and is the cause of most heart attacks and "sudden deaths." CAD is a major cause of mortality in divers. Since sudden death from CAD occurs in half a million Americans yearly, it is to be expected to cause some in-water accidents, particularly in people over 50. Sudden death from heart attack seems to occur under conditions of hypothermia or stress, and has been attributed to an irregularity of the heart beat (Eldridge 1979).

Victims of sudden cardiac death could just as easily die while bicycling, jogging or hang gliding, so scuba diving per se is not the actual cause (the deaths are not from air embolism or DCS, but from drowning). Even so, deaths from heart attack while diving are included in DAN's annual statistics.

In its report on 1995 scuba diving accidents and deaths. Divers Alert Network noted: "Cardiovascular disease has been a significant cause of death in fatal diving mishaps for as long as DAN has been collecting data. This should come as no surprise since cardiovascular disease is the number one cause of death for both men and women in the United states and most other developed nations. The diver with atherosclerosis [hardening] of the coronary arteries is at an increased risk of suffering a myocardial infarction [heart attack] or sudden cardiac death." (DAN 1997)

Of the 64 cases for which DAN had autopsy information (of the 104 scuba deaths during calendar year 1995), 20 had cardiovascular disease as the primary cause of death or the contributing factor which lead to the primary cause of death. This finding is in contrast to other medical conditions such as diabetes and asthma, which don't show up as causes of scuba deaths reported to Divers Alert Network. (DAN 1997)

A patient with known coronary artery disease who requires medication, or for which surgery has been recommended, should not dive. One author has suggested that a history of heart attack does not preclude diving if: 1) more than a year has passed since the heart attack; 2) there is no chest pain or arrhythmia on maximal exercise; 3) the patient has a normal stress test; and 4) the physical exam is normal (Millington 1988). Doubtful cases (when the patient insists on diving) should be referred to a cardiologist for a more complete evaluation, which might include stress testing or coronary angiography (injection of dye into the coronary vessels).

Smoking. Organizations promoting scuba diving are united in their no-smoking policy. One editorialist wrote: "There is no choice for the diver. He or she should quit smoking now - or consider giving up diving." (Tzimoulis 1986) Apart from the likelihood of developing airway disease, which increases the risk of pulmonary barotrauma from air trapping, the greatest immediate hazard from smoking is excess blood carbon monoxide (CO) and decrease in arterial oxygen content (see Section I).

Diving can be quite stressful and any physiologic impairment increases its inherent risks. Based on half-life of excess CO in the blood (about six hours), and typical CO-hemoglobin levels of smokers (5%-10%), scuba divers who cannot break the smoking habit should abstain at least 12 hours before any dive. However, many divers do smoke, and sometimes just before a dive. Sadly, it is not uncommon to see dive professionals - divemasters and instructors - smoke during the surface interval between a two-tank dive. For a more detailed discussion of the potential hazards of smoking and diving, see Martin (1996).

For discussion of other conditions see one or more of several reviews: (Becker 1983; Hickey 1984; Davis 1986; Dembert 1986; Millington 1988; Davis 1990; Linaweaver 1990, Mebane 1993; Twarog 1995). For a discussion of Divers Alert Network, see Section R.

REFERENCES AND BIBLIOGRAPHY

References with * are especially recommended.

Becker GD, Parell GJ. Medical examination of the sport scuba diver. Otolaryngol head neck surg 1983;91:246-50.

Brouhard BH, Travis LB, Schreiner B, et al. Scuba diving and diabetes. (Letter). Amer Jour Dis Child 1987;141:605-6.

Davis JC, Bove AA, Struhl TR. *Medical Examination of Sport Scuba Divers*, 2nd edition, 1986. San Antonio, Tx: Medical Seminars, Inc.

*Davis JC. Medical evaluation for diving. In Bove AA, Davis JC, eds. *Diving Medicine*, 2nd Edition. W.B. Saunders Co., Philadelphia, 1990.

Dear G, Dovenbarger J, Stolp BW, Moon RE. Diabetes among recreational divers. Undersea Hyperbaric Med 1994; 21 (Suppl.);94.

Dear, G. The DAN Diabetes Survey. Alert Diver, May/June 1994; p. 28.

Dembert ML, Keith JF. Evaluating the potential pediatric scuba diver. Am J Dis Child 1986;140:1135-41.

Dembert ML, Keith JF. Scuba diving and diabetes. (Letter). Am J Dis Child 1987;141:605-6. Brouhard BH, Travis LB, Schreiner B, et al. Scuba diving and diabetes. (Letter). Am J Dis Child 1987;141:605.

Divers Alert Network Report on Diving Accidents and Fatalities. Divers Alert Network, Box 3823, Duke University Medical Center, Durham, NC 27710: Published yearly since 1987.

Dreifuss FE. Epileptics and scuba diving. (Letter). JAMA 1985;253:1877-8.

*Edmunds C, McKenzie B, Thomas R. *Diving Medicine for Scuba Divers*. J.L. Publications, Melbourne, 1992.

Farmer JC, Jr. Ear and sinus problems in diving. In Bove AA, Davis JC, eds. *Diving Medicine*, 2nd Edition. W.B. Saunders Co., Philadelphia, 1990.

Goldman RW. Scuba diver standards (letter). J Am Board Fam Pract 1988;4:295.

Greer HD. Epilepsy in diving. Pressure. March/April 1992, pages 5-6.

Hickey DD. Outline of medical standards for divers. Undersea Biomed Res 1984;11:407-432.

Hill RK. Should epileptics scuba dive? (Letter). JAMA 1985;254:3182.

Linaweaver PG, Vorosmarti J. *Fitness to Dive*. Thirty-fourth Undersea and Hyperbaric Medical Society Workshop, May 1987. Undersea and Hyperbaric Medical Society, Bethesda, Maryland.

*Linaweaver PG, Bove AA. Physical examination of divers. In Bove AA, Davis JC, eds. *Diving Medicine*, 2nd Edition. W.B. Saunders Co., Philadelphia, 1990.

*Martin L. Smoking and Diving - Is It Really Dangerous? Skin Diver Magazine, May 1996, p. 22.

Martindale JJ. Scuba divers with asthma. (Letter). Brit Med J 1990;300:609.

*Mebane GY, McIver NKI. Fitness to Dive; Chapter 4, in Bennett P. Elliott D. *The Physiology and Medicine of Diving*. W.B. Saunders Co., Philadelphia, 1993.

Meckelnburg RL. Should epileptics scuba dive? (Letter). JAMA 1985;254:3183.

Millington JT. Should epileptics scuba dive? (Letter). JAMA 1985;254:3182-83.

Millington JT. Physical standards for scuba divers. J Am Board Fam Pract 1988;1:194-200.

REFERENCES AND BIBLIOGRAPHY

(continued)

Smith RM, Neuman TS. Elevation of serum creatine kinase in divers with arterial gas embolization. N Engl J Med 1994;330:19-24.

Twarog F. Discussion of risk of scuba diving in individuals with allergic and respiratory diseases. J. Allergy Clinical Immunology 1995; 96:871-873.

Tzimoulis P. If you smoke, don't dive. Skin Diver Magazine, June 1986, page 8.

Williams JA, King GK, Callanan VI, Lanskey RM, Rich KW. Fatal arterial gas embolism: detection by chest radiography and imaging before autopsy. Med J Austral 1990; 153:97-100.

Wedman B. Diabetes and scuba diving. (Letter). Diabetes Educator 1987;13:267-8.

DIVING ODDS N' ENDS

Deepest Dives on Compressed Air

For many years the record for deepest dive on compressed air was the October 14, 1968 dive by John J. Gruener and R. Neal Watson, to 437 feet off Freeport, Grand Bahama Island. On February 14, 1990, Bret Gilliam dove 452 feet off the coast of Honduras (Roatan). He descended in 4 minutes 41 seconds and stayed at depth one minute 40 seconds. Then on March 18, 1994, Daniel J. Manion, M.D. dove to 510 feet on Clifton's Wall, Nassau, The Bahamas. The dives by Gilliam and Manion were solo dives and, as reported by the divers, went without a hitch. Both men made many dives prior to achieving their records. Both made decompression stops before surfacing.

Finally, both men acknowledge the extraordinary danger in diving to such depths on compressed air. Although the dives are necessarily short, death can occur as result of oxygen toxicity, nitrogen narcosis, air embolism or decompression sickness. Many deep divers have never returned.

SECTION O

Should Asthmatics Not Scuba Dive?

This question is commonly asked in the diving community. Not surprisingly, there is no simple answer. In this chapter I will present background information on the question and offer some general recommendations. The final answer in all cases should rest with an informed patient, the patient's physician and, for open water students, the scuba instructor.

Asthma is probably the most controversial medical condition affecting recreational divers. An estimated 10% to 15% of children have some history of recurrent wheezing, and an estimated 5% to 8% of adults are diagnosed as "asthmatic." Added to these statistics are an estimated several million certified scuba divers, with several hundred thousand newly certified every year, and it is no surprise that many current and would-be divers have some history of asthma.

Asthma is a disease of the airways. Patients prone to asthma can develop intermittent attacks of cough, wheezing, chest tightness, and/or shortness of breath. These symptoms are due to narrowing of the air tubes (bronchi) within the lungs. One major cause of the narrowing is excess mucous in the airways. Because symptoms occur episodically, and often unpredictably, there is no way to know when someone with an asthma history will have an "asthma attack."

Scuba divers breathe compressed air underwater, so they must have unobstructed flow of air in order to equalize air pressures. Unequal air pressures are the cause of all barotrauma, including ear and sinus squeeze, and air embolism. Since asthmatics may develop air flow obstruction in the lungs at any time, the question of when, if ever, asthmatics may safely dive is problematic. For reasons which I will discuss,

Some recommendations and opinions from the medical literature about asthma and scuba diving

"A history of bronchial asthma is disqualifying if there have been any attacks within 2 years, if medication is needed for control, or if bronchospasm has ever been associated with exertion or inhalation of cold air."(Strauss 1979)

'Never'- "Once an asthmatic, always an asthmatic" (Linaweaver 1982) "Absolute contraindications: [Asthma] attacks within the past 2 yr. Medication is required to prevent or treat episodes of dyspnea. Effort- or cold-induced asthma." (Hickey 1984)

"Any patient with currently active bronchial asthma should be strictly forbidden to dive. Any patient with a history of childhood asthma, symptoms suggestive of asthma within the past year, suspicion of exercise or cold air-induced asthma should be referred to a pulmonary medicine specialist for evaluation to include challenge testing." (Davis 1986)

"No diving by individuals...who have had clinically significant bronchospasm within the last five years, whether or not they take medications and irrespective of the precipitating event" (Neuman 1987)

"...a conservative recommendation is that any asthmatic with frequent flareups or continuous need for medication to control symptoms, should refrain from diving. Conversely, an adult who has "grown out" of asthma, or has been asymptomatic for some time ...with normal lung function, may participate in recreational diving. In all instances, of course, the potential risks should be explained to the diver." (Martin 1992)

"Divers using bronchodilators are disqualified. The bronchodilator itself leads to increased risk of arrhythmias." (Millington 1988)

"Well-controlled, mild asthmatics should be allowed to dive during remissions, but be particularly advised about the risks of rapid ascent." (Denison 1988)

"All individuals who have current active asthma are advised not to dive. Any individual who seems to have outgrown his asthma and has not had any bronchospasm, wheezing, or chest tightness and has not used any bronchodilator recently may be a candidate for diving if a complete battery of PFTs are normal." (Neuman 1990)

'Never' - "Childhood asthma never goes away and continues to be a hazard to divers, even if apparently arrested and asymptomatic in adulthood." (Greer 1990)

"If the person ever has had bronchospasm associated with exercise or inhalation of cold air, diving is contraindicated." (Harrison 1991)

"...not to dive within 48 hours of wheezing is safe [reasonable]" (Farrell 1990)

(Continued)

Some recommendations and opinions from the medical literature about asthma and scuba diving *(continued)*

"In principle, diving is absolutely contraindicated in those with air-trapping pulmonary lesions or bronchial asthma." (Melamed 1992)

Not with: "History of asthma over the last 5 years; use of bronchodilators over the last 5 years; respiratory rhonchi or other abnormalities on auscultation."(Edmonds 1991, Edmonds 1992)

"Intending divers with a past history of asthma and asthma symptoms within the previous five years should be advised not to dive." (Jenkins 1993)

"The recommendation that an asthmatic patient not dive should be determined by the history and severity of the disease." (Neuman 1994)

"Asthmatics may dive if they have allergic asthma, but not if they have cold-induced, exercise induced, or emotion induced asthma. . . Only well-controlled asthmatics may dive. Asthmatics should not dive if they have needed a bronchodilator in the last 48 hours or have any other chest symptoms." (Farrell 1995, quoting the UK Standard)

"The asthmatics who we like to clear [for diving]are those who have well-defined triggers and who are unlikely to get significantly worse underwater. And that well-defined trigger can be definied in any way that you want, as long as you know what the trigger is." (Neuman, 1995)

"Despite the impetus to disseminate more liberal recommendations, there is no strong evidence with which to challenge the traditional recommendation that asthmatics should not scuba dive." (Moon, 1995)

"Nil" symptoms or signs for at least 12 months. (Gorman 1996)

there are many opinions and no uniform agreement. Quotes in the following table, taken from the medical literature, reflect this difference of opinion. Note that recommendations range from 'never' to 'not with a history of asthma over the previous five years' to 'no diving within two days of wheezing.'

WHY IS THERE A WIDE RANGE OF OPINION ON ASTHMA AND DIVING?

There are three basic explanations, which are summarized below and then discussed at length in the following pages.

1. Asthma is a condition with a wide range of both the frequency and severity of symptoms such as wheeze and chest congestion; when used without precise definition or description, the term "asthma" may mean different things to different people.

2. Despite sound theoretical objections as to why asthmatics should not dive, there is no solid evidence that scuba-diving asthmatics have an in-creased accident rate.
3. There are differences in philosophy among physicians and scuba professionals about personal risk-taking.

1. *Asthma is a disease with a wide range of frequency and severity of symptoms.*

Some authors have recommended that anyone "with asthma" not go scuba diving. However, such a broad prohibition flies in the face of reality, since it includes a large group of people with a history of asthma who, in fact, dive often and without any problem.

On the other hand, any asthmatic who is constantly wheezing and coughing should obviously not scuba dive. So where should the line be drawn between remote history of asthma and active disease? It seems that most experts would draw the line at some arbitrary point, usually denoted by patient symptoms and need for medication (see quotes in table). However, none of the guidelines for deciding who should not dive is established by any studies of which I am aware; they are all "best guess" recommendations. If there is a line to draw somewhere, and I believe there is, it should be based on individual evaluation as opposed to something as arbitrary as "5 years" or "2 days" without symptoms. (In contrast to many earlier recommendations, the importance of an open mind and individual assessment are becoming increasingly recognized; see Neuman, et. al., 1994, and Neuman 1995.)

To demonstrate variability of the label "asthma," I have made up 10 different scenarios for a hypothetical 30-year-old man with some history of asthma (next page). Each scenario is ranked for severity of the asthma, from 1 (least) to 10 (most). In each case the subject might legitimately check "yes" to a scuba diving questionnaire asking if he ever had asthma. If the questionnaire is for a certification course, a "yes" answer in each case would result in the requirement that the applicant obtain "medical clearance."

The consensus among dive medicine physicians would probably be to say "yes" to scenarios 1-3 (he may dive), and a clear "no" to scenarios 8-10 (he may not dive). Nos. 4-7 are problematic; most likely the percentage of diving physicians saying "no" would increase as we go from number 4 to 7.

The point is that there is asthma and there is asthma. The worse the asthma, in terms of need for medication, symptoms, or degree of air flow obstruction, the riskier the diving (at least physicians perceive it this way). There can be no rule about diving that fits all asthmatics, except

10 SCENARIOS FOR A 30-YEAR-OLD MAN WITH A "HISTORY OF ASTHMA," RANKED FROM LEAST (1) TO MOST SEVERE (10)

1. Had asthma as child; grew out of it at age 12; no symptoms or trouble since. No symptoms when exercising.

2. Had asthma as child. No problem at all except very rarely, with heavy exertion, such as running in cold weather, patient has noted a slight cough and shortness of breath. The last time was about five years ago. Symptoms always went away without treatment.

3. No asthma as child. Seven years ago patient had to use an asthma inhaler. Occasionally feels "chest congestion" with a cold, but it always abates without any specific treatment. Last asthma treatment was seven years ago.

4. No asthma as a child. About once a year, with a cold, patient has a little wheezing. Uses an asthma inhaler for a day at most, and always gets better. Exercises regularly with no difficulty.

5. No asthma as a child. About once a year gets a mild attack, and takes medication for a few days, including both pills and an inhaler. Between attacks feels well.

6. Had asthma as a child. Grew out of it at age 10, then at age 25 asthma recurred. Now carries an asthma inhaler and uses it about once a month, at most. In the past five years has had two bad asthma attacks, both requiring steroid medication.

7. No asthma until age 22. Now uses an asthma inhaler regularly, but feels well controlled except for occasional exacerbations. Lung function is normal when tested between attacks.

8. Uses prednisone tablets and an inhaler to control asthma symptoms. Doctor adjusts prednisone dose, sometimes to as low as only 5 mg a day, other times as high as 40 mg a day. Lung function is near normal when tested between attacks.

9. Has been hospitalized about once a year for past five years for a severe asthma attack. Has breathing machine (nebulizer) at home for inhalation of bronchodilator, which he requires regularly. Lung function shows modest impairment when tested between attacks.

10. Hospitalized several times a year for asthma. Lung function always abnormal when tested.

for the no-brainer that if you never dive you'll never have a diving accident. Ultimately the "line" for diving vs. no diving should be based on a thorough evaluation of the individual, and not on any arbitrary and unproven criteria.

2. *Air trapping can lead to fatal air embolism, yet many asthmatics do dive, and without any definite evidence for increased accident rate.*

The major theoretical concern is an increased risk of air embolism. This can occur if an area of the lungs traps air underwater. In theory, mucous in the airways may allow air to pass by as the diver descends, but then trap the air on ascent. On ascent the trapped air will expand and could rupture the lungs, putting bubbles into the circulation. The result can be a non-fatal or fatal stroke (see Section F). Other theoretical asthma-related problems, all of which may lead to drowning, include:

• the possibility of asthma exacerbation from physical exertion, inhalation of hypertonic saline (seawater), or from breathing dry, compressed air (Edmunds 1991);

• increased work of breathing due to increased air density at depth;

• increased risk of heart rhythm disturbance in people using a bronchodilator (the most common type of asthma medication) (Millington 1988); potential of bronchodilator drug to cause enlargement of blood vessels in the lungs. These blood vessels normally capture small venous bubbles and keep them from entering the arterial circulation. Drug-induced dilation may allow the venous bubbles to enter the arterial circulation as gas emboli (Edmunds 1992, Jenkins 1993);

• increased risk to diving companions if the asthmatic gets into trouble. Despite all these theoretical objections, many asthmatics do dive, and without mishap. Information in this area is based mainly on surveys of active divers and retrospective compilation of accident data.

This information appears in bits and pieces in the medical literature, in Divers Alert Network's annual accident reports, and in surveys of diving asthmatics (see box). There is no statistically valid, published study that definitively answers the question heading this chapter (and there may never be). What follows is a summary of data and information relevant to the question.

A survey of responders to a British dive magazine questionnaire found that: 89 of 104 had asthma since childhood; 70 wheezed less than 12 times a year; and 22 wheezed daily (Farrell 1990). The entire group had cumulatively made 12,864 dives and not suffered any instances of pneumothorax or gas embolism; only one diver reported decompression sickness. Interestingly, 96 of the divers reported using an asthma inhaler just before diving and some were also using preventive medication such as steroids. The authors' conclusion that "the British Sub Aqua Club's recommendation to divers - not to dive within 48 hours of wheezing - is safe" met with strong disagreement in subsequent letters to the medical journal (Martindale 1990, Watt 1990). In a clarification, the authors of the original paper stated the word "reasonable" should have been substituted for the word "safe," and reaffirmed their recommendation (Glanvill 1990).

Of 10,422 responders to a survey in Skin Diver, 870 (8.3%) answered yes to the question "Have you ever had asthma?"; 343 (3.3%) indicated they "currently have asthma"; 276 (2.6%) stated that they dive with asthma (Bove 1992). Diving accident experience among the asthmatics was not reported.

Of responders to a questionnaire in Alert Diver, DAN's bimonthly magazine published, 88.7% (243 divers) reported taking some medication for asthma, and 55.8% took medication just before a dive (Corson 1992). Of this group, 73 (26.4%) had a history of hospitalization for asthma. A total of 56,334 dives were reported by 279 individuals. Eleven cases of "decompression illness" (AGE or DCS) were reported in 8 individuals, or one in 5100 dives, "significantly exceeding" the estimated risk for unselected recreational divers by a factor of 4.16. The authors concluded that "the risk of decompression illness is higher in the surveyed asthmatics than in an unselected recreational diving population" (Corson 1992).

Data Related to Asthma and Diving

Surveys of Diving Asthmatics

British survey (Farrell 1990)
Survey of *Skin Diver* readers (Bove 1992)
DAN survey of *Alert Diver* readers (Corson 1992)

Reviews of Accident/Mortality Statistics

DAN retrospective review (Corson 1991)
DAN 1994 Accident Report (DAN 1994)
University of Rhode Island Accident Statistics (McAniff 1991)
Review of Accidents from early 1980s (Neuman 1987)
L.A. County Coroner's Cases, 1985-1990 (Schanker 1991)
Australia/New Zealand Experience (Edmunds, 1991, 1992)

Admittedly, there are problems with reader surveys.

- Surveys presumably include only asthmatics who continue to dive and maintain enough interest to read scuba periodicals; as a result, they may *under-represent* asthma-related problems because they don't count asthmatics who quit diving (Watt 1990). However, it is also true that many current asthmatics choose not to admit that they scuba dive (Lin 1987), so by not counting all scuba-diving asthmatics the surveys may *over-represent* asthma-related problems.
- The survey data don't permit comparison of scuba diving asthmatics with and without accidents as to severity of asthma, level of control with medication, and reason for any pre-dive medication (prevention vs. treatment of symptoms).
- The surveys don't reveal the character of the dives, e.g., the depths achieved, episodes of rapid or uncontrolled ascent, and the water conditions.

A retrospective review to assess the risk of asthma for arterial gas embolism (AGE) and type II decompression sickness (neurologic impairment from nitrogen bubbles) was made by DAN for the four years 1987-1990 (Corson 1991). Fifty-four out of 1213 divers reported to DAN with AGE or type II DCS had a history of asthma, of which 25 were currently asthmatic (defined as having an asthma attack within one year or taking bronchodilator therapy). For a control population, 1000 questionnaires were sent to a ran-domly selected group of DAN members, of which 696 were returned; 37 control divers admitted a history of asthma, of which 13 were currently asthmatic. There was no statistically significant increase in risk for type II DCS in the asthmatics. The data for AGE suggested an approximately two-fold increase in risk for asthmatics, but did not reach statistical significance (Corson 1991).

The 1994 DAN Accident Report confirmed 465 cases of decompression illness (including DCS and AGE) among North American divers during 1992 (DAN 1994). Of this group, there was a history of current asthma in eight and past asthma in 20, representing 1.7% and 4.3% of the total, respectively. Except for the comment that "two individuals were using over-the-counter inhalers for asthma," no information is provided about disease severity or the role of asthma in any specific accident (DAN 1994).

Scuba diving *deaths* linked to asthma are infrequent. In the 1970s and 1980s the University of Rhode Island's National Underwater Accident Data Center kept dive fatality statistics on U.S. divers. Asthma was not noted as a cause of death in any of the 1183 autopsies recorded during this period (McAniff 1991). A review of scuba death reports from the early 1980s found that, whenever asthma was mentioned, there was either no explanation of the circumstances, or another, and preventable, cause of death was present, such as out-of-air-at-depth or uncontrolled ascent (Neuman 1987).

A review of 18 consecutive scuba diving fatalities at the Los Angeles Coroner's office between 1985 and 1990 found "apparent air embolism or lung barotrauma" in four patients; in none was death linked to asthma (Schanker 1991).

One autopsy report has been published of an asthmatic who died from scuba diving. She was an obese, 40-year-old diver with a history of: asthma for four years; an emergency room visit for asthma three months before her demise; using an asthma inhaler eight times a day; breathing difficulties on the day of her dive. The autopsy confirmed arterial gas embolism and asthmatic bronchitis (Marraccini 1986). (It is noteworthy that the deceased had denied respiratory problems on her written dive school application.)

DAN also keeps data on all recreational scuba diving deaths among North American residents. Ninety-six recreational scuba diving fatalities were reported for 1992 (DAN 1994). DAN's analysis found that "Cardiovascular disease is a prominent immediate cause of death...diabetes mellitus and bronchial asthma do not appear prominently in this series." In its 1997 report of 1995's 104 scuba deaths, DAN again did not find asthma to be a significant factor (in contrast to cardiovascular disease; see Section N).

In contrast to the U.S. and British experience, asthma was found to be a contributing factor in 8% of 124 scuba diving deaths in Australia and New Zealand (Edmunds 1991, Edmunds 1992). Most of these deaths were in clinically mild asthmatics who were otherwise physically fit young men. In a number of cases the diver was returning to obtain a bronchodilator spray; in others, medication had been used immediately before the dive. Edmonds has provided several case histories of asthmatics who have died during or just after a scuba dive (Edmunds 1991, Edmunds 1992).

I cannot explain the difference in mortality data between Australia/New Zealand and the rest of the world. Certainly in England and the U.S. there appears to be no conclusive evidence for an increased accident *or* mortality rate among asthmatics who dive. This does not mean that diving can be considered "safe" for asthmatics; it would be a foolish reader who interprets the data this way. It only means that available information does not confirm a statistically significant increase in accidents among divers who admit to having asthma. As with diabetes, it is quite possible that asthmatics who would get into trouble scuba diving (for all the theoretical reasons listed) have 'selected' themselves out of the activity, for one reason or another.

3. *Differing opinions may be based on differences in personal philosophy.*

This is the third explanation for varying opinion about asthma and scuba diving. I mentioned this reason in discussing the 10 asthma scenarios; for scenarios in the middle group (4-7), the difference between saying "yes" and "no" to scuba diving may be attributable to philosophical differences over "taking risks."

Recreational scuba diving is an inherently risky activity for anyone; physicians believe that any condition characterized as "asthma" might well add some extra measure to the sport's inherent risk. But how much extra risk? No one knows, of course. Surely the answer must largely depend on the vagaries of a *particular diver's* asthma. But even if some precise measurement of extra risk were known, there is no agreement over what would constitute *unacceptable additional risk* for scuba diving.

For example, according to DAN, in the last 10 years an average of 98 Americans have died each year while engaging in recreational scuba diving (DAN 1997). There are a variety of explanations for these deaths, including diver error and stupidity, but overall the figure is an accepted fact of recreational diving; no one seeks to ban the sport because of these deaths, only to make it safer for all participants. Now, if one out of these approximately 98 scuba diving deaths per year could be blamed on asthma, would that be sufficient to ban all asthmatics from diving? Two? Three?

Similarly, there are an estimated 800 non-fatal accidents a year reported to DAN, of which about half are confirmed as DCS or AGE. Again, this is an accepted aspect of the sport and no one seeks to squelch recreational scuba diving because of its inevitable accident rate. When it comes to asthma, however, statistics are examined for some justification to recommend that asthmatics as a group not dive. But how many accidents attributable to asthma would trigger this recommendation? Fifteen? Ten? Five?

I doubt there would be any consensus in answering these questions. Instead, there would likely be more questions about the statistics. For example, some might want to know: 'Why did these divers get into trouble, and not all the other asthmatics who also dive? Was their asthma worse? Their dive profiles more extreme? Was there some pattern of behavior that could be identified and perhaps changed?'

Interpretation of statistics can be subjective, so even as more studies accumulate the issue will likely remain unsettled and argued. At the June 1995 meeting of the Undersea and Hyperbaric Medical Society, two eminent dive medicine physicians took opposite sides of the debate, "Should asthmatics not dive?" Both physicians know all the literature, and have had experience treating dive accident victims. With similar knowledge and backgrounds the two doctors argued opposite sides of the issue. (There was no "winner" but the emerging consensus from the 1995 UHMS meeting seems to be a more liberal attitude, as was expressed in the 1994 article by Drs. Neuman and Bove. The proceedings of the 1995 symposium is available in print from UHMS [Elliott 1996]).

Future debates might focus on the methodology of the studies or the validity of the statistics, but the real argument is likely to be over something more subtle: philosophical differences in personal risk taking. Simply put, any given study on the subject may be interpreted in different ways, depending on inherent biases. As a result, for people with mild and non-limiting asthma, the answer to the question "Should asthmatics not dive?" will largely depend on who you ask.

WHAT ARE SPECIFIC RECOMMENDATIONS?

My recommendations are presented here for the recreational scuba diver and would be diver. These recommendations, based on both the theoretical risk of AGE and the information at hand, are not to be construed as specific for any given individual.

"ACTIVE" ASTHMA. If the asthma is "active" - requiring daily or frequent medication to control symptoms - I would advise against diving altogether. This is particularly true for any *prednisone-dependent* asthmatic. Prednisone is a corticosteroid in pill form, widely used to treat asthma symptoms. Prednisone-dependent asthma suggests a severe degree of impairment, and would probably disqualify for diving.

On the other hand, an asthmatic who is well-controlled on an *inhaled* steroid (generic names include beclomethasone, budesonide, flunisolide, triamcinolone, and fluticasone) is likely using the drug not to treat symptoms but to prevent them, and may be able to dive safely.

I would also classify as "active" any asthmatic with a demonstrably abnormal test of vital capacity (standard pulmonary function test, called *spirometry*), physical examination (wheezing) or chest x-ray. "Demonstrably abnormal" means there is no doubt as to the abnormality. This is an important qualification because sometimes changes are noted on tests which don't really reflect any significant abnormality, but instead only a normal variation. If there is any doubt or question about an abnormality, the patient should be referred to a diving medicine specialist.

For anyone classified as having "active asthma" the theoretical risks seem too great for what amounts to a purely recreational activity. Although some asthmatics do use a bronchodilator inhaler just before a dive (Farrell 1990, Lin 1987, Corson 1992) this practice is certainly not recommended by physicians. Thus, there is an admitted paradox: "active" asthmatics do engage in a theoretically risky recreational activity without apparent mishap, but physicians (myself included) are not willing to condone it. Nor are we willing to provide sanction for "active" asthmatics to begin scuba diving as a new activity.

At some point it must be acknowledged that diving is different from swimming or jogging; any asthma exacerbation underwater could lead to panic and drowning. I would advise people in this group to go snorkeling instead, or take up some other water sport such as swimming, sailing or windsurfing.

"CHILDHOOD-ONLY" ASTHMA. If someone had childhood asthma, and as an adult has had no asthma symptoms or required asthma medication, and is otherwise in good physical condition, there should be no medical restriction to scuba diving. I would not require an examination for people in this group, but if one is done it should reveal no wheezing. A breathing test and chest x-ray, if done, should be normal. While this recommendation for childhood-only asthma appears to reflect a consensus among diving-trained physicians (see quotes at beginning of section), in the past some physicians wrote that even remote asthma poses an unacceptable risk for diving-related barotrauma (Linaweaver 1982, Greer 1990).

"INACTIVE" ASTHMA. The person in between the "childhood only" and "active asthma" groups presents the most difficult problem: the asthmatic who wheezes infrequently, or uses a bronchodilator or steroid medication occasionally, or who feels normal and well controlled with routine inhaled medication (i.e., not taken for symptoms). This might include the asthmatic with exercise-induced asthma who has learned to prevent symptoms with inhalation steroid medication. On theoretical grounds, this person should probably not take up scuba diving, although there are no compelling data to support this position. Patients with inactive asthma who wish to dive should have a physical exam, chest x-ray and a test of vital capacity (spirometry). As explained above, these tests should show no demonstrable abnormality.

Some physicians recommend specialized pulmonary function tests, including exercise tests and something called "inhalation challenge," which involves inhaling an asthma-provoking drug in the pulmonary function lab. Only people susceptible to asthma attacks react to this drug; the rest of the population does not. The idea with both tests is to induce a potential asthmatic to have an attack under stressful or abnormal conditions; if an attack occurs under stressful conditions in the lab, diving would then be considered too risky an activity.

That is the theory, but I don't believe these asthma-provoking tests are particularly useful for answering the question about diving. Simulation of what may happen in the water cannot be had by exercising someone on a treadmill or having them inhale a noxious agent in the lab. There are no studies showing that these "stress" tests are any more useful in answering the asthma question than are the basic tools available to all doctors: a test of vital capacity (spirometry), a careful history and a good physical examination. (However, it should be pointed out that some physicians at the UHMS asthma symposium felt exercise testing to be an important tool [Elliott 1996]. Since the issue is unsettled either way, some doctors may choose to rely upon stress tests to reach a decision.)

WHAT IS THE INFORMED CONSENT APPROACH?

For the inactive asthmatic who wishes to take up scuba diving, I recommend an "informed consent" approach. He or she should receive an explanation of the theoretical risks. I have already explained that many people with "inactive asthma" do dive, but that doesn't mean it is safe. The would-be diver needs to understand that air flow obstruction might increase the risk of barotrauma, and that stressful conditions (cold water, strenuous activity) could trigger an asthma exacerbation. Particularly, the potential diver should understand that open water conditions are very different from the swimming pool (where scuba training initially takes place), and may lead to problems not encountered in the more benign pool environment (Martindale 1990).

Ultimately, the decision should be left up to the individual. How is this done? After the risks are explained, he or she must reaffirm their wish to dive. Then, if a note is required by the training agency, the examining physician should not sign or offer any statement that diving "is safe" for the individual, but instead write a brief note summarizing the patient's condition. The note should state that the patient's asthma history is not a prohibition to diving and that the potential diver understands the risks. Diving is inherently a risky activity anyway, so this type of informed consent makes sense. One possible example of such a note is shown on this page.

It is important to emphasize that the physician should never approve an asthmatic for "shallow water diving only." Barotrauma is actually more apt to occur closer to the surface than in deeper water. This is because the greatest pressure changes occur near the surface. From 33 feet depth to the surface, ambient pressure decreases 100%, whereas from 66 to 33 feet the pressure decreases only 50%.

If a note is not required for the training agency, the patient might still be asked to sign such a statement to keep in the medical file. This will indicate that the physician and the patient discussed the issues, and that an informed decision was made by the patient.

Some people have criticized this approach, on the grounds that individuals referred to a doctor deserve a medical decision on whether they should or should not dive. One doctor stated, "Either you are going to take responsibility for the situation or you are not. To try and leave the decision up to the individual or agency is not only inappropriate but not serving the patient very well."

I strongly disagree with this attitude, and believe it is one reason most doctors seem reluctant to get involved in this issue. For a doctor to simply tell a patient with asymptomatic asthma that he or she can or cannot scuba dive, given all the data I have presented, implies that the physician has a crystal ball. The patient could rightly infer that "Dr. X said it is OK to dive so I assumed it was safe." This approach would place an impossible burden on the examining doctor, especially when the activity is inherently risky.

I believe this critic's comment reflects an outdated, paternalistic attitude, one that the practice of medicine has moved away from over the years. In fact, if a patient with inactive or childhood-only asthma is clueless as to the risks, seems unable to accept his or her own responsibility for diving, and has a "You're-the-doctor-tell-me-what-to-do" attitude, I would not be able to write the kind of letter shown above. Such a patient would simply not receive my sanction for scuba diving.

In summary, a patient with inactive asthma, who wishes to scuba dive, should be approached with an open mind. The theoretical risks should be explained. A physical exam, detailed medical history, and perhaps a chest x-ray and simple test of lung function (spirometry) may be all that are needed to reach a reasonable assessment; the exam and basic tests should be normal. If desired, spirometry can also be measured after exercise (using either a treadmill or stationary bicycle). If there are any questions regarding subtle abnormality, the applicant should be referred to a diving medicine specialist.

I realize the safest approach (for doctor and patient) might be to "just say no." However, such a dogmatic response might lead some people to seek a more favorable second opinion, or to file a new medical questionnaire with a different dive shop and omit the asthma history. A dogmatic response won't necessarily prevent the asthmatic from diving, but will keep him or her from a proper medical evaluation

WHAT ABOUT MEDICOLEGAL CONCERNS?

Underlying any evaluation for diving fitness is concern about legal liability. The agency and scuba instructor are wary of being sued if one of their trainees has a mishap. The trainee signs all kinds of waivers, but pieces of paper don't always eliminate the possibility of lawsuit.

Doctors, of course, are always concerned about malpractice suits and protect themselves with malpractice insurance. But nobody wants to be sued; it is painful even when you are insured and have done nothing wrong. Doctors win about 80% of all malpractice cases that come to trial, but each "won" case still leaves a trail of stress, lost work time, and a demoralized feeling. Even when a doctor is named in a lawsuit from which he or she is eventually dropped (50 out of every 100 initial claims are dropped with no further action), the whole process takes from one to three years and costs thousands of dollars. Until the suit is dropped against the doctor, he or she must report the existence and nature of the lawsuit on *every professional application, such as for hospital staff privileges, renewal of existing privileges, licensure renewal, etc.* For the sloppy lawyer who files a meritless lawsuit, there is no penalty.

Understandably, some doctors figure it is not worth "taking a chance" on a lawsuit by passing judgment on a patient for scuba diving. Other doctors feel that "just saying no" is the safest route, since that stance surely eliminates any legal risk. This is unfortunate, because the risk in most cases should be with an informed diver, not with the training agency or the doctor.

Surely, if the training agency lies to the trainee, or the doctor gives false assurances, that might be actionable. Such is rarely, if ever, the case. Agencies are explicit in explaining to trainees the potential hazards of scuba diving, and all trainees sign informed consent waivers of one sort or another. Physicians certainly have nothing to gain monetarily or otherwise by inducing someone to dive.

This is not to say that concern about liability is misplaced. Even if the doctor does his or her best to fully inform about the risks, an accident is an accident, and an enterprising lawyer will look for someone to blame (except the diver, of course). So medicolegal concerns are real and something we all have to live with. For the doctor, there are three options: stay out of the arena altogether; say "no" without performing a thorough evaluation; or evaluate and fully inform the patient about the potential risks (preferably in a face to face meeting, with clear documentation about the communication).

For the potential diver, I believe there is only one option: become fully informed about the risks of diving, not dive when ill or unfit, and strive to make every dive as safe as possible.

REFERENCES AND BIBLIOGRAPHY

References with * are especially recommended.

Bove AA, Neuman T, Kelsen S, Gleason W. Observations on asthma in the recreational diving population. (Abstract). Undersea Biomedical Research 1992;19(Suppl.):18.

Butler BD, Hills AB. Transpulmonary passage of venous air emboli. J Appl Physiol 1985; 59:543-47.

Corson KS, Dovenbarger JA, Moon RE, Bennett PB. Risk assessment of asthma for decompression illness. (Abstract). Undersea Biomed Research 1991;18 (Suppl.):16-17.

Corson KS, Moon RE, Nealen ML, Dovenbarger JA, Bennett PB. A survey of diving asthmatics (Abstract). Undersea Biomed Research 1992;19 (Suppl.):18-19.

DAN 1992. Fitness for Diving. Divers Alert Network, Duke University, 1992.

Davis JC, Bove AA, Struhl TR. *Medical Examination of Sport Scuba Divers,* 2nd edition, 1986. San Antonio, Tx: Medical Seminars, Inc.

Denison D. Disorders associated with diving, in Murray JF, Nadel JA, eds., *Textbook of Respiratory Medicine,* W.B. Saunders Co., Philadelphia, 1988.

Divers Alert Network 1992 Report on Diving Accidents & Fatalities. Divers Alert Network, Box 3823, Duke University Medical Center, Durham, NC 27710; 1994.

Edmonds C. Asthma and diving. SPUMS Journal 1991;21:70-74.

Edmonds C, McKenzie B, Thomas R. *Diving Medicine for Scuba Divers.* J.L. Publications, Melbourne, 1992.

Edmonds C, Lowry L, Pennefather J. *Diving and Subaquatic Medicine.* Butterworth Heinemann, Oxford, 1992.

*Elliott DH, editor. *Are Asthmatics Fit To Dive?* Symposium at UHMS Annual Meeting, June 1995. Undersea and Hyperbaric Medical Society, 10531 Metropolitan Avenue, Kensington, MD 20895-2627.

Farrell PJS, Glanvill P. Diving practices of scuba divers with asthma. Brit Med J 1990; 300:166.

*Farrell PJS. Assessment of asthmatic divers in the UK, in *Are Asthmatics Fit To Dive?,* DH Elliott, editor. Symposium at UHMS Annual Meeting, June 1995. Undersea and Hyperbaric Medical Society, 10531 Metropolitan Avenue, Kensington, MD 20895-2627.

Glanvill P, Farrell PJS. Scuba divers with asthma. (Letter). Brit Med J 1990;300:609-10.

Gorman D. Asthma and diving. A review of emergent attitudes and society policies. The Undersea Journal, First Quarter, 1996, pages 81-83.

Greer HD. Neurological Consequences of Diving. Chapter 19 in: Bove AA, Davis JC, eds. *Diving Medicine,* 2nd Edition. W.B. Saunders Co., Philadelphia, 1990.

Harrison LJ. Asthma and diving. Florida Med J 1991;78:431-33.

Hickey DD. Outline of medical standards for divers. Undersea Biomed Res 1984;11:407-32.

Jenkins C, Anderson SD, Wong R, Veale A. Compressed air diving and respiratory disease. Med J Austr 1993;158:275-79.

Lin LY. Scuba divers with disabilities challenge medical protocols and ethics. The Physician and Sports Medicine 1987;15:224-35.

Linaweaver PG, Jr. Asthma and diving do not mix. Pressure, June 1982, pages 6-7.

Linaweaver PG, Vorosmarti J. *Fitness to Dive.* Thirty-fourth Undersea and Hyperbaric Medical Society Workshop, May 1987. Undersea and Hyperbaric Medical Society, 10531 Metropolitan Avenue, Kensington, MD 20895-2627.

Linaweaver PG, Bove AA. Physical examination of divers. Chapter 25 in: Bove AA, Davis JC; *Diving Medicine,* 2nd Edition, W.B. Saunders Co., Philadelphia, 1990.

Marraccini JV, Friedman PL. Scuba death due to asthmatic bronchitis, air embolism, and drowning. Forensic Pathology No. FP 86-6 (FP-149) 1986;28:1-4.

Martin L. The medical problems of underwater diving. (Letter). New Engl J Med 1992;326:1497.

Martindale JJ. Scuba divers with asthma. (Letter). Brit Med J 1990; 300:609.

McAniff JJ. *United States Underwater Diving Fatality Statistics, 1989.* Report No. URI-SSR-91-22. University of Rhode Island, National Underwater Accident Data Center, 1991.

Melamed Y, Shupak A, Bitterman H. Medical problems associated with underwater diving. New Engl J Med 1992;326;30-5.

Mellem H. Emhjellen S, Horgen O. Pulmonary barotrauma and arterial gas embolism caused by an emphysematous bulla in a SCUBA diver. Aviat Space Environ Med 1990:61:559-62.

Millington JT. Physical standards for scuba divers. J Am Board Fam Pract 1988;1:194-200.

*Moon RE. The case that asthmatics should not dive, in *Are Asthmatics Fit To Dive?*, DH Elliott, editor. Symposium at UHMS Annual Meeting, June 1995. Undersea and Hyperbaric Medical Society, 10531 Metropolitan Avenue, Kensington, MD 20895-2627.

Neuman T. Pulmonary Considerations I, in Linaweaver PG, Vorosmarti J. *Fitness to Dive.* Thirty-fourth Undersea and Hyperbaric Medical Society Workshop, May 1987. Undersea and Hyperbaric Medical Society, 10531 Metropolitan Avenue, Kensington, MD 20895-2627.

Neuman TS, Moon RE. Are people with asthma fit to dive? Pressure, November/December 1991, page 3.

Neuman TS. Pulmonary Disorders in Diving. Chapter 20 in: Bove AA, Davis JC; *Diving Medicine,* 2nd Edition, W.B. Saunders Co., Philadelphia, 1990.

*Neuman TS, Bove AA, O'Connor RD, Kelsen SG. Asthma and Diving. Annals Allergy, 1994;73:349.

*Neuman TS. The case for allowing asthmatics to dive, in *Are Asthmatics Fit To Dive?*, DH Elliott, editor. Symposium at UHMS Annual Meeting, June 1995. Undersea and Hyperbaric Medical Society, 10531 Metropolitan Avenue, Kensington, MD 20895-2627.

Schanker H, Spector S. Relationship between asthma and scuba diving mortality. (Abstract). J Allerg Clin Immunol 1991;81:313.

Smith TF. The medical problems of underwater diving. (Letter). New Engl J Med 1992; 326,1497-8.

Strauss RH. State of the art: Diving medicine. Am Rev Resp Dis 1979;119:1001-23.

Watt SJ, Gunnyeon WJ. Scuba divers with asthma. (Letter). Brit Med J 1990;300:609.

DIVING ODDS N' ENDS

Eugiene Clark and Sylvia A. Earl

Oceanography and underwater exploration have long been make-dominated activities, but two women stand out as giants in the field.

Eugiene Clark, born in 1922, is a world famous diver and among the world's top oceanographers. With a Ph.D. in zoology, she pioneered research on sharks and has published several books on the subject. Her personal memoir, *Lady With a Spear*, appeared in 1953 (out of print). Dr. Clark has dived in everything from scuba gear to helmet suits, from submarines to one atmosphere JIM suits. She is the subject of numerous articles and books, including two written for children by Ann McGovern: *Shark Lady: The Adventures of Eugene Clark*, and *Shark Lady II: The Further Adventures of Eugene Clark*.

Sylvia A. Earle, born in 1936, is a world famous marine biologist who made her first dive at age 16; she borrowed a friend's copper diving helmet and made a compressed air dive in a Florida river. Since then she has led or participated in expeditions totaling more than 6000 hours underwater. In 1970, for two weeks she led the first team of female aquanauts to live underwater, in a U.S. Navy experiment called Project Tektite. After Tektite she had a ticker tape parade and a visit to the White House. Dr. Earle has held many important positions in the field of oceanography, and was at one time the chief scientist of the National Oceanographic and Atmospheric Association. Her 1995 book *Sea Change: A Message for the Oceans*, reviews the history of ocean exploration and warns about the precarious state of the seas. She writes: "If the sea is sick, we'll feel it. If it dies, we die. Our future and the state of the oceans are one."

DIVING ODDS N' ENDS

"Pipin" Ferreras and the Deepest Breath-hold Dive

On December 17, 1994, Franciso "Pipin" Ferreras, a Cuban-born immigrant to the U.S., dove to an incredible depth of 417 feet with a single breath of air. He was underwater for 2 minutes, 28 seconds. The dive, which took place near Pipin's home in Key Largo, Florida, bested his previous world breath-hold record of 413.3 feet.

Then on March 10, 1996, Pipin achieved another world record breathhold dive, descending to 428 feet (128 meters) off Cabo San Lucas, Mexico. He surfaced in less than three minutes.

Prior to these dives Pipin had already accomplished more than 500 breath-hold dives to greater than 350 feet, and has stated that his ultimate goal is 500 feet!

There are four main categories of breath-hold diving, and only the first three are recognized as a sport for world competition:
1) totally unassisted;
2) constant ballast, whereby the diver descends with the aid of a weight belt and ascends still carrying the belt;
3) variable ballast, whereby the diver descends with a weight belt, then drops the belt and ascends under his own power; and
4) "no-limit" breath-hold diving.

To reach such fantastic depths (and come back alive), Pipin and other no-limit breath-hold divers descend with the aid of a heavily weighted sled, then ascend with the aid of a lift bag.

During these dives Pipin is able to slow his heart rate from 60 to 8 beats/minute, decreasing his body's need for oxygen and allowing him to survive. Less understandable is how his lungs and chest cage are able to withstand the immense water pressure at 400+ feet.

But Is Recreational Scuba Diving Safe? The Great Debate

IS SCUBA DIVING SAFE?

Is scuba diving safe? Anyone who has read *Scuba Diving Explained* to this point would be justified in replying: "What a dumb question!" You, the reader, have reviewed the potential diving complications of DCS and AGE, and examined the controversy surrounding diving with diabetes, asthma and other conditions. It should be clear by now that apart from the bends and gas embolism, divers also risk running out of air or drowning in other ways. You also know that each year there are a small number of diving accidents and deaths among the millions of people who participate in recreational scuba diving. In short, you know the question belies a simple 'yes' or 'no' reply, and that the answer greatly depends on what the question really means, what the questioner is really asking. Safe compared to what? To never diving? To sitting on a couch? To playing golf? To mountain climbing? To jumping out of an airplane? To driving a car on the freeway?

So why do I bother asking the question? My reason is that the question - as simplistic as it may be - is asked all the time, by many people, and it almost always elicits a heated debate. Simplistic, perhaps, but it is not a dumb question.

Like the debate on many other difficult-to-answer questions, this one seems to be 90% over semantics and personal philosophy (e.g., What do you mean by "safe"?), and only 10% about hard data (e.g., accident rates in scuba vs. other activities). As a result, participants often end up talking at cross purposes. Consider the following portion of an on-line conversation about the safety of scuba diving.

Diver A: Scuba diving is SAFE, and we shouldn't go around teaching otherwise.

Diver B: If you check your dictionary, you'll see that the definition of safe is ". . . without risk." Diving is not without risk.

Diver C: Excuse me, but SAFE and RISK FREE do not have the same meaning. Diving is safe, but it is not risk free.

Diver A: Just what I said, diving is safe. You should not tell students starting a course that diving is unsafe, since that is not true.

Diver B:	How can you say it's safe, when there are risks? We are obligated to explain the risks involved.
Diver A:	Yes, but there are risks in everything we do in life, including just sitting still or sleeping. Take driving, for example. Diving is certainly safer than driving a car.
Diver B:	Where are your data that show diving is safer?
Diver A:	I don't have any, but diving must be safer considering all the people killed on the roads each year. Driving is definitely not safe.
Diver C:	I don't know, you guys seem to be locked in a semantic struggle not over an activity, but over a word.

This is not idle chit chat, since the debaters are all instructors who teach scuba, and who can be expected to impart their feelings to open water students. Whether or not semantics is a factor, we must acknowledge important differences of opinion, and realize that the opinions and attitudes of the most experienced will affect newcomers to scuba diving.

In the mid 1990s, the scuba diving safety debate even extended to concern about long-term, sub-clinical problems, i.e., bubble-related disease that might be found only with magnetic resonance imaging (MRI) of the brain and spinal cord. Researchers in Germany published an article in the respected British journal Lancet, titled "Central nervous system lesions and cervical disc herniations in amateur divers" (Reul 1995). Fifty-two amateur divers (at least 40 dives per year for 4 years) were compared with 55 athletic non-divers.

The divers had more abnormal "bright spots" on their MRI scans than the non-divers. In addition, the divers had much more degenerated intervertebral disc disease than the non-divers. The authors postulated that the abnormalities were due to silent bubble formation occluding small blood vessels without causing symptoms (only one diver had any history of decompression sickness). Unexplainedly, there was no statistically significant correlation between occurrence of bright spots and years of diving experience, or with the number, mean duration or depth of the dives.

Despite the study's lack of correlation with diving depth or intensity, it was picked up by the lay press and widely publicized, prompting more debate and concern on the safety issue. Unfortunately, the study was far from convincing in its conclusions. While the study raised the question of silent bubble damage, it certainly did not provide a satisfactory answer. Letters to Lancet (Wilmshurst 1995; Hovens 1995; Rogers 1995) pointed out some of the study's major weaknesses (such as the way the two groups were selected). An official response by Divers Alert Network also pointed out the study's faults and sought to assure divers (DAN 1996). To quote from DAN's response:

The supposition of any damage to the brain rests on the occurrence of so called silent bubbles occurring in the blood or brain and spinal cord. That such bubbles do exist has been well demonstrated by Doppler technology in blood and tissue studies of animals' spinal cords. Whether or not, however, these silent bubbles are the cause of changes in the brain is unproved.

. . .Divers should not be unduly concerned about [the Lancet study]. More research is needed, but the world is filled with many divers who have been diving for over 40 years who show no unusual deterioration in their abilities which would affect their quality of life.

. . .Certainly, [the study's] results should not be discounted. However, in the absence of neurological decompression illness, many other studies in which divers were compared with non-divers, have failed to demonstrate that diving causes long-term neurological impairment or any functional abnormalities.

Since the provocative Lancet article, another study reported an abnormal number of MRI brain leisons in asymptomatic recreational divers with a large patent foramen ovale (Knauth 1997; Wilmshurst 1997). Importantly, the volunteers for this study had no history of DCS. (This study and the subject of patent foramen ovale are discussed in Section G.) The extent to which abnormalities found on MRI scans might be from silent bubbles traversing a patent foramen ovale is an ongoing area of research.

Debate about safety has been going on since the sport of scuba diving began and will likely continue as long as people dive, perhaps because the sport attracts such a diverse group of people. In fact, anyone who attempts to answer the question "Is Scuba Diving Safe?" will probably have a particular bias, whether it is commercial, academic, medical, political or otherwise. For example, a manufacturer of scuba gear (always wishing to sell merchandise) might respond YES to the question, and then qualify the answer with "proper training and high quality equipment are required for safe diving."

A training agency (always seeking to gain new members) might also respond YES but emphasize that one must be in good health to enter their training program.

A physician experienced in treating dive accident victims, and seeking to prevent more, might respond NO, scuba is not safe and that "you dive at your own risk." So might an accident victim or a victim's family respond to this question.

A politician seeking to prevent scuba diving accidents in his district (and the attendant bad publicity) might respond NO, not without further legislation he is currently proposing.

A non-profit agency like DAN might respond with neither YES nor NO, but instead emphasize the importance of continuing research to understand the nature and causes of diving accidents, and on how to make the sport safer.

And I might respond with: "Read my book!" That's not an entirely fair response, however. I may have provided you enough information in the preceding sections to form your own opinion, but I have not really provided any direct, specific answer of my own. So my answer to the question is provided below and on the next page.

Is Recreational Scuba Diving Safe?

Scuba diving subjects people to altered ambient pressures. These changes in pressure create the risk of developing two important problems, decompression sickness and arterial gas embolism. In addition, being in or under the water presents the possibility of drowning from pressure-related problems or from other causes, such as running out of air or a panic attack. However, in the context of millions of recreational dives a year, the incidence of diving accidents and deaths is considered very small.

The comprehensive data collecting methods of Divers Alert Network assure that most, if not all, scuba diving deaths and serious accidents are reported to it. According to DAN, about 100 North Americans die while scuba diving each year (in 1995, 104 deaths [DAN 1997]). A large percentage of these deaths occurred in people who somehow exceeded recreational guidelines, such as: diving deeper or longer than called for by dive tables; entering overhead environments without proper training or equipment; diving with medical illnesses which should have prohibited the dive.

In addition, DAN receives notice of approximately a thousand non-fatal diving injuries each year, and reports on those that contain sufficient information for diagnosing a true scuba diving accident (in 1995, 590 cases [DAN 1997]). Most of these are cases in which the diver was ill enough to require referral to a hyperbaric chamber facility.

(continued)

Is Recreational Scuba Diving Safe?
(continued)

Based on this information, scuba diving must be considered to present a finite, albeit small, risk to those who participate. Comparing the *amount of risk* with other outdoor sports (e.g., mountain climbing, snow skiing, bicycle riding) is difficult, if not impossible, for two reasons: 1) the number of people actually participating in any popular sport is unknown, as is the frequency of their activity; and, 2) the nature of accidents varies from sport to sport, and any given injury can affect the victim to a varying (and unpredictable) degree. For example, breaking a leg on the ski slopes or suffering a concussion while bike riding cannot be meaningfully compared with a non-fatal case of the bends.

Similarly, comparing risks of scuba diving with essential but risky activities like driving a car is also difficult, since the number of miles driven, the type of driving, etc., are all unknown variables.

Anyone engaging in scuba diving must accept that the sport presents certain risks that would not otherwise be present (though another sport might present a different set of risks). Accepting this fact, the diver should understand that risks can be significantly minimized by such common sense steps as obtaining proper training, diving in good health, staying physically fit, adhering to established dive tables, and not participating in dives that exceed the limits of the individual's training.

In summary, for the vast majority of participants, recreational scuba diving seems to be a very safe activity. For the vast majority, recreational diving has been, and will continue to be, accident-free. However, as in any sport that carries inherent risks - whether it is bicycling, mountain climbing, snow skiing, kayaking, football, or a myriad others - accidents will continue to happen to a small number of participants.

It is up to the individual, through proper training and diving common sense, to minimize the risks to himself or herself. Taking everything into consideration, a wholly satisfactory answer to this question can only be provided *by the individual diver*, based on his or her own expectations and frame of reference.

References

Annual Report on Diving Accidents & Facilities, Divers Alert Network, Box 3823, Duke University Medical Center, Durham, NC 27710; 1997.

DAN responds to Lancet Article - Long-term consequences of diving. The Journal of Underwater Education, Fall 1996, pages 27-28.

Hovens MMC, Riet G, Visser GH. Long term adverse affects of scuba diving (letter to the editor). The Lancet 1995;346:384.

Knauth M, Ries S. Phoimann S, et. at. Cohort study of multiple brain lesions in sport divers: role of a patent foramen ovale. BMJ 1997;314:701-703.

Reul J, Weis J, Jung A, Willmes K, Thron A. Central system lesions and cervical disc herniations in amateur divers. The Lancet 1995;345:1403-1405.

Rogers G. Long term adverse affects of scuba diving (letter to the editor). The Lancet 1995;346:385.

Wilmshurst P, Edge CJ, Bryson P. Long term adverse affects of scuba diving (letter to the editor). The Lancet 1995;346:384.

Wilmshurst P. Brain damage in divers (editorial). BMJ 1997;314:689-690.

GLOSSARY

air - a gas mixture containing 21% oxygen, 78% nitrogen, and 1% other gases (mainly argon); compressed air is used for recreational scuba diving.

air compressor - a machine that compresses or pressurizes air; for scuba purposes, air is compressed from the atmospheric level (14.7 psi at sea level) to the capacity of the tank, usually between 2500-3000 psi.

air embolism - see arterial gas embolism

air pressure - the force per unit area exerted by the weight of air; at sea level the air pressure is 14.7 psi. Air pressure decreases with altitude.

algorithm - a set of equations incorporated into diving computers in order to compute nitrogen uptake and elimination from changes in depth and elapsed time.

ambient pressure - the surrounding pressure; on land, comes from the weight of the atmosphere (see air pressure); at depth, comes from the weight of the water plus the weight of the atmosphere.

argon - an inert gas that makes up less than one percent of air.

arterial gas embolism - the condition characterized by bubble(s) of air from a ruptured lung segment under pressure; the bubbles enter the pulmonary circulation and travel to the arterial circulation, where they may cause a stroke.

asthma - a common condition manifested by narrowing of air passages within the lungs (the bronchi); one reason for the narrowing is excess mucous in the airways.

ata - atmosphere absolute; 1 ata is the atmospheric pressure at sea level; is measured with a barometer.

atmosphere - the blanket of air surrounding the earth, from sea level to outer space. Also, a unit of pressure; "one atmosphere" is pressure of the atmosphere at sea level, i.e., 760 mm Hg. Two atmospheres is twice this pressure, 1520 mm Hg, etc. Abbreviated atm.

atmospheric pressure - pressure of the atmosphere at a given altitude or location.

barometric pressure - same as atmospheric pressure.

barotrauma - any disease or injury due to unequal pressures between a space inside the body and the ambient pressure, or between two spaces within the body; examples include arterial gas embolism, pneumomediastinum, and pneumothorax.

bathyscaphe - literally, deep boat; a vessel that can descend and ascend under its own power, but is not designed for horizontal travel. The bathyscaphe *Trieste* set the world depth record in 1960.

bathysphere - a round, heavy walled vessel that can be lowered to great depths in the ocean via a tether from the surface ship; does not ascend or descend under its own power.

BC - see buoyancy compensator.

bends - a form of decompression sickness caused by dissolved nitrogen leaving the tissues too quickly on ascent; is manifested by pain, usually in the limbs and joints; "the bends" is sometimes used to signify any manifestation of decompression sickness.

bleb - an abnormal pocket of air in the lungs, usually under the lining of a lung, that can rupture with ascent and lead to barotrauma.

bottom time - variable definition; in square wave diving, the time between descending below the surface to the beginning of ascent. In multi-level diving, the time between descending below the surface and beginning the safety stop. (Other definitions may apply depending on the specific type of diving.)

Boyle's law - at a fixed temperature and for a fixed mass of gas, pressure times volume is a constant value.

breath-hold diving - diving without life support apparatus, while holding one's breath.

bubble - a collection of air or gas surrounded by a permeable membrane through which gases can enter or exit.

bulla - similar to bleb; an abnormal pocket of air or fluid; sometimes found in the lungs of patients with emphysema.

buoyancy - tendency of object to float or sink when placed in a liquid; objects that float are positively buoyant, those that sink are negatively buoyant and those that stay where placed are neutrally buoyant.

buoyancy compensator - an inflatable vest worn by the diver that can be automatically or orally inflated to help control buoyancy; abbreviated BC.

carbon dioxide - CO_2; an odorless, tasteless gas that is a byproduct of metabolism; is excreted by the lungs in exhaled air.

carbon dioxide toxicity - problems resulting from buildup of CO_2 in the blood; they may range from headache and shortness of breath, all the way to sudden blackout.

carbon monoxide - CO; odorless, tasteless, highly poisonous gas given off by incomplete combustion of hydrocarbon fuels.

carbon monoxide toxicity - illness from inhaling excess CO; problems may range from headache to unconsciousness and death.

- at a constant volume, the pressure of a gas varies inversely with absolute temperature.

chokes - a form of decompression sickness caused by enough bubbles entering the lungs to interfere with gas exchange; manifested by shortness of breath and can be fatal.

closed circuit scuba - apparatus designed to allow divers to re-breathe exhaled air after removal of CO_2 and addition of supplemental O_2. In contrast to "open circuit," closed circuit scuba is noiseless and produces no bubbles.

compartment - a theoretical division of the body with an arbitrarily assigned half-time for nitrogen uptake and elimination. In designing decompression tables the body is divided into a finite number of compartments for purposes of making calculations, e.g., five, six or more.

computer - see dive computer

Dalton's Law - the total pressure exerted by a mixture of gases is equal to the sum of the pressures that would be exerted by each of the gases if it alone were present and occupied the total volume.

decompression - any change from one ambient pressure to a lower ambient pressure; always results in a reduction of gas pressures within the body.

decompression dive - any dive where the diver is exposed to a higher pressure than when the dive began; the decompression occurs as the diver ascends.

decompression stop - on ascent from a dive, a specified time spent at a specific depth, for purposes of nitrogen off-gassing; when not mandatory it is called a safety stop.

decompression illness - DCI; a relatively new term to encompass all bubble-related problems arising from decompression, including both decompression sickness and arterial gas embolism.

DCI - see decompression illness.

DCS - see decompression sickness.

decompression sickness - DCS; a general term for all problems resulting from nitrogen leaving the body when ambient pressure is lowered. Can be divided into Type I (musculoskeletal and/or skin manifestations only) or the more serious Type II (neurologic, cardiac, and/or pulmonary manifestations).

dive computer - a small computer, carried by the diver, that constantly measures water pressure (and hence depth), and time; based on a pre-programmed algorithm, the computer calculates tissue nitrogen uptake and elimination in several theoretical compartments and provides a continuous readout of the dive profile, including: depth, elapsed time of dive, duration at current depth before decompression becomes mandatory; and a warning if the rate of ascent is too fast.

dive tables - a printed collection of dive times for specific depths, by which the diver can avoid contracting DCS. Most tables are based on Haldanian theory for nitrogen uptake and elimination.

dry suit - a water-tight garment that keeps the diver's body warm by providing insulation with a layer of gas, such as air; for diving in waters that are too cold for comfortable wetsuit protection, usually below 65°F.

EAN - enriched air nitrogen; nitrox.

eustachian tube - a short, muco-cartilaginous tube connecting the back of the nose to the middle ear. The anatomy of this tube is such that it tends to close naturally when ambient pressure is higher than middle ear pressure (as on descent in a dive), and tends to open naturally when ambient pressure is lower than middle ear pressure (on ascent).

first stage regulator - regulator attached to the scuba tank that lowers the tank pressure to ambient pressure + a pre-determined pressure (e.g., ambient + 140 psi).

free diving - variably defined; in some usage, diving without any scuba or other equipment and synonymous with breath-hold diving; in other usage, diving without any attachment to the surface, and therefore includes scuba diving.

fsw - feet of sea water; used to indicate either an actual depth, or just a pressure equal to that depth (e.g., in a hyperbaric chamber).

gas embolism - see arterial gas embolism

gas laws - laws that predict how gases will behave with changes in pressure, temperature and volume.

gauge pressure - pressure exclusive of atmospheric pressure; when diving, gauge pressure is due solely to the water pressure.

half-time - half the time it takes for a dissolved gas in a tissue (such as nitrogen) to equilibrate to a new pressure, or to reach full saturation at a new pressure. Theoretical tissue half-times are used in designing dive tables and algorithms for dive computers.

Haldanian - related to Haldane's theory that nitrogen is taken up and given off in exponential fashion during a dive, and that there is some safe ratio of pressure change for ascent (originally, 2:1).

heliox - mixture of helium and oxygen, used for very deep diving.

helium - second lightest gas; does not cause problems of narcosis seen with nitrogen, and is therefore used for very deep diving.

Henry's Law - the amount of any given gas that will dissolve in a liquid at a given temperature is a function of the partial pressure of the gas in contact with the liquid and the solubility coefficient of the gas in the liquid.

high pressure nervous syndrome - convulsions or seizure-like activity arising from high gas pressure at depth, especially with helium.

hookah - a surface-supplied compressed air apparatus, for use in shallow diving in calm waters. The air is delivered to one or more divers through a long hose.

hydrogen - an inert gas, and lightest of all the elements; has been used in experimental diving situations.

hyperbaric chamber - air-tight chamber that can simulate the ambient pressure at altitude or at depth; is used for treating decompression illness.

hypercapnia - a higher than normal PCO_2 level in the blood.

hyperthermia - a body temperature warmer than normal; less common in diving than hypothermia, but can occur from overheating in a wet suit.

hyperventilation - over breathing to the extent that the blood carbon dioxide level is owered; may lead to tingling in fingers and dizziness.

hypothermia - a body temperature colder than normal (37°C/98.6°F); severe problems start to manifest when body temperature reaches about 35°C (95°F).

hypoventilation - under breathing to the extent that the blood carbon dioxide level is elevated; may be manifested by carbon dioxide narcosis.

hypoxemia - lower than normal PO_2 level in the blood; insufficient oxygen in the blood.

hypoxia - same as hypoxemia; terms are often used interchangeably.

liveaboard - a dive boat with sleeping and eating accommodations. Commercial liveaboards are usually between 50 and 130 feet long, and can carry anywhere from 10 to 30+ divers for a week or more.

middle ear - air-containing space of the ear bordered on one side by the tympanic membrane, which is exposed to any change in ambient pressure. Air pressure in the middle ear space can only be equalized through the eustachian tube, which connects the middle ear to the back of the nose.

mixed gas - variously defined; basically, any non-air mixture (e.g., nitrox), although some authors use the term only for mixes that contain a gas in addition to (or in place of) nitrogen (e.g., helium).

nitrogen - inert gas that makes up 78% of air. Nitrogen is inert in that it does not enter into any chemical reaction in the body, but it can cause problems under pressure (see nitrogen narcosis, decompression sickness).

narcosis - depressed mental state, anywhere from confusion or drowsiness to coma.

nitrogen narcosis - depressed mental state from high nitrogen pressure; usually does not begin to manifest on compressed air until below 80 fsw.

nitrox - any mixture of nitrogen and oxygen that contains less than the 78% nitrogen as found in ordinary air.

NOAA - National Oceanic and Atmospheric Administration.

OEA - Oxygen enriched air; nitrox.

open circuit scuba - apparatus used in recreational diving; exhaled air is expelled into the water as bubbles; no part is rebreathed by the diver. Compare to closed circuit scuba.

otitis - inflammation or infection of any part of the ear; otitis media involves the middle ear, otitis externa the outer ear (ear canal).

oxygen - O_2; gas vital for all life on this planet; makes up 21% of air by volume.

oxygen therapy - administration of any gas, for medical purpose, that contains more than 21% oxygen.

oxygen toxicity - damage or injury from inhaling too much oxygen; can arise from either too high an oxygen concentration or oxygen pressure. The first manifestation of oxygen toxicity while diving can be seizures.

oxygen window - difference between total gas pressures in arterial and venous blood; exists because oxygen is partly metabolized by the tissues, so venous oxygen pressure is lower than arterial oxygen pressure.

partial pressure - pressure exerted by a single component of a gas within a gas mixture, or dissolved in a liquid.

partial pressure, carbon dioxide - PCO_2; pressure exerted by carbon dioxide in any mixture of gases, or dissolved in a liquid.

partial pressure, nitrogen - PN_2; pressure exerted by nitrogen component in any mixture of gases, or dissolved in a liquid.

partial pressure, oxygen - PO_2; pressure exerted by oxygen in any mixture of gases, or dissolved in a liquid.

pneumomediastinum - abnormal collection of air in the middle part of the chest, between the two lungs (mediastinum); often a consequence of barotrauma.

pneumothorax - abnormal collection of air outside the lining of the lung, between the lung and the chest wall; often a consequence of barotrauma.

pressure - any force exerted over an area; see atmospheric pr., ambient pr.

psi - pounds per square inch; a common measurement of air pressure.

recreational scuba diving - diving to prescribed limits, including a depth no greater than 130 fsw, using only compressed air, and never requiring a decompression stop; abbreviated RSD.

regulator - in scuba, any device which changes air pressure from one level to a lower level. See first and second stage regulator.

repetitive dive - any dive done within a certain time frame after a previous dive; variable definition exists as to what time frame constitutes "repetitive." With some tables any dive within 12 hours of a previous dive is considered repetitive; when using a computer, any dive whose profile is affected by a previous dive is considered repetitive.

residual nitrogen time - the time it would take to off-gas any extra nitrogen remaining after a dive; in dive tables, RNT is designated by a letter A through Z. Residual nitrogen time is always taken into consideration in determining the safe duration for any repetitive dive.

reverse squeeze - pain or discomfort in enclosed space (e.g., sinuses, middle ear, inside face mask) on ascent from a dive.

RSD - see recreational scuba diving.

safety stop - on ascent from a dive, a specified time spent at a specific depth, for purposes of nitrogen off-gassing; by definition it is not mandatory for safe ascent from the dive. Compare with decompression stop.

saturation - the degree to which a gas is dissolved in the blood or tissues; full saturation occurs when the pressure of gas dissolved in the blood or tissues is the same as the ambient (surrounding) pressure of that gas.

saturation diving - diving performed after the body is fully saturated with nitrogen; to become fully saturated the diver must stay underwater for a much longer period than is allowed in recreational scuba diving tables.

scuba - self-contained underwater breathing apparatus.

sea level - the level of the world's oceans; all oceans are at sea level.

second stage regulator - the regulator that follows, in line, the first stage regulator, and delivers compressed air to the diver.

shallow water blackout - a sudden unconsciousness, from hypoxia, that occurs among some breath hold divers. Often occurs near the surface after a deeper dive, hence "shallow water."

sinuses - air spaces within the skull that are in contact with ambient pressure through openings into the back of the nasal passages.

sinusitis - inflammation or infection of the sinuses in the head.

skin diving - another term for breath-hold diving; diving without the use of scuba equipment.

squeeze - pain or discomfort in an enclosed space (sinuses, middle ears, inside a face mask) caused by shrinkage of that space; occurs on descent. See reverse squeeze.

submarine - heavy walled vessel that can withstand pressures underwater and allow occupants to breathe air at sea level pressure; can travel under its own power.

surface interval - length of time on the surface, usually out of the water, between two consecutive dives.

surface-supplied compressed air diving - diving with the air continuously supplied by a compressor on the surface; can be used for both sport and professional diving.

supersaturation - an unstable situation where the pressure of a gas dissolved in the blood or tissues is higher than the ambient pressure of that gas. Supersaturation is always present to some degree with every decompression.

thermocline - intersection between two layers of water of that are of distinctly different temperatures; usually the colder layer is deeper. A diver can easily feel a thermocline.

tissue - a part of the body characterized by specific characteristics, such as muscle, bone, or cartilage. The term is also used to refer to any part of the body with a specific half-time for loading and unloading nitrogen; in this latter context a tissue may be contiguous or non-contiguous, or even a theoretical compartment.

trimix - mixture of helium, nitrogen and oxygen, used for very deep diving.

water pressure - force per unit area exerted by the weight of water; each 33 feet of sea water exerts a pressure equivalent to one atmosphere, or 14.7 psi.

wet suit - any suit that provides thermal protection in or underwater by trapping a layer of water between the diver's skin and the suit; see dry suit.

All About DAN, or: Where are the Hyperbaric Chambers?

DAN, or Divers Alert Network, is a non-profit organization established in 1980 to promote diver safety. Affiliated with Duke University Medical Center, DAN's headquarters are in an office building in Durham, North Carolina, a short distance from the campus (see address at end of this Appendix). DAN is supported by membership dues, sponsoring corporations, and the sale of dive-safety-related materials such as textbooks, videos, and oxygen equipment. Since its founding, DAN has gained world-wide reputation as the pre-eminent source for information on diving safety, and as an aid for divers in need of immediate help and/or referral to a hyperbaric chamber. DAN's activities include the following:

1) **HYPERBARIC CHAMBER REFERRAL.** DAN maintains an up-to-date list of all functioning hyperbaric chambers in North America and the Caribbean. DAN does not publish this list, since at any one time a given chamber may be non-functioning, or its operator(s) may be away or otherwise unavailable. Current information is regularly phoned into DAN by chamber personnel. Through Duke, DAN operates a 24-hour emergency phone line for anyone (members and non-members) to call and ask for diving accident assistance. Dive medicine physicians at Duke Medical Center carry beepers, so someone is always on call to answer questions and, if necessary, make referral to the closest functioning hyperbaric chamber. (The emergency HOT LINE phone number is at the end of this Appendix.)

2) **OXYGEN FIRST AID.** DAN offers oxygen first aid courses around the country. DAN tirelessly promotes the importance on having oxygen on dive boats *and* teaches divers how to use it.

3) **DAN CHAMBER ASSISTANCE PROGRAM.** DAN provides funding for recompression chambers and training for their staff in key diving regions throughout the world.

4) **YEARLY STATISTICS.** DAN keeps statistics on all accidents in North Americans that occur while scuba diving, and publishes a

yearly compendium. This information is useful to track the rate of deaths and non-fatal accidents, to analyze their causes, and to show ways in which diving can be made safer.

5) **ALERT DIVER.** Dan publishes *Alert Diver*, a bi-monthly magazine mailed at no extra charge to all DAN members. Non-technical and oriented to the recreational diver, *Alert Diver* contains articles relating to dive safety, health and medicine, plus information on DAN membership benefits and activities.

6) **MEDICAL EDUCATION.** DAN conducts several courses a year on medical aspects of diving, held at the Duke University campus and also at popular dive resorts around the world. These medical courses are open to anyone with an interest in diving related injuries.

7) **INSURANCE PROGRAM.** DAN offers an excellent insurance program for members. All DAN members receive automatic medical evacuation assistance; this is not insurance for self-arranged transport, as DAN makes all the arrangements after receiving a telephone call. This service provides global medical evacuation for a DAN member needing assistance 100 or more miles from home. For a moderate annual fee, DAN members can also receive supplemental medical coverage for any water-related accident (not just diving) anywhere in the world; this program covers up to 95% of hyperbaric chamber and other forms of medical therapy not otherwise covered by the member's regular medical insurance.

8) **RESEARCH.** Not least, through its university-appointed medical staff DAN does research in diving medicine and diving-related accidents.

DAN'S ADDRESS: P.O. Box 3823
                      Duke University Medical Center
                      Durham, NC 27710
    Internet Address http://www.dan.ycg.org

MEDICAL INFORMATION LINE   919-684-2948

For information on DAN, or to   800-446-2671
sign up for membership   FAX: 919-490-6630

DAN Diving Emergency Hot Line (24 Hours): 919-684-8111

<u>NOTES</u>

U.S. Scuba Training Agencies

The first category includes all U.S. agencies that certify for recreational scuba diving. The next two categories include agencies that certify for technical diving and cave diving. In each category agencies are listed by alphabetical order. Where available, a web site address is also provided. (Section U lists comprehensive internet web sites that may also link to scuba training agencies.) Please note that certification policies are constantly evolving; many traditional recreational diving agencies now offer training in "technical" diving skills, particularly nitrox diving.

Recreational Diving Certification

Handicapped Scuba Association (HSA)
1104 El Prado
San Clemente, CA 92672-4637
Phone & Fax: 714-498-6128
Publication: Squid
http://ourworld.compuserve.com/homepages/hsahdq/weare.htm

International Diving Educators Association (IDEA)
PO Box 8427
Jacksonville, FL 32239-8427
Phone: 904-744-5554
Fax: 904-743-5425
Publication: Newsletter
http://www.touristguide.com/idea.html

International Scuba Educators Association
PO Box 17388, 1475A Belcher Rd.
Clearwater, FL 34624
Phone: 813-539-6491
Publication: Newsletter

Multi-National Diving Educators Association (MDEA)
PO Box 3433
Marathon Shores, FL 33052
Phone: 305-743-6188
Fax: 305-743-7499
Publication: Multi-National Diving News

National Academy of Scuba Educators (NASE)

1728 Kingsley Avenue, Suite 6
Orange Park, FL 32073
Phone: 904-264-4104
Fax: 904-269-2283
Publication: Divelog
http://www.nasescuba.com

National Association of Scuba Diving Schools (NASDS)

1012 South Yates
Memphis, TN 38119
Phone: 800-735-3483; 901-767-7265
Fax: 901-767-2798
Publication: Diving Retailer
http://www.divesafe.com

National Association of Underwater Instructors (NAUI)

PO Box 14650
Montclair, CA 91763-1150
Phone: 800-553-6284; 909-621-5801
Fax: 909-621-6405
Publication: Sources, The Journal of Underwater Education
http://www.naui.org

Professional Association of Diving Instructors (PADI)

1251 East Dyer Road, Suite 100
Santa Ana, CA 92705-5605
Phone: 800-729-7234; 714-540-7234
FAX: 714-540-2609
Publication: The Undersea Journal
http://www.padi.com

Professional Diving Instructors Corporation (PDIC)

1554 Gardner Avenue
Scranton, PA 18509
Phone: 800-642-9434; 717-342-9434; 717-342-1480
Fax: 717-342-1276; 717-342-6030
Publication: PDIC NEWS
http://www.pdic.intl.com

Scuba Schools International (SSI)

2619 Canton Court
Fort Collins, CO 80525-4498
Phone; 800-892-2702; 970-482-0883
Fax: 970-482-6157
Publication: Dive Business International
http://www.ssiusa.com

National YMCA Scuba Program (YMCA)
5825-2A Live Oak Parkway
Norcross, GA 30093-1728
Phone: 770-662-5172
Fax: 770-242-9059
Publication: Buddy Lines
http://www.webcom.com/~cscripts/-ymca/ymca.html

Training for Technical Diving
(Including Nitrox Certification)

American Nitrox Divers International (ANDI)
74 Woodcleft Avenue
Freeport, NY 11520
Phone 516-546-2026
Fax: 516-546-6010
Publication: Newsletter
http://www.andihq.com

International Association of Nitrox and Technical Divers (IANTD)
9628 NE 2 Ave., Suite D
Miami Shores, FL 33138-2767
Phone: 305-751-4873
Fax: 305-751-3958
Publication: I.A.N.T.D. Journal
http://www.iantd.com

Professional Scuba Association (PSA)
9487 NW 115th Ave.
Ocala, FL 34482-1007
Phone: 407-896-6294
Fax: 407-896-4542
Publication: Newsletter
http://www.travelbase.com/activities/scuba/pro-scuba

Technical Diving International (TDI)
9 Costal Plaza, Suite 300
Bath, ME 04530
Phone: 207-442-8391
Fax: 207-442-9042
Publication: Newsletter
http://www.techdiver.com

Cave Diving Certifying Agencies

Cave Diving Section of the National Speleological Society (NSS-CDS)
P.O. Box 950
Branford, FL 32008-0950
Publication: Underwater Speleology
http://iquest.com/cds

National Association for Cave Diving (NACD)
P.O. Box 14492
Gainesville, FL 32604
Phone: 352-332-0738; 352-495-3348
Fax: 352-495-3348
http://www.afn.org/nacd

U.S. Scuba Newsletters, Magazines, and Journals

This section includes most U.S. periodicals with national circulation, and aimed at the recreational diver or those who teach recreational diving. Any list of current periodicals is bound to change frequently, as new magazines enter the market and others fold. Some scuba magazines are also available on the internet; see Section U for a list of some comprehensive scuba web site addresses.

The list is divided into four categories: 1) newsletters without any advertising or organization affiliation (only one is available); 2) periodicals produced by clubs, organizations or training agencies; 3) general circulation periodicals, which includes all the popular scuba magazines; 4) technical journals (only one is included, the UHMS journal). In most cases information has been verified by the periodical; when information could not be verified, the category has been left blank. Circulation is for most recent year available; address is for the main editorial office. Within each category, listing is alphabetical. Any omissions or errors should be called to the attention of the author.

1) Newsletters

Ben Davison's In Depth/Undercurrent
Address: P.O. Box 90215, Austin, TX 78709 (Editorial)
Phone (editorial): 512-891-9812
Phone (subscription): 800-326-1896 *Fax:* 415-461-7953
In print since: 1975
Circulation: 10,000
Comment: In Depth/Undercurrent is the amalgamation of two newsletters, the older Undercurrent (founded in 1975 by Ben Davison) and the more recent In Depth (founded in 1986). In Depth/Undercurrent, which bills itself as "Consumer reviews for sport divers", accepts no advertising and has no organizational affiliation. Articles are about travel and scuba equipment. The newsletter welcomes letters and reports about good and bad dive experiences from its readers.

2) Periodicals Produced by a Club or Organization and Available to the Public

Except as noted, subscription is available through membership in an organization or club; periodicals are not sold on newsstands. In some cases the target audience is specialized, but all of these periodicals carry articles that should interest the general scuba diver.

Alert Diver
Parent organization: Divers Alert Network
Address: Box 3823, Duke University Medical Center, Durham, NC 27710
Phone (editorial): 919-684-2948, ext. 626
Phone (subscription): 919-684-2984, ext. 333
Fax: 919-493-3040
In print since: 1980
Circulation: 180,000
Comment: Bimonthly magazine with emphasis on medically-related topics of interest to recreational divers.

Calypso Log
Parent organization: Cousteau Society
Address: 870 Greenbrier Circle, suite 402, Chesapeake, VA 23320
Phone (editorial): 757-523-9335
Phone (subscription): 800-441-4395
Fax: 757-523-2747
In print since: 1974
Circulation: 150,000
Comment: Distributed to members of the Cousteau Society, which charges a yearly membership fee. Emphasis is on travels of *Calypso*, Cousteau's famous ship, and on ocean preservation & conservation. Organization also publishes a similar periodical for children, *Dolphin Log*.

Dive Business International
Parent organization: Scuba Schools International (SSI)
Address: 2619 Canton Court, Fort Collins, CO 80525-4498
Phone (editorial): 303-482-0883
Phone (subscription): Same
Fax: 303-482-6157
In print since: 1980 (name changed from "The Bulletin" in 1993)
Circulation: 5,200

Comment: The monthly periodical for dive professionals associated with SSI, including "resorts, dive store owners and managers, instructors and dive control specialists."

Dive Report
Parent organization: Watersport Publishing, Inc.
Address: P.O. Box 83727, San Diego, CA 92138
Phone (editorial): 800-776-3483, 619-697-0703
Phone (subscription): Same
Fax: 619-697-0123
In print since: 1993
Circulation: 5,200
Comment: A monthly periodical for "dive store owners and managers, instructors, scuba manufacturers and their representatives, dive resort and boat owners, and dive travel representatives." *Dive Report* functions as de facto trade journal for the scuba industry, and includes articles on legal issues. It is available free to anyone in the target audience.

Pressure
Parent organization: Undersea & Hyperbaric Medical Society
Address: 10531 Metropolitan Avenue, Kensington, MD 20895
Phone (editorial): 301-942-2980
Phone (subscription): Same
Fax: 301-942-7804
In print since: 1972
Circulation: 2,400
Comment: UHMS is "an international nonprofit professional association servicing the diving and hyperbaric communities." Pressure is a bimonthly newsletter with non-technical articles on diving and hyperbaric medicine. Non-physicians with an interest in scuba diving medicine or hyperbaric therapy can become associate members of UHMS and receive the periodical. It may also be available in some medical libraries.

Sources, The Journal of Underwater Education
Parent organization: National Association of Underwater Instructors (NAUI)
Address: 4650 Arrow Highway, suite F-1, P.O. Box 14650, Montclair, CA 91763-1150
Phone (editorial): 909-621-5801
Phone (subscription): Same, Order Dept. X
Fax: 909-621-6405

In print since: 1989 (Replaced NDA News)
Circulation: 14,000
Comment: Sent to professionals in NAUI, including divemasters, instructors, and dive store operators.

Squid
Parent Organization: Handicapped Scuba Association
Address: 1104 El Prado, San Clemente, CA 92672
Phone (editorial): 714-498-6128
Phone (subscription): Same
Fax: 714-498-6128
Circulation: 1,500
In print since: 1984
Comment: Published biannually

The Undersea Journal
Parent organization: Professional Association of Diving Instructors (PADI)
Address: 1251 E. Dyer Rd. Suite 100, Santa Ana, CA 92705
Phone (editorial): 800-729-7234; 714-540-7234
Phone (subscription): Same
Fax: 714-540-2609
In print since: 1967
Comment: Sent to professionals in the PADI organization, including divemasters, instructors, and dive store operators.

3) General Circulation Periodicals

Except as indicated, all periodicals in this group are printed on glossy paper and come out four or more times a year. Larger-circulation magazines will be found on many newsstands; others may be found only on selected newsstands, and in some dive stores. All are available by subscription.

Discover Diving
Address: Watersport Publishing Co., P.O. Box 83727, San Diego, CA 92138
Phone (editorial): 800-776-3483; 619-697-0703
Phone (subscription): Same
Fax: 619-697-0123
Circulation: 85,000

In print since: 1982
Comment: A general dive magazine, with articles on dive travel, photography, history and sea creatures.

Dive Training
Address: 1200 South Federal Highway, Suite 301, Boynton Beach, FL 33435
Phone (editorial): 407-731-4321; 800-683-3483
Phone (subscription): 800-444-9932
Fax: 407-369-5882 (editorial)
Circulation: 95,000
In print since: 1991
Comment: Aimed at the newly certified diver, and scuba instructors. Contains many useful articles for these two large groups.

Dive Travel Magazine
Address: P.O. Box 1388, Soquel, CA 95073
Phone (editorial) and Fax: 408-462-0158
Phone (subscription): 800-676-7254
Circulation: 40,000
In print since: 1983
Comment: Issued quarterly. As its name indicates, emphasis is on dive travel (including live-aboards) and diving destinations.

Immersed
Address: F.D.R. Station, Post Office Box 7934, New York, N.Y. 10150
Phone (editorial): 718-545-1325
Phone (subscription): same
Fax: 718-545-3889
Circulation: 15,000
In print since: 1996
Comment: A quarterly journal for technical diving, e.g. deep, cave, and mixed gas diving, "without the jargon." Contains many interesting articles on emerging technology not found in other general magazines, such as rebreathing circuits.

Ocean Realm Magazine
Address: P.O. Box 6953, Syracuse, N.Y. 13217
Phone (editorial): 210-824-8099
Phone (subscription): 800-681-7727
Fax: 210-820-3522
Circulation: Approx. 30,000

In print since: 1985
Comment: Emphasis is on ocean environments and sea creatures; a slick, glossy quarterly with many beautiful photos.

Rodale's Scuba Diving
Address: 6600 Abercorn St., Savannah, GA 31405
Phone (editorial): 912-351-0855
Phone (subscription): 800-666-0016
Fax: 912-351-0735
Circulation: 200,000
In print since: 1992
Comment: In 1992 Rodale, a large magazine company (Prevention Magazine) bought out the periodicals *Fisheye View* and *Pacific Diver*, and started *Scuba Diving*. Emphasis is on dive travel and Consumer Reports-style equipment reviews.

Scuba Times
Address: 14110 Perdido Key Drive, Suite 16, Pensacola, FL 32507
Phone (editorial): 800-234-0060
Phone (subscription): 800-950-7282
Fax: 904-492-7807
Circulation: 50,000
In print since: 1979
Comment: A general scuba magazine, published bi-monthly. Each issue has a special section called Advanced Diving Journal, with articles on technical and medical aspects of diving.

Skin Diver Magazine
Address: 6420 Wilshire Blvd., Los Angeles, CA 90048-5515
Phone (editorial): 213-782-2960
Phone (subscription): 800-800-3487
Fax: 213-782-2121
Circulation: 200,000
In print since: 1951
Comment: The largest-circulation and oldest scuba magazine in print. Every issue contains articles that run the gamut from dive travel and dive medicine to equipment reviews and wreck diving.

Sport Diver
Address: World Publications, 330 W. Canton Ave., Winter Park, FL
32789-3195
Phone (editorial): 407-628-4802
Phone (subscription): 800-394-6006
Fax: 407-628-7061
Circulation: 70,000
In print since: 1992
Comment: Aim is to publish general interest articles for the more active
and well traveled recreational scuba diver.

Sub Aqua Journal
Address: 150 Marine St., City Island, New York 10464
Phone (editorial): 718-885-3332
Phone (subscription): 718-885-3332
Fax: 718-885-9002
Circulation: 22,000
In print since: 1991
Comment: Emphasis is on wreck diving and advanced diving.

4) Technical Journals

This journal, for health professionals in the field of underwater medicine, is available through any medical library.

Undersea and Hyperbaric Medicine
Address: 10531 Metropolitan Avenue, Kensington, MD 20895
Phone (editorial): 301-942-290
Fax: Same
Circulation: 2,000
In print since: 1993
Comment: Journal formed in 1993 from merger of two older journals,
Undersea and Biomedical Research, and Journal of Hyperbaric
Medicine, each of which has been in print since the early 1970s. All arti-
cles in these journals, and its successor Undersea and Hyperbaric
Medicine, are abstracted in Medline, the national medical journal data
base.

NOTES

Distributors of Dive Books and Videos, and Internet Addresses for additional information

The first list in this Section is of dive book distributors; write or call for a free catalog. Some companies on this list also publish their own scuba books. The second list contains internet addresses of comprehensive scuba sites; in turn, each site contains many links — to books, dive shops, on-line magazines, scuba resorts, news groups, etc. Like all web sites, the ones listed here are subject to a change of address. However, since they are all inter-linked in some fashion, by starting at any one site you should be able to "surf" the web and retrieve large amounts of scuba-related information.

Book Distributors

Aqua Explorer Publications

Address: P.O. Box 116, East Rockaway, NY 11518
Phone: 516-868-2658; 800-695-7585
Fax: 516-868-2658
Catalog emphasis: Wreck diving, underwater life, diving guides; also distributes wreck videos.

Aqua Quest Publications, Inc.

Address: P.O. Box 700, Locust Valley, NY 11560-0700
Phone: 516-759-0476; 800-933-8989
Fax: 516-759-4519
Catalog emphasis: Wreck diving, underwater life, deeper diving. Aqua Quest also publishes its own series of Diving Guides to popular dive sites, ranging from Hawaii to the Caribbean and Bermuda.

Bennet Marine Video
Address: 8436 West 3rd Street, Suite 740, Los Angeles, CA 90048-4100
Phone: 800-733-8862
Fax: 213-951-7595
Catalog emphasis: Underwater videos on all subjects, from underwater photography to dive boat etiquette to how to use dive tables.

Best Publishing Company
Address: P.O. Box 30100, Flagstaff, AZ 86003-0100
Phone: 520-527-1055; 800-468-1055
Fax: 520-526-0370
Catalog emphasis: Over 300 books on dive medicine, advanced diving (commercial and scientific), history of diving, photography, dive vacations and more. Best distributes and publishes books on diving and hyperbaric medicine.

Divers Alert Network
Address: Box 3823, Duke University Medical Center, Durham, NC 27710
Phone: 800-446-2671
Fax: 919-490-6630
Catalog emphasis: Dive medicine, diving safety and first aid. Catalog also contains DAN-promoted non-book products such as oxygen equipment, T-shirts, decals, etc.

Watersport Publishing, Inc.
Address: P.O Box 83727, San Diego, CA 92138
Phone: 619-697-0703
Catalog emphasis: Company's own dive books, which span gamut from *When Women Dive* to *Mixed Gas Diving*.

Some Comprehensive World Wide Web Sites On Scuba Diving (in alphabetical order)

Aqueous Scuba
http://www.aqueous.com/aq65.html

Best Publishing
http://diveweb.com/best

The CyberSea Scuba Journal
http://www.scubajournal.com/scuba/webmate/cybersea/page/cybersea/cs-index

The Dive Shop
http://www.nadnet.com/ds/divelink.htm

e.Diver
http://www.empg.com/ediver.htm

Rodale's Scuba Diving
http://www.scubadiving.com

Scuba Central
http://www.scubacentral.com

ScubaDuba
http://www.scubaduba.com

Scuba On-Line
http://www.scubaon-line.com

Underwater Sports World & Virtual Dive Shop
http://www.uwsports.com

Yahoo-Scuba
http://www.yahoo.com/recreation/outdoors/scuba

SECTION V

INDEX